The Prison Counsellor

Caring Was Her Only Crime

Sarah Templeton

Edited by Sara Donaldson
Cover Design by Izzie @ Izmade
Layout by Oliver Tooley

Published 2025 by Gemini Publishing Ltd.

This book is dedicated to one very special boy.

He's one I couldn't contact to ask if I could tell his story, because he is no longer with us.

Anthony Thomas, thank you for loving me unconditionally for ten years.

And thank you for helping so many people.

I will forever love you millions.

A word from the author about confidentiality

This is usually the bit where the author tells you that to maintain confidentiality everything about each character has been changed, and some people have been amalgamated.

Interestingly, when I approached them, nearly every client who appears in this book said I could use their real name – the ones I could trace or I'm still in touch with anyway. I haven't because they might not feel that way in ten years' time!

But I have used a name that is in some way related to each of them. Only they will know this. It might be their middle name, it might be a variation of their surname, but it will definitely be linked to them. Because they wanted it that way. And some of them even chose the name they wanted to be known as in the book.

And, very importantly, each story is most definitely one person's story. Nobody has been amalgamated with anybody else.

Every single boy and man you are going to read about exists. Their stories are all true.

And I am grateful to each and every one of them for allowing me to tell their story. I just hope I have done all of them justice.

My first glimpse of a 'criminal'

I've always been fascinated by crime, Prisoners, Prisons and absolutely anything to do with the criminal justice system. I can trace this back to when I was just eight years old. On many a weekend trip down from Buckinghamshire, where I lived, to visit my nan in Sussex we would sometimes get diverted. I loved those diversions because it meant we actually drove through HMP Ford – an open Prison near Arundel.

I can remember the shiver of delight when my mum told me, with exasperation, that we were going to be late for Sunday lunch AGAIN because 'we were being diverted'. I knew that meant passing excitingly close by to who I then thought of as 'criminals' working in the grounds of this open Prison.

I remember getting more and more excited as we drew closer and then craning my neck out of the window to look at these men in their navy blue boiler suits tending to the gardens.

And I distinctly remember meeting the eyes of some of them, who were actually smiling and waving at me! This had me very perplexed. I thought criminals were all evil people? Really, REALLY bad people. And yet here were these smiley, friendly men taking the time to wave back to an eight-year-old peering through the back window of a Ford Escort, openly gawping at them.

Our journey to Sussex diversions happened two or three times a year and every time I grew more fascinated by these men who certainly didn't look evil to me. Some of them had the kindest faces and warmest smiles and the biggest shock to me, at that time, was they looked perfectly normal. My eight-year-old self had expected criminals to be snarling, angry, vicious and very obviously sinister characters. Bill Sikes in *Oliver!* was all I had to go on.

Coupled with watching *Crown Court* on telly, at every opportunity I could, this was as close as I came to the criminal justice system as a child, but the fascination was there.

If only I had known then where that fascination would take me.

When helping people became important

By the time I was in my early 30s, I had been self-employed, running my own employment agency for many years, was earning good money and adored the 'helping people' aspect of my work. Yes, the money was nice, but I felt a much bigger buzz from actually helping people. Some of them in dire circumstances.

There are thousands of examples, but one that has always stuck in my mind is a girl who rang me on a Monday morning about 11 a.m. sobbing. It was difficult to hear what had happened through the sniffles and tears, but I eventually understood she had been made redundant from her job and was beyond terrified – primarily because on the Friday of that week she had bought, and was moving into, a brand-new house with her first ever mortgage and now she was jobless.

I remember doing my best to calm her down, assuring her I would bust a gut to help her, and talking her through several jobs I was currently trying to fill for local companies, several of which I thought were ideal for her.

By the Wednesday afternoon not only had I kept her busy with several interviews but she had been offered a permanent job paying around £5,000 a year more than her previous one. She phoned me, crying again, but this time with happiness and gratitude.

This was what I found satisfying. Helping people. Taking away their sadness and making them happy again.

After working in recruitment, making people happy for fifteen years, I was itching to find a way to help people more. Yes, I could find people jobs but I knew I could help more people in different ways. I just didn't know how.

The answer came to me very unexpectedly on the London Underground.

I was a huge theatre lover at the time and had once fancied myself as a professional actor. I'd been 'spotted' by RADA – The Royal Academy of Dramatic Art – the Holy Grail for anybody wanting to take acting seriously. Somebody important from RADA had come to see me in a play and took me aside afterwards and asked me why I wasn't acting professionally. I had explained I was now twenty-three and had a mortgage. I had also had those opportunities taken away from me by a mother who insisted I do a secretarial course rather than the A-Levels in English, Drama and Theatre Arts I had been accepted to study at the sixth form of a highly respected school with a thriving drama department.

It all seemed too late to do anything about it by then so I carried on working in recruitment, opened my own agency aged twenty-five and resented the fact that I'd never been able to act professionally for the next twenty years!

But the one thing I could do was go to London's West End and watch professional theatre shows, which I did avidly from the age of seventeen onwards. There wasn't a show in the West End for the next fifteen years that I hadn't seen at least once and some up to five times. I was a huge fan of musicals and spent many glorious hours walking up and down London's Shaftesbury Avenue looking for a new show to see.

I would also see a lot of homeless people on the streets and the guilt I felt would cut me to the quick. I would look into the eyes of these people and see the desperation and hopelessness, and found myself dishing out £20 notes on a regular basis, stopping to chat to those who wanted to. I felt an immediate rapport with these people, but I had no idea why.

Going home on the train one night – feeling guilty at shoving £20 notes into homeless peoples' hands and then returning to my comfortable, warm three-bedroomed flat – an advert jumped out at me. It asked if you cared about people? Did you have compassion? Did you want to help people who found themselves homeless? Were you non-judgmental and did you have time to help those who needed it?

I couldn't write the phone number down quickly enough. Something told me this was 100% what I had been looking for.

What I didn't know then, but found out very soon afterwards, was this advert was for *The Big Issue* magazine's first ever mentoring scheme and I was just about to sign up for it.

One step away from finding my vocation

Entering the world of the London homeless was very new to me but instantly gratifying. All my fellow trainees were lovely, as was our instructor. I knew immediately I was in the right place and, more importantly, with the right people. People who cared about some of the most judged and looked-down-on members of society.

We had some hugely informative training on 'homeless culture'. I was like a sponge. I soaked up every snippet of information because I was so desperate to start helping people in the greatest need – and even more desperate to get it right.

I soon found out that some of the other trainees worked for big international banks in the City of London and were allowed one or two days a month 'to volunteer and do good work in the community'. It was their choice as to how they spent this time and these very young people had decided that helping the London homeless was paramount. I loved them for that.

I was soon assigned my first mentee, a girl in her 30s, and set about changing her life! She was very religious and loved volunteering at her church and had written a CV which frankly horrified me. It was all about her church volunteering and writing poetry. Yet she wanted a job in an office! Now this is where I knew my stuff. We ripped up that CV, rewrote it and within weeks she was back working in an office.

I found out afterwards that she had written her CV with the help of staff at *The Big Issue*. Much as I adored everything about *The Big Issue* I couldn't have this! How could they be sending someone out with a CV detailing their church work and how good they were at writing poems when I had uncovered fifteen years' previous experience working in offices?

This was probably the first time I put my head above the parapet, but it definitely wasn't going to be the last! I had a little word with my instructor and before I knew it I was training the entire *Big Issue* staff team on how to write CVs.

For the next seven years I mentored homeless people, moving onto The Depaul Trust Charity when *The Big Issue*'s mentoring scheme became too big for them to manage. During those years I mentored numerous homeless people, including two girls who have gone on to become extremely good friends of mine. One of them nearly didn't make it past our introductory meeting because I couldn't understand most of what she was saying and she spent most of our 'exploratory' meeting in the toilet!

It turned out she was Italian, with a very strong accent, which is why I could only understand one word in three. And instead of taking drugs in the toilets, which I had very naïvely thought she was doing – having been told in the introductory notes that she was a heroin addict – it turned out she had hepatitis C and terrible kidney problems hence spending a good hour in the ladies. I so very nearly turned her down purely because I couldn't understand most of what she was saying but something in me just couldn't. How could I turn down somebody who wanted help?

And I thank God for that every day because twenty-five years later she is one of my very best friends and I adore her.

I had some good successes as a mentor. The Italian girl being one of them. She went on to gain a second degree, got off the heroin for good, moved into a beautiful flat I was envious of, and started working as a lecturer at the university she had studied at.

The third girl I ever mentored had been told by her teachers (who needed sacking) that 'she would end up on the streets'. Well guess what? She did. Don't you just love inspiring teachers like that? Not. I'm hoping they don't exist anymore.

By the time I met her she had a two-year-old daughter and a three-year-old son and was homeless. But she had a big dream and that was to be a teacher. So we set about finding a college that had a crèche. She found one and three years later was the proud owner of her own degree and living in a spacious flat with her gorgeous son and daughter.

I loved mentoring and The Depaul Trust started to use me to help train new mentors. And then came that defining moment – my fabulous supervisor, Joe, said to me one day, 'Would you like more of a challenge?'

Of course my eyes lit up. 'What sort of challenge are we talking about?'

Joe carried on, 'Mentoring recently released Prisoners. We have a separate division that helps Prisoners when they come out of Prison. It's a much tougher job because the vast majority of them go back to Prison, but I'd like to see if you can keep one out for six months.'

You can imagine my reaction. Oh yes! I was up for this. And I wanted to know more. Apparently the person they had in mind for me had been in Prison pretty much solidly from the age of nineteen to thirty-one, but he was due for release and they wanted to see if I could keep him out for longer than he had ever been free as an adult.

And so it began. I met this highly entertaining character and after managing to keep him out for six months, which was the standard mentoring period, they asked me to do something they said they had never done before.

Joe again, 'Er, nobody thought he would ever be out of Prison for six months so would you mind trying to keep him out for another six?'

I could never say no to Joe. I had so much respect for him because, like me, he cared. So began months seven to twelve of keeping this, what I now know to be very-obviously-ADHD, character on the straight and narrow. It wasn't a completely straight road. In fact, it became very rocky at times.

There was the occasion when I stupidly took him to a riverside pub for lunch, instead of the standard coffee shop, and he, ordering two pints at a time, very quickly became rolling drunk. Totally my mistake.

Then he found a job driving a lorry. All good until he had a nasty attack of road rage one day and was banned from driving. But bar these hiccups he was still out of Prison twelve months later.

I spent many hours with him in various London parks talking about his childhood and time in Prison. I learnt so much about how he couldn't stop doing what he did, although he hated himself for it. He was angry at how he'd ruined his 20s by spending all of it in Prison. He was ashamed of how he had very little relationship left with his family who had despaired of him years ago – only his mum would have anything to do with him now and she was fast losing patience herself. How, until he met me, he had assumed that this was how his life was going to be and he really hadn't thought there was an alternative.

I knew absolutely nothing about ADHD at this point or I would've known to fast-track this boy towards a diagnosis and medication, which would have changed his life completely. But as it was, I said goodbye to him after the twelve months, wished him the very best of luck and knew that this was a turning point not only for him, but for me as well.

I had always wanted to help those in the MOST need and to me that seemed to be people who are locked away from the rest of the world because they are so 'bad' they are not even allowed to mix with the general public. Those men at HMP Ford had never left my mind. They didn't look evil to me. There had to be good in them, didn't there?

I had just spent a year working with an ex-Prisoner who I had become very fond of and I knew what I had to do next. There was absolutely no question in my mind.

I had to get into these Prisons.

Who knew getting IN
was just as difficult
as getting OUT

Once I'd made my mind up that I wanted to do something inside a Prison, I thought the next step would be relatively easy. Surely these places were crying out for volunteers and help? I'd never had any trouble getting into all the homeless charities I had volunteered with, which included many years with Crisis and several other big London homeless charities. How wrong could I be?!

It took several weeks of never-ending Googling, researching different Prisons, emailing random people, and investigating charities who might be involved in specific Prisons and could be a potential route for me getting behind those walls.

This is when I learnt for the first time how all Prisons work independently. Up until that point, along with possibly a lot of other people, I had thought that the Ministry of Justice had a system! A system whereby all the Prisons were run in the same way with the same structure.

I threw that idea out of the window straight away because every Prison I was contacting within driving distance of me seemed to have a very different way of gaining access.

Some suggested I should volunteer through Chaplaincy. Others suggested that I start as a Visitor Centre Helper, serving tea and coffee to wives, girlfriends and parents visiting Prisoners. Every Prison seemed to have a different system and it was proving harder than I had expected to infiltrate it. I was prepared to do anything, literally anything, to get my foot in the door but finding anybody to even respond was almost impossible.

I wasn't about to give up. This was my life's dream and surely somebody could make use of me? Eventually, one of my Google searches threw up NACRO – The National Association for the Care and Resettlement of Offenders. I had literally emailed dozens of people offering my help so when NACRO came back to me and invited me for an interview I leapt on it. Soon after, I found myself in a kitchen in Hemel Hempstead with a very elderly lady who was a representative of this organisation.

Over tea and biscuits we had a good chat about my past and, much as she spent a lot of the time looking wistfully out of the window in the kitchen, eventually she decided that because of all my recruitment experience I would probably be of most use on a six-week pre-release course at the local Prison, HMP The Mount.

I didn't care what they did with me. I was at the point of desperation thinking, 'Do something, ANYTHING with me for God's sake.' Here I was with all this passion, compassion and empathy and I needed somewhere to direct it.

Wistful kitchen lady did as she said she would do. She contacted the Prison and very soon I was invited in for an interview with the head of the six-week pre-release course.

When first arriving at the Prison, I knew I hadn't been wrong. I had known pretty much all my life that this was my destiny. As soon as I was let through the airlock and double security gates and into the Prison I felt an incredible adrenaline rush. Excitement beyond compare. I absolutely knew this was where I belonged. It was utterly overwhelming, exciting and terrifying all at the same time. Only terrifying because I didn't know what I was doing. I was never terrified of the boys and men I met.

This Prison seemed huge. HMP The Mount at Bovingdon, near Hemel Hempstead in Hertfordshire, was literally a twenty-minute drive from my house. A category C Male Prison, relatively new and in extremely good condition. Just walking from reception to the workshop was adrenaline fuelled. I couldn't help but smile at the Prisoners walking towards me and to my delight they all smiled back and gave me a nod and a 'hello'.

Finally arriving in the six-week pre-release course workshop I was led to meet Dena, the Course Lead Tutor, and from the minute we met I knew things were going to go well. Dena loved the fact that I had fifteen years of recruitment experience and thought her course, where they were preparing men for release, was going to be absolutely perfect for me. She explained how they were helping men with CVs, writing letters to companies requesting interviews, honing their interview techniques and training them in how to use computers, spreadsheets and other IT skills and she thought my experience would be in invaluable.

At the end of the interview, it was decided that I would come in one afternoon a week and spend two and a half hours helping the Tutors with various aspects of the course. My heart sang as I left the Prison that day knowing that FINALLY I was on the right path.

Getting started

Before I could start, there was a bit of admin that needed sorting. I had to clear a Disclosure and Barring Service (DBS) check, which thankfully was okay, and it was only a few weeks later I found myself in a contained Perspex classroom within the pre-release workshop.

Suddenly I was in front of sixteen men, the vast majority of whom were in their 20s and 30s. One thing I hadn't expected was how much fun I would have with these men. And just how much I would laugh during our sessions. They were very accepting of me right from the beginning, and quickly had me in stitches with their wit and sarcastic humour. Only two weeks later it was decided that I didn't need an Officer in the room with me during our two and a half hour classes. Dena felt I was capable of taking the sessions on my own. I readily agreed. I could relate to these men so easily and they seemed to like me. I certainly liked them.

With hindsight, I now believe this was because they could tell I genuinely didn't see myself as any different to them. I found all of them fascinating, interesting and I didn't for one second think I was any better than any of them. Plus, they made me laugh and I've always been a sucker for anybody who can do that!

So I was more than delighted at the prospect of not having an Officer sitting watching me – I've never liked being watched, but before that something had to change. And that was they had to pay me!

At the time my own employment agency was making good money and I really didn't feel the need to take any of the Prison service's money (oh my! how that would change in future years, but for now I was more than happy working for free). However, it was Prison regulation that I had to be taken on as staff, on an hourly rate, and be called a 'Tutor' rather than a 'Volunteer' if I was to work with these men on my own. All be it in a see-through classroom with Prison Officers and Tutors just the other side of it.

That was sorted very swiftly and then I was really ready to get started with these fabulous characters, who I was warming to more and more by the minute.

Finally, I had a whole bunch of them to myself for two and a half hours a week and I was determined to make a difference to their lives.

I was largely left to my own devices for two and a half hours on a Monday afternoon for the next eighteen months! As long as I was doing something to prepare these men for release and the world of work, rather than returning to their previous dodgy activities, I was trusted to make the best use of that time.

We began with interview technique and role play, which threw up some hysterical scenarios where we would all be weeping with laughter at the intended incompetence of the interviewee and the outrageously rude arrogance of the interviewer.

There were some men who initially sat at the back of the room, slouched in their chairs, determined not to get involved, but before long all of them joined in, not wanting to miss out on the fun.

Using humour, which I now realised was so important to these men, I managed to quite quickly help them realise they had more power and choice than they had thought.

Initially they had assumed the interviewer held all the power. I made it very clear to them that they were there to interview the employer just as much as the other way round. Was this company good enough for them? Did they treat their staff well enough? What was the staff turnover like? How would their role develop within the next five years? All stuff I had been utilising with my employment agency clients for donkey's years by now.

When they realised they had some power and control, their attitude towards interviews changed. I could see it physically in them. Their shoulders would go back, their heads would be held just that little bit higher and I could see some of them performing and presenting themselves extremely well at interviews.

These boys and men took great joy in educating ME and I was all ears. They told me how their blotted DBS's and criminal records were going to stand in the way of getting into the armed forces, working for the post office and certain other jobs. I hadn't thought of this before. How annoying. There was I trying to prepare them for everything and anything, promising them the world was their oyster once they were released, and here were they telling me that a lot of their options were already closed off.

I also noticed that not one of them liked being told what to do. So before long we were moving onto how they could go about setting up as self-employed sole traders.

Some had been self-employed before Prison and between us we came up with numerous other career ideas on my whiteboard with my coloured pens.

Gardening, landscape gardening, window cleaning, car valeting, taxi driving, patio cleaning – it was all possible, on a self-employed basis.

The prospect of this seemed to excite them much more, so having set up my own business I cracked on with sessions on how to start working for yourself. They were all ears when it came to how to get an accountant and why you needed one, what information needed to go on a business card, how to create promotional and marketing material, and what and when you needed to notify the Inland Revenue to keep yourself legal.

I could tell this floated their collective boat much more than working for somebody else's company.

And it was during these eighteen months that the first seeds were sown for me thinking about training to be a counsellor. This all came about from the men, not from me. One by one they would come up to me and ask if they could talk to me privately. I never said no to any of them. We were short of time, but we managed fifteen to twenty minutes at coffee break halfway through class and then again after we had finished, before the Officers came to collect them to go back to their cells.

It was during these one-to-one sessions that I knew I had been right all along. These men weren't evil. All of them had a story. And some of the stories were absolutely tragic.

One man in his early 40s had worked for The Royal Opera House in London as a Production Manager for twenty years. He had a completely unblemished record till he was off sick for the first time in two decades. He had his pay docked, which he didn't agree with so had challenged it. At the point he wasn't able to feed his kids anymore, with no money coming in, he very temporarily became involved in dealing drugs, literally to feed his family. He was immediately caught. Probably due to his incompetence and not knowing what he was doing.

Another man had been a Management.Consultant in the international food transportation industry – a professional and educated man in his 50s who had never committed a crime in his life. Until the day a large client of his went bust, owing him a lot of money. He had a shipment due to leave and, finding himself short of cash for the first time ever, took up one of the many offers to include drugs in his shipment, which for the last thirty years he had always refused to do. There was a large amount of money on offer and, only due to the client going bust, he felt he had no choice. He was caught almost immediately and found himself in Prison.

Another young lad, aged about twenty-six, had set up a post-pub delivery service. I thought this was ingenious. Bearing in mind we were still in the mid 2000s, before online 24-hour deliveries. He had a team of vans and drivers ready to supply anything and everything to customers who had come home from the pub too drunk and over the driving limit to go out and get it themselves!

He and his team had a full menu of 'purchasables' from alcohol – including wine, beer and the most popular spirits – to kebabs, cigarettes, chocolate and fast food, and he and his business partner were expanding the business and making very good money. He actually said to me one day, quietly when nobody else was listening, 'I shouldn't be in here, Sarah. I come from a good family. My mum and dad both work, my brother is an accountant and my sister is manager of a building society. I feel really bad because I know I didn't need to end up in here, whereas I can see so many of these others were destined for this life.' I cannot remember what he was in Prison for, but I truly hope he never went back.

I also met a lovely French man who was calm, polite, quite gentle and sophisticated. I couldn't think for the life of me what would've put him behind bars, until he told me one day.

He'd been in a pub with his sister. A drunk man had been pestering the sister all evening and just would not leave her alone. Eventually, my man had lost patience with this drunk and pushed him away from his sister. The drunk had fallen backwards, hit his head on the pub fire hearth, cracked his head open and a purely protective brother had been sentenced to Prison.

My heart broke for each and every one of these boys and men.

My eight-year-old self had been so right. They weren't evil. Life had been going very well for most of them until one slip-up had had catastrophic consequences.

Trouble of the Gemini kind ... and the BIG decision

Every six weeks I would be given a new bunch of sixteen men. As the second lot arrived for the first class, rowdy and raucous, I left them to their own devices for ten minutes, sorting my own pens and notes out, knowing they had only just been let out of their cells and had a lot of excess energy to release.

Suddenly, crashing through the door, came one of my 'course one' lads, outraged and bellowing at all of them. I don't know who was more shocked, me or them. But in no uncertain terms he told them to 'SHUT the FUCK up,' that, 'She's alright this one', and that they needed to show me a lot of respect. God love him!

Suitably subdued, we started the second group. In it was a young man aged twenty-six. In years to come – because Prison etiquette says you never ask anybody what they are in Prison for – I would find out that he had been, in his own words, 'a crap armed robber'. He hadn't ever bothered to go further than ten miles away from his hometown so within quite a short time was caught.

It turned out this boy and I both came from the same Buckinghamshire town. I didn't live there anymore but had been to junior and senior school there and spent a lot of my younger years in the town he had been born in and still lived in. I also drove through it on my way to and from the Prison.

He was desperately homesick, so in every session he spent a few minutes asking which shops were still there, which takeaways were still open, if this pub or that pub was still open ... and anything else he could think of about his town. His eyes would mist over when I'd tell him that our joint favourite takeaway was still there and thriving! I kept to myself the sad thought of how long a time it was going to be before he would be wolfing down another of their burgers.

It brought it home to me, hard, that while I drove through this town an hour later on my way back home, somebody could be in Prison literally six miles away, but hadn't seen his own hometown for four years. How bloody difficult must that be? I thought this every time I drove through it and passed our joint favourite burger bar. This alone taught me never to take my freedom for granted again.

Not only did we share a connection to the town but we soon found out that we shared a birthday. And it so happened that one of my working days was on our joint birthday.

As I walked into the Perspex classroom that day he had his arms raised in the air, and with a big grin and a very loud "APPY BIRTHDAY' greeted me along with a big, but brief, bear hug.

This brought my very first telling-off in a Prison. Sadly, it's not going to be the last! But this one was handled beautifully.

I was told by one of the Officers at the end of the day, 'We saw what happened – just don't touch them.' I explained it was both our birthdays and he had taken me off-guard. The Officer said he completely understood but just to bear it in mind in future.

I would come to respect how this 'mistake' was handled. It was an honest mistake and not one I would ever make again.

For the next eighteen months, I adored my Monday afternoons at HMP The Mount. I worked with hundreds of different young and older men and I can honestly say I enjoyed every single second. The one-to-ones continued weekly, when I just hoped and prayed I was doing and saying the right things. I was listening. Not judging. Trying to keep Prisoners positive about their futures and DEFINITELY steering them away from criminal activities.

I like to think I was opening their eyes to a crime-free future and giving them the confidence to know that only THEY had the choice of whether to bring their past into their future. Or leave it where it belonged. Behind them.

I was adoring the Prison environment and loving my work, but I still knew I could do more. These snatched one-to-ones weren't long enough. I needed to sit with these men for much longer than fifteen minutes. To get to know them, their stories, their hopes and fears on a deeper level and to have the time and tools to help them.

And then I had it. The lightbulb moment. I needed to train to be a counsellor. I might have been one year off my 50th birthday but that was never going to hold me back. I knew I had to train professionally to help these Prisoners, so with a very heavy heart I asked for a meeting with Dena.

She had been nothing but supportive from day one and carried on being so. She thought me training to be a counsellor was a brilliant idea. She had often remarked that I seemed to have a noticeably easy rapport with every Prisoner I came across and she had seen how they would open up to me.

Dena asked me if I would please come back and do my placement at her Prison. At that point I had absolutely no idea what a 'placement' was, but I assured her that I would! I would've done anything for this woman as she had given me such a fantastic opportunity and the freedom to run my sessions with the men however I wanted. She knew I had their best interests at heart and gave me complete autonomy to manage myself and do the job as well as I possibly could.

As I climbed into my car in the Prison car park after my last session there were tears, but I was also very motivated and excited because I knew I could do more to help these boys and men. And if that meant leaving the Prison temporarily so I could focus completely on training to be a counsellor, I would do it knowing as soon as I possibly could, I would be back.

Counselling training, pipe cleaners and bloody Carl Rogers

Once I've decided to do something I need to do it straight away. So I was immediately back onto Google trying to find the most local college to start my counselling training. This was in the October and annoyingly I had just missed the September start. There was no way I was waiting till the following September, so I found a course that started in the January.

For those of you who know nothing about counselling, and at that point that very much included me, I made a horrific mistake. I started on a course that was for 'person-centred' counselling. I didn't actually know that there were any different 'modalities' or versions of counselling. I was that naïve. I just thought you trained to be a counsellor and that was the end of it.

But no, apparently there are theoretically different forms of counselling and I had stumbled over the least appropriate for me! Somewhat typical. I can be incredibly gormless at times and I'm the first to admit it.

Person-centred counselling is the least pro-active of any of them. There's no delving into peoples' pasts, there's no giving them tools to help themselves in the future, and it's all just a matter of sitting there listening, reflecting back to the client what they have said, asking them 'How does that make you feel' on a very regular basis and doing not a lot else.

The bloke who invented this style of counselling was Carl Rogers. I despised him. I was most often heard saying that 'if he wasn't dead, I'd kill him myself'. I found his theory, what little there was of it, so deathly dull, boring and massively lacking in tools to help people.

If I had done my research, which I hadn't, I would've known that a humanistic, psychodynamic, Adlerian, integrative or transactional analysis course would've been far better suited to me. But no. Zero research. I just flung myself on the first course I could find, assuming that all counselling training was the same.

I put myself through this torture for five and a half years. I had a wonderful Tutor who humoured me when I lost the plot every time she pulled pipe cleaners out of the cupboard and made us get on the floor with a big piece of paper and crayons. This wasn't what I wanted to do! I wanted theory. I wanted to know how to help these very complex boys and men in Prison. Sticking a pipe cleaner on a piece of paper wasn't going to help any of them.

Only the last year was useful. After I had qualified in this person-centred nonsense, in 2015, I knew I had to do more training as I had bugger all tools to help people with. A year of cognitive behavioural therapy (CBT) training sorted that out and I finally felt ready to see clients once I had started my CPCB Level 5 in CBT.

But before I could get to Level 5 I had the torture of Level 4. This two-year diploma, which I honestly think I could've learnt in a month, involved getting the hallowed placement Dena had talked about and invited me to go back to her Prison to do.

A placement consisted of you nearly always working for free for a charitable organisation and gaining your 100 hours that were needed to pass this wretched and torturous Level 4.

So everybody else was flicking through the college-provided pamphlet with possible placements, which primarily seemed to be for Cruse the bereavement charity, Place 2 Be for kids and a few random others. None of which appealed to me.

I knew where I was going. Straight back to my beloved Prison, HMP The Mount. Just as Dena had asked.

That was until I encountered the Head of Counselling. This woman was abrasive and blunt to say the least. She told me, in no uncertain terms, that I had done 'the wrong sort of counselling to work in a Prison' and there was no way she was letting me loose on her clients. I couldn't believe it. I had only done counselling training to work in a Prison and now it turned out, because I had sweated through a namby-pamby counselling course, she wouldn't entertain the idea of me volunteering there. I begged, I pleaded, I wrote emails, I spoke to her on the phone several times, but no, she was absolutely adamant I was not going back to HMP The Mount to do my placement. I was heartbroken but not deterred.

At college the next evening I grabbed hold of this placement pamphlet and happened to see on one page there was mention of Aylesbury Young Offender Institute. Young Offenders? Nothing horrified me more. I had images of arsey, arrogant eighteen-year-olds, whereas I had been used to lovely men in their 20s, 30s and 40s. But it was no good. There were no other

Prisons within an hour's driving distance so I had to apply to do my placement at HMP YOI Aylesbury.

It really didn't fill me with joy and I was deeply disappointed I couldn't go back to HMP The Mount but if I was going to get into a Prison, it had to be Aylesbury Young Offenders. So the application process began.

Yet again, getting into a Prison was just as hard as getting out but nothing was going to stop me. I was going back inside a Prison and nothing, absolutely nothing, was going to hold me back.

Sex offenders
and paperclips

There was a lot more frustration getting into this Prison than any of the others before or after. I had been given a name to email and apparently they were the only person who could interview me and see if I was suitable to work with these snotty teenagers! I was still not happy about the prospect of working with arsey kids but I wasn't doing my placement anywhere other than a Prison, so Aylesbury it had to be.

There followed approximately three months of utter frustration, emailing this email address I'd been promised was the right one then not hearing from them for weeks. It was so difficult to know how often to email as I didn't want to come across as annoying, but it was infuriating hearing back from them with no offer of an interview – just a random question and then silence for weeks. Eventually, and God knows I could've given up because most people would've done, I had an email from the Prison saying, 'Oh, I'm sorry, I thought you were a trainee Psychologist.'

For heaven's sake! I had sent my CV and been very clear all along that I was a Trainee Counsellor. Eventually, they did offer me an interview time and I was thrilled to have half a foot in the door. Although, because everything had been so haphazard and disorganised, I wasn't sure it would happen until I actually arrived on the day.

On the afternoon of the interview I was stomach-churningly anxious and hugely excited in equal measures. Stepping through the gate and walking through the Prison I could feel the adrenaline coursing through my veins again.

I knew everything hung on this meeting. I had to make a good impression and I had to get over the fact that I had already been shocked at how incompetent this numpty had been at simply arranging an interview. It really shouldn't take three months when somebody is offering to help in a Prison for free.

Anyway, I was now there. Walking through the crumbling old Victorian Prison to the Admin block.

I didn't immediately warm to my interviewer but I had to get over that, and quickly, because I desperately needed to impress them.

We sat in a tatty, cluttered office. The sun was streaming onto my face, but no thought was given to how comfortable I was – and then came the first question. 'How entrenched are you in person-centred theory?'

Damn. For the first time in my life, I paused before I answered. I knew so much hung on this. One Prison hadn't wanted me simply because I'd studied this mind-numbing theory and now I was being asked by another what I thought of it.

I'm usually very impulsive when I reply, and words pour out of my mouth before I think, but this time there was definitely a pause, a big one, as I desperately gathered my thoughts. I decided the best answer was – 'I like it as far as it goes, but for me personally, it doesn't go far enough.'

I waited. Had I just blown my chances completely? By telling someone I had spent the last five and a half years learning something that another Prison wouldn't even entertain? Could they be a massive Carl Rogers and person-centred counselling fan and expect me to be more passionate about that theory? I really didn't know, as I sweated and dripped in the sun.

'Right answer, because it doesn't cut it here,' came back the reply.

Thank GOD. I'd got it right AND I'd been honest. Phew.

The interview only went on for about fifteen minutes as I spoke about my volunteering experience with ex-Prisoners in the community and my eighteen months at HMP The Mount.

Then it was decided we would go on a tour of the Prison but before we did my escort put a large silver paperclip in their fringe to hold it back. I thought that was slightly odd but didn't say anything.

Before we left the office, I was pointed to one of the caged areas where a group of boys were lolling around. I'll never forget these words. 'That's the sex offender Wing. They aren't allowed out when the others are out. Most of them are in here for sleeping with their sisters.' Not sure what I was supposed to say to that so I think I just mumbled an 'okay'.

We then went on a very short tour of some of the Prison and it couldn't have been more different to the clean and relatively new-build HMP The Mount. It was old, damp, walls were crumbling and the whole place looked like it needed knocking down, but for me this was still heaven and where I wanted to be.

Meeting some random person I had just been introduced to, as we departed, I was admonished for not telling my interviewer about the paperclip they had put in their own hair! I thought this extremely strange. Why would I comment on the paperclip when they had put it there? Maybe this was a version of humour, but I didn't find it funny.

However, back in the office it seemed I had passed the test because I was told I could have the placement, but before I did I had to do some of the obligatory Prison training. I was euphoric but tried not to show it. This interviewer didn't seem to have emotions. So I thanked them very much for their time and was walked to the gate and told to wait to hear about the training.

This couldn't have been more different to my first meeting with Dena, but I could get over that because I had just been told I could do my placement in a Prison and that had been my one and only goal.

I was happy. And gagging to start.

Guns, knives and toothbrushes

Surprisingly, bearing in mind the lengthy delays before, it was only a matter of two or three weeks before I was back in the Prison to do my training.

This was very exciting and as I settled into my seat in the back row it was easy talking to my neighbours, who all seemed to be nurses, admin staff or Prison Officers who were either redoing the training or there for the first time, like me. One timid, nervous Officer, thirty-five-ish, had been off sick for six months after being stabbed in the Prison and he was gently easing himself back in by doing the training again. These people were warm and friendly and couldn't have been more different to the strange, cold, paperclip oddball. I was soon chatting with several lovely nurses and was relieved to see that there were nice people working at the Prison who I could actually relate to.

I have to say, in my whole HMPS career this training was the best. I learnt about all the innovative ways Prisoners turned simple everyday objects into dangerous weapons. The one that fascinated and horrified me the most was a simple toothbrush. Prisoners would melt an area of the toothbrush head and ram into it two razor blades, approximately one centimetre away from each other. I was told this was because when you slashed somebody's face the gashes were too close together to be stitched up properly, so their victim would be left with a very obvious scar.

I'm sure I wasn't supposed to be, but I was secretly quite impressed at the innovative ideas these Prisoners had, but equally hoped I was never on the receiving end of any of them! Especially when we came to knife and gun training. This was serious stuff. We all had to stand up in pairs, with one pretending to hold a knife or a gun, and we were instructed on the best ways to get out of the situation.

Luckily for me, I was told the best way is with your mouth. Talking and reasoning was always the best option. This pleased me because if there's one thing I could do, it was communicate with Prisoners. I wasn't quite so hot on the physical side of things, but I did manage to very deftly remove a gun from my partner when she was pointing it at me. I'm not sure I would be anywhere near as confident to do this if it was a real gun, but I managed it several times with my partner holding her fake gun.

The next training was even better. This was run by the Prison department, 'Safer Custody'. The role of this department is to keep Prisoners safe. To stop them self-harming and most definitely to stop suicides in Prison. It's a hugely valuable department and we were due two days training by them.

Aylesbury's disorganisation and the chaos I had experienced so far was still lingering, because the first day I turned up for training, after sitting there for an hour and a half with two other trainees, we were informed, 'The Tutor has forgotten and the training won't be happening, so go home.' This was infuriating when you have arranged cover for your business and paid someone to work for you, just to be turned away because somebody had forgotten to put it in their own diary.

But when I finally did get my two days training it was excellent. I was particularly impressed with the suicide awareness section. Although we had touched on suicide during my counselling diploma this was by far more in-depth. I still remember, to this day, so much of what I learnt in those sessions and they were incredibly valuable.

And then I was done. I had passed the training, my DBS was still clear, and I was given the first date when I would be starting my placement.

It was agreed I would go in once a week at the beginning, but I made it clear I was more than happy to go in two afternoons a week and see six clients. Three each day.

I can't possibly describe to you how excited I was to be finally going to work in a Prison, one-to-one with a Prisoner. It was just a shame it was going to be a snotty teenager, but at that point I didn't care. I just wanted to get my hands on somebody in Prison who wanted help, because I had so much help to give. It was literally exploding out of me.

The disorganised paperclip interviewer told me that they would leave referrals in a certain pigeonhole and I would need to go there on my first day to find out who my number one client was.

To say I couldn't wait was an understatement, but nothing could've prepared me for the first client I was allocated.

Finally – a Prison Counsellor, albeit a Trainee

It was August 2013 by the time I was first on shift and itching to see my very first arsey teenager!

That morning I'd chosen my clothing very appropriately, now considering myself an old hand at the Prison system after eighteen months at HMP The Mount. I arrived in my low-heeled black flat boots, 'regulation' dark denim jeans (no rips), a dark top with absolutely no flesh showing between the top and the jeans, and a waterproof knee-length jacket, because most of the time it pissed it down with rain in Prisons. I don't know if they have their own particular weather system, but I've encountered more rain in Prison yards than anywhere else!

The 'no flesh between the top and the bottom' seemed to be particularly important bearing in mind one poor volunteer at The Mount had been attacked. And the reason given? She had had an inch of flesh exposed beneath her crop top and her bottoms. Seems that one inch of flesh got the better of one sex-starved Prisoner, who had launched himself at her and managed to get her the sack and him removed to another Prison. I hadn't been in that day so annoyingly I'd missed the drama, which had happened in our pre-release workshop.

I wasn't making that mistake – not that anybody would've wanted to see my muffin top. Mine wasn't young, tight and firm like hers had apparently been. It wasn't so much one muffin as a small bakers with several rolls and they weren't going on display for anybody.

So I arrived at the gate, in the ever-present rain, having left absolutely everything in my car apart from a pen and a notebook, triple checking that I hadn't brought my mobile phone, chewing gum or anything with me that would get me into trouble before I even started.

I was registered and signed in by an Officer sitting in a hut, who then approved my entrance to the Prison but not before passing through Security.

Security was a much bigger and brighter office where they patted me down and made me remove everything from my pockets, somewhat like security at an airport. Once I was through there I was in the Prison good and proper, complete with, for the very first time, a Prison belt and Prison keys. Oh my, did I feel official now.

It was at this moment I realised I hadn't a clue how to find the Admin block. This had never been a problem at The Mount because I was escorted everywhere, but at Aylesbury I was to be trusted with my own keys and belt. I was on my own.

Everywhere looked the same and the only reason I knew to turn left or go straight forward was because the right was blocked off with red and white no-entry tape as that section of the Prison had collapsed and was now a rotting, sodden and dangerous 'no-go' area.

I plumped for left, as this seemed a bigger pathway leading round the back of the Prison, and used my keys for the first time. This was terrifying because not only did each 'pass' have two gates and two locks, which you had to find two keys for, but then on the other side you had to remember to lock both gates and both locks with the same two keys.

Luckily on the other side of this first set of gates I found two cheery looking Officers who pointed me in the direction of the Admin block. I arrived sweating with anxiety but relieved to have found the place, and even more relieved to see that the paperclip fruit loop wasn't in the office, so I didn't have to encounter them today.

I found the huge wall of pigeonholes they had referred to and eventually found the tiny tatty sticker saying 'counselling'. I reached my hand in and as promised there was my envelope.

I opened it with excitement and found my first client had a completely unpronounceable name! It also announced he was on A Wing so there came my next problem. How in God's name did I find A Wing?

Back out into the torrential rain and there, like a shining beacon on my right, on the other side of the big concrete Association area, was a plain white sign announcing 'A & B Wings'. I strode over there as quick as I could, dodging puddles and used my keys to open the huge metal gates onto A Wing.

Finding a friendly Officer holding a clipboard, I assumed he might know and asked him if he had, per chance, a 'Dante' on his Wing. I'd settled on the pronunciation as 'Don-Tay' and it seemed I was right. I will never forget his words, 'Oh yes, there is only one Dante in this Prison,' (*Thank Christ for that*, I thought but didn't say. I was already dripping wet without having to go and find another Wing) and he trundled off to get him for me. I stood there twiddling my thumbs, taking in everything around me.

This was a big Wing. There were a lot of what looked like eighteen to twenty-two-year-olds out of their cells. The noise levels were deafening – boys shouting at each other, being shouted at by Officers, and all the boys looking bored, with a few of them playing table tennis. There was tension in the air. Most people would've run a mile, but I knew I was in the right place and was back in my favourite environment. I loved it from the start. I could've done without the shouting, but the adrenaline was once again pumping through my veins.

Shortly afterwards, my friendly Officer was walking back towards me with a boy behind him. I was about to meet my first arsey teenager.

Together we were shown to a strange room, which was certainly nothing like the 'calm, tranquil, confidential and safe space therapy rooms' we had been taught were the norm at college. This was the junction of A Wing and B Wing, at right angles with each other, and was literally the room in the corner which passed for a corridor between the two Wings! It had two grey metal chairs that had definitely seen better days, one very small table and two doors. One leading onto A Wing and one leading onto B Wing.

Me and Dante took our seats, with me giving him the one behind the table as I thought taking it would make me look like the person in control and that was the last thing we wanted in a counselling relationship – again drummed into me at college.

The Officer locked the door and was gone, and there I was with my very first arsey teenager. Except he wasn't. What he was was extremely embarrassed and self-conscious.

Hmmm. Had to get over this. I did the usual counselling introduction of telling him who I was, how long the session would last, that everything was confidential (unless it caused concern that he was a risk to himself or to others), that he was in charge of the session and what we talked about was his choice – and how would he like to start?

Feeling rather relieved for remembering all that after having the 'standard intro' pummelled into my brain for the last five and a half years, I was person-centred through and through and ready for him to unload.

I was met with silence. Then what happened was he laid his head down on the table with his arms stretched wide either side and said, 'Well this is awkward.'

It seemed Dante and I might have something in common. I knew this drippy person-centred theory wasn't going to be enough for working with these boys and was no help in building rapport, so quickly I said, 'Look, would you rather I asked you questions and we did it that way?'

He nodded so vehemently I knew I was on the right track. And we were off.

What I didn't know yet was how much I was going to need to help this boy. Had I known in advance I think my brain would have exploded there and then.

Paris, London and Kevin

I soon found out why somebody with the name of Dante had found himself in Prison in Buckinghamshire. This boy had been born in Paris, France, and told me very early on he had been taken off his mother in Paris and given to an aunt to bring up in Hertfordshire. As had his older brother.

My inquisitive brain immediately wanted to know why but it soon became clear this was a very touchy subject for Dante. He had never asked and he didn't want to know. Neither did his brother.

Even more bizarrely, his aunt in Hertfordshire had renamed him Kevin. Kevin for heaven's sake! But Dante had found out his real name when he was thirteen and reverted to it. With all due respect to the Kevins out there – who wouldn't!

Once we had thrown person-centred theory out of the window, and decided to just talk, I started to find out so much more about him. The more I did the more I realised I had been hideously pre-judgmental about Young Offenders and this was the very start of me adoring the whole lot of them and, without a shadow of a doubt, of Young Offenders becoming my absolute favourite client group! I'm the first to admit when I'm wrong and I'd been very wrong about this.

Dante might have been born in France but his beautiful golden skin and chocolate brown eyes told me he wasn't a native. It turned out his family were from what had originally been the French Republic of Congo in Africa.

Dante had been brought up in Hertfordshire by his aunt who had had Dante, a newborn baby of two weeks, and his two-year-old brother thrust upon her before she went on to have three children of her own. The poor woman must've been run ragged and didn't notice when Dante, aged fourteen, had been enticed off to Norwich for a week to be trained as a drug dealer.

This made me think of myself at fourteen. If I was ten minutes late home from school my mother would've worried and been fretting on the front doorstep and she certainly would've noticed if I had evaporated for a day, never mind a week. But apparently this boy wasn't missed for the seven days he spent up in Norfolk. And this is really where it all began to go horribly wrong for him.

It ended tragically when his uncle, who he considered his father, died. His aunt was in hospital at the same time as his uncle, both of them with pneumonia, and the whole family were thrown into panic. Dante had been arrested just previous to them both becoming seriously ill and hospitalised. He had been on the run, as he told me, 'not very far because I was only staying with my girlfriend', but by the time he snuck in to the hospital to say goodbye to his subjugate dad, he had already passed away.

Dante couldn't forgive himself for this. He credited his uncle with keeping him on the straight and narrow and had been desperate to impress him. He felt he had ruined everything and was still grieving for the man he considered his father.

Time already spent on remand, and serving 50% of the sentence behind bars and the rest on licence, meant

Dante was due to serve eleven months. But he was still absolutely livid with himself about this and beating himself up spectacularly well.

During our sessions, Dante told me constantly how he considered he was now 'behind' his peers. How he desperately wanted to make his family proud of him, and how he was now wasting time and getting behind everybody else who was out there achieving in life.

One thing Dante kept repeating, which would come back to haunt me, was how he knew he thought differently to other people. He must've told me this at least ten times and at the time I thought little of it.

He adored his girlfriend Katie and absolutely did not want to spend his life in Prison. These were the recurring themes.

He told me he had spent summers in France and it was only during those summer holidays he had realised his real mum was actually French.

I felt we did some good work from the August to the Christmas as Dante was due to be released at the very beginning of January.

I managed to help him accept that in the great scheme of things eleven months wasn't a terribly long time. Many people took a gap year and he could just consider that this was his. We made so many plans for the future. Dante did as many courses in Prison as he possibly could, and I hoped I had helped him re-frame his misdemeanours as a teenager, knowing he could start life again aged nineteen. And he really wasn't that far behind anybody.

Dante and I had no choice but to get used to the constant tap-tap on the door as an Officer came through, usually followed by a boy carrying a large clear plastic bag with all his worldly goods in it, as he moved Wing. These interruptions happened anywhere between two and five times during our one-hour sessions.

Anybody in the counselling profession would have a coronary about this but it's something you get used to in Prisons. Dante and I became very used to stopping mid-sentence and picking up again as soon as yet another boy and an Officer had moved from one Wing to the other.

Dante had been incredibly hurt when his aunt had booked a visit and then not turned up. He had to phone home that night to find out she'd actually gone to France for a wedding and forgotten all about him.

This is about the most cruel thing you can do to somebody in Prison. Sitting in the Visit Hall waiting for your visitor who doesn't show has to be the most crippling rejection somebody can feel, and my heart broke for him when he told me this. Not only had he been let down, but all the other Prisoners in the Visit Hall had seen his humiliation.

As autumn came, Dante told me that he was being visited by a UK Border Rep due to him being born in France, but as he had only been there for two weeks he had been told by everybody and their dog that it wouldn't be a problem. Nobody thought he would get deported.

Dante's main concern was that he wouldn't be released on 4 January as planned while they fannied around at the Foreign Office. He was itching to get on with his new life.

The meetings with the UK Border Rep threw up a faint chance of the Foreign Office trying to deport him and he had been told to find himself an immigration solicitor. This is not easy when you are eighteen, stuck inside Prison with very little credit on your phone, no access to the internet and getting very little help from anybody in the Prison.

So drumroll ... fanfare! This is the very first time I 'stepped outside the bounds of counselling'. Much more about that later, but how could I not help this boy? We were now at the end of October, it was Halloween, and I had been working with him since the height of summer. He mattered to me and I wanted to do everything I could to help him.

I soon found Dante an immigration solicitor actually based in Aylesbury. When I went to meet the man, he told me there was very little chance of Dante being deported because he had lived in the UK longer than 50% of his life.

Too right he had! He'd been in Paris for literally two weeks and in Hertfordshire for eighteen years! I was assured this was just the Foreign Office ticking boxes and he really had nothing to worry about.

So we carried on our sessions knowing the immigration solicitor was doing the necessary. Dante was moved to D Wing, which was fine for him but not so great for me when I walked out of the gate and came crashing down onto hard concrete. I'd fallen off a huge step that I swear was illegal. But everybody in the Prison was used to it except me! Bloodied knuckles, ruined jeans and injured pride was the only damage done. And I never went out of that particular gate again!

My last session with Dante was on 17 December 2013. I was so sad to say goodbye to this boy, who I'd become very fond of, but I knew that was what counselling was all about. We had done whole sessions on 'endings' at College and I hadn't realised at the time that this was something I was going to be absolutely appalling at! But I said goodbye to him. Wished him all the very best. Reassured him that he had not wasted any time, had instead done a huge amount of training in Prison and, importantly, I didn't want to see him in Prison ever again. He was far too intelligent and driven for that.

That was in the December. Dante was due for release on 4 January, before I was back in the Prison after the Christmas break.

Guess who was the first person I saw when I returned in January?

New Year surprises, Solicitors and baby books

Back into the Prison on 7 January, on my way to meet a new client, I suddenly, and very unexpectedly, heard my name being called again and again and again. I couldn't see anyone among the sea of grey sweatshirts and sagging grey jogging bottoms, not to mention hear much above the extreme shouting levels that were ever-present at Aylesbury. But eventually I saw somebody waving what looked like white papers in the air and realised it was Dante.

I was due to see another client in fifteen minutes, but I was never going to ignore this one. So I scuttled down the Wing as quick as I could to find out what was going on.

Dante looked scared and anxious as he showed me a letter from the Foreign Office. He hurriedly told me that he had already filled in the appeal, which I was very impressed with, although I had always known he was a bright boy. But he said he still needed my help.

What's a girl to do? A girl who cares anyway. Stand there and tell him, 'I'm sorry this falls outside the boundaries of counselling.' I don't think so. I threw my bag down on the nearby table-tennis table and started to read the letter he'd been waving at me.

I noticed a very strange plopping noise as I was reading and I asked him what it was. 'Oh don't worry about that, that's just the rain.' Really? Rain was dripping onto a table-tennis table, just outside his cell, and Dante was obviously so used to it meant nothing to him. I was appalled. Dear God. At least the Prison service could keep them dry, couldn't it?

This letter looked pretty serious to me. It told Dante that he was going to be deported to France as soon as he left Prison. There was also a letter from the UK Border Agency, full of inaccuracies. It was quite clear that his Offender Manager hadn't notified these authorities of any of the courses he had done or the certificates he had gained. Instead it looked like Dante had done absolutely nothing in the eleven months inside, whereas I knew he had done every course he could in a bid to not waste any more of his life and not fall any further behind his mates on the outside.

I knew how much this would be affecting Dante. I knew he would be terrified of losing his girlfriend and being forced away from everything he had ever known.

We had laughed in many a session about how crap his French was. The boy wasn't even going to be able to speak the language if they plonked him in Paris.

Anyway, he had appealed and now we just had to wait to hear what would happen next. I so felt for him. I couldn't imagine how anyone could have no choice as to which country they lived in.

I managed to carry on seeing Dante once a week (unbeknown to the paperclip prawn who would probably have had something to say about that) until on 28 January Dante told me he was due in court on the Friday. He looked absolutely terrified. He was frantically giving me his girlfriend's number, his mum's number, his sister's and his brother's.

I asked him very tentatively, as I had no idea if it was actually possible, whether he would like me to speak on his behalf. He literally threw his arms up in the air and shouted, 'Yes, please!' That was nice validation to receive. If I could do it or not was another matter.

Meanwhile, I had work to do. I had to prove that this boy had more connection with England than he did France. And for that we had to go right back to when he was a baby, aged two weeks. I spoke to his sister, who was extremely helpful, and then spent the next few days dashing between Hertfordshire and Buckinghamshire trying to get hold of his Red Baby Book, to show that Dante had been inoculated in the UK, and his school reports, to show he had been educated in England. But just as I was gathering everything I possibly could Dante had another letter notifying him he wasn't needed in court on the Friday. Panic over. It was just 'procedural', whatever that meant.

It was during these 'in-between' sessions I finally found out why Dante had been given away as a baby. Bearing in mind he was born in 1990, towards the end, but still very much in the AIDS epidemic. It turned out his French mother was HIV positive. Dante mentioned this in passing not realising the relevance of it until I explained that in those early days of AIDS/HIV it was thought that you could easily pass the infection on. I told him as gently as I could that I didn't think his French mother gave him away at all. I think he and his brother were taken off his French mother. I could see him taking this in but he wasn't convinced. Not at first. That perceived rejection was going to be hard to shake off.

As January rolled into February, I continued to see Dante, gathering as much evidence as I could of his links with the UK and on 11 March he and I met with his immigration solicitor. The solicitor agreed I could speak on his behalf. Dante showed me the statement he had written stating why he should be allowed to stay in the UK. I showed him the one I had written and we both read the one his girlfriend had written. All three of them were powerful in my view, but what hope did we have against the Foreign Office?

It was during this time that Dante asked me if I could test him for autism. He had always said he knew he 'thinks differently to other people' and he wondered if this was due to autism. I brought in a simple screener from the outside, but he didn't screen anywhere nearly high enough for autism so we left it. We had more important things to deal with, including correspondence between the solicitor and the Foreign Office.

When I went into the Prison on 8 April, I had the shock of my life. He had gone. Evaporated. Thank the heavens I had those phone numbers. I couldn't wait to get out of the Prison that day to call his solicitor, his sister and his girlfriend, only to find out that all four of us were desperately trying to find him.

In the afternoon, I had a phone call from a strange phone number. I could've cried. It was Dante. It turned out he had been shipped to an Immigration Removal Centre at Colnbrook near Heathrow Airport. He was desperate to see me so we arranged that I would go over the next afternoon. But not before one of the strangest conversations of my life. When I asked him if there was anything he needed he said, 'Yes, pants.' This was definitely going outside the bounds of counselling! However, pants he needed so pants he would have.

The next day, when I had battled through the traffic to get to Heathrow and pulled into one of the two Immigration Removal Centres bang next to the airport, clutching the pants, I walked into this very strange building. Nothing like a Prison, but also nothing like any other building I had been into before.

And there was my boy. No more grey tracksuit. He was looking incredibly smart in his own clothes. It was shocking to see him in anything other than his Prison-issue sweatshirt and jogging bottoms. But there he was in pristine white trainers, dark navy blue jeans, a crisp white, obviously expensive, T-shirt and a navy blue padded jacket. I've never hugged anybody so hard in my life as I did Dante that day. I just didn't want to let him go. Hadn't life been hard enough for him up to now? How could they do this to somebody who had only been in France for two weeks and in England for the other now nineteen years?

That was the first of many trips to the Immigration Removal Centre as we now knew he was definitely going to go to court and I was going to be allowed to speak on his behalf. As was his girlfriend, who was seventeen and absolutely petrified of going to court but was determined to help Dante. I'd never met her, but I'd spent most of the last year talking about Katie so I was fascinated to meet her.

We were ready for this. The preparation had been done. The solicitor had been fantastic. We had gathered as much evidence as we possibly could that Dante belonged in England, not in France, and now all we had left to do was face a Judge and take on the Foreign Office!

The final time I left Dante I hugged him even tighter, not knowing what lay ahead and terrified for him and the uncertainty of it all.

The one thing I did know was I was going to throw everything I had at this Judge because the Foreign Office was trying to rip this boy away from everything he knew and the thought of it broke my heart.

Life-changing decisions and life and death situations in court

We were a full team now supporting Dante. His English mum/aunt was involved, pointing me in the right direction to get every scrap of evidence to prove everything and anything about this boy who had been living in England from the age of two weeks.

His sister was fantastic and had a better memory of his childhood so she came in very handy. I had yet to meet the brother or his girlfriend Katie, but when we were given the date for the hearing, at a very grotty West London Court, I knew I was about to meet the entire family. I suspect I was about a hundred miles outside the bounds of counselling by now.

I will never forget that day as long as I live. I don't do mornings but I was there early for the 10 a.m. start. It was just me and the court-appointed solicitor initially and I set to work straight away briefing her. The poor woman had only found out about the case the night before, as somebody else had pulled out, but she seemed to understand the desperation and urgency of the situation.

Next to arrive was English mum with older brother, who had also been brought over from France to England. Katie his girlfriend was nowhere in sight. This had me worried, because I knew she was a key witness to show how Dante had a stable and reasonably long-term relationship in the UK. At this point they had been together four years, and if she didn't show up that was going to weaken his case.

Eventually, about one and a half hours late, this tiny little girl arrived with her friend. They'd got lost on the bus. Katie looked absolutely terrified out of her wits. I immediately felt so sorry for her. Not only was she having to go to court and speak in public but she was also potentially losing her long-term boyfriend, who the Foreign Office would have on a plane to Paris pretty much instantly.

We couldn't even see Dante. He had been brought from the Immigration Removal Centre in a Prison van at the crack of 6 a.m. and was with two Prison Guards locked in a room far away from us. The next time I would see him he would be standing in the dock, but that wasn't coming till much later on in the afternoon.

The morning saw the solicitor spend most of her time in court and when it came to lunchtime I somehow managed to find myself in the local Tesco café with her for company. I had no idea where the rest of the family had gone, as we had all managed to lose each other leaving the court building.

Over a baguette the solicitor was not hopeful. She said the Judge didn't like anybody and was being snappy and intolerant of anything anybody had to say. Nothing was impressing her apparently.

Gathering after lunch, it was time for Dante's supporters to appear and I was due to go in last. The whole day had a feeling of doom about it as the solicitor had told us in the morning that the Judge was a woman and an absolute harridan. I could see Dante's girlfriend sinking further and further into her seat and I knew she wished she was anywhere but there. I was the opposite.

I wanted my say in that court and was determined to give the Judge a piece of my mind!

After lunch a couple of members of the family were called in and all came out saying that the Judge was an absolute cow. His girlfriend went in mid afternoon and came back out saying it had gone 'okay'. I think she was so terrified she could barely speak.

Then it was time for me. I'm absolutely sure I was seen at the time as being pretty much irrelevant, but as they had said I could speak they would have me in. Little did they know that when I start speaking I rarely stop, especially when I'm very passionate about something.

The first thing I saw when I walked into the court was Dante. But there was to be no hugging this time because he was in a glass dock. Attached to two Prison Officers, and in handcuffs.

I finally came face-to-face with this Judge, expecting the worst as nobody who had been in before me had a good word to say about her.

She was in her mid 40s and a very sensible, no-nonsense sort of woman. She asked me who I was and what I did and I explained in full, including how Dante had done nothing but try to improve his life in Prison for eleven months.

At this point, she asked the tall, lanky, and quite frankly drippy, Foreign Office representative to stand and asked him again how many courses and qualifications Dante had gained while he was in Prison. The poor man looked very flustered, shuffling papers in his Manila file, but said very clearly, 'none'.

As I had just regaled the Judge with all the different qualifications and courses Dante had completed, she then very pointedly said to me, 'Are you calling the Foreign Office liars, Sarah?'

Ruddy heck. Was I? I loathe liars and I was determined to tell the truth, so I answered, 'I'm not necessarily calling them liars but Dante has told me that his Offender Manager had never updated his Offender Assessment System (OASys) Report, which is what the Foreign Office will be basing their information on. To my knowledge he has thirty-three certificates for courses he has taken and passed in eleven months.'

I thought I would throw in a bit of reality, so added, 'And I know for certain he did numerous of those because when I turned up to see him, several times, I had been dumped in favour of Bricks.' What you and I might call Construction Training, but was known in the Prison as simply 'Bricks'.

Soon after this, I could see the Judge not looking at me anymore, but to my right and behind me. I thought I must be boring the woman to death, but no, other people then started to look behind me. Eventually, I turned around myself only to see Dante's English mother flat on her back on the floor with family members flapping around her. The woman was unconscious. This caused absolute uproar as you can imagine. The Judge ordered for an ambulance to be called. Dante was desperate to get out of the dock to get to his potentially dying English mother, but was denied the right to, so was trapped in the dock and everybody else, including me and the man from the Foreign Office, were swiftly ushered into a court next door.

This whole palaver took at least an hour and Dante was now in another dock, with his English mother in an ambulance and nobody knowing what on earth had happened, but we had to carry on.

Maybe this softened the Judge but all of a sudden she seemed very interested in why I was so passionate about helping this boy. She asked me why I did what I did. I told her I had mentored homeless people and ex-Prisoners for the best part of twenty years by this point. She actually relaxed on her bench, put her head on her hands in front of her, really looked me in the eye and talked directly to me rather than the whole court.

I wasn't about to let this opportunity drop. Plus, I was beginning to like this Judge. I told her how passionate I was about boys like this who had not the best of upbringings. How he had been allowed to disappear at the age of fourteen and be trained as a drug dealer. And how he had never felt he belonged anywhere, knowing he had been given away at the age of two weeks. I told her how I had worked with him for the best part of a year and I absolutely knew this boy had no intention of going back to Prison and I had every intention of supporting him, when he finally got out.

The Judge asked me why I did this if I wasn't paid for it. I said for one pure and simple reason – I cared about him. I cared about what happened to him and no, I didn't want a penny for doing that. It would just give me huge satisfaction to keep Dante on the right path and ensure that he had a happy crime-free life in England and NOT in France, where he would be much more at risk without his steady girlfriend, network of friends, family, and me to support him. Me and the Judge had a good twenty-minute chat about all this and then I left the court.

Unknown to me at the time, the two Prison Officers had said to Dante, 'You want to thank her – she's just won your case.' As I left the courtroom, I felt hopeful but still clueless as to which way the Judge was going to go.

One thing we did all know by the end of the day was that English mum had passed out because she hadn't had any lunch. It wasn't the heart attack we had all worried about and instead was just lack of food and a fainting fit. No wonder I hadn't seen her in the Tesco café when I was sharing a baguette with the solicitor. She hadn't been near a sandwich, let alone anything more substantial, and this had been one long, draining day.

Aeroplanes, painful waiting and bricks

By 4:30 p.m. we were finished. There was to be no answer today. I had absolutely zero idea about this whole process and we were given no feedback whatsoever. The solicitor could give us no idea how it had gone, nor what the outcome would be.

Dante was taken by Prison transport back to the Immigration Removal Centre without any of us being able to say a proper goodbye to him and I then had to drive from West London to Poole in Dorset. I don't think I had ever been so tired or emotionally drained in my life.

Although I was still seeing my counselling clients in HMP YOI Aylesbury every week, nothing would come between me and them, I had had to uproot myself suddenly following an unexpected house sale. I was living temporarily in a flat I owned in Poole in Dorset. I cried most of that hundred mile journey home as my boy was still locked away, on his own. He was still only nineteen. We had no clue whether he was going to be sent back to France and here was I driving mile upon mile away from him. Exhaustion and high emotion collided and I sobbed pretty solidly all the way down the motorway.

For another six weeks, Dante sat in that wretched Immigration Removal Centre, right next to Heathrow Airport, with planes flying over his head every two minutes, which I thought was the most cruel thing a government could do. I can see the logic of putting people who are about to be deported near an airport, but what does that do for your mental stability when you are fighting to stay in the only country you have ever known? Hearing aeroplanes take off every two minutes, knowing that you could be on one within a couple of hours. Torture. Pure torture.

Six weeks after the court date came the news we had all been waiting for. The Judge wasn't such a cow after all! I knew she was taking on board everything I was saying to her. She was going to let Dante stay in the UK! Dante told me in an emotional phone call that he was going home – to Hertfordshire.

The Foreign Office wasn't quite done with him yet though. They were still going to make Dante register with his local Police station weekly for the next year. Which I thought was a bit excessive, but he did it. And it took another year before he received a letter from the Home Office telling him he had the indefinite right to remain in England.

Dante used all that 'Bricks' training to get himself work straight away on a building site, which is where he has been pretty much ever since. He's risen through the ranks from being a labourer to a bricklayer and now specialises in scaffolding.

His girlfriend had asked me at the court if I meant it when I said I would carry on supporting him and make sure he stayed on the straight and narrow? I said I absolutely did mean it, but only if he and she wanted it. She very quickly assured me that they definitely did.

It was at this point I remembered my Tutor always saying, 'There are boundaries – and then there are Sarah boundaries.' Her partner had worked in a Prison for many years so she understood my passion to help more than most.

Dante has since become the biggest supporter I have of counsellors staying in touch with their clients. He cannot understand the logic of cutting all contact from somebody who has supported you and cares about you. As he says, 'You know me better than anyone, so of course when anything goes wrong, why wouldn't I come back to you?' And I quite agree with him. And frankly, if you don't care about your clients then I firmly believe you are in the wrong job.

Having been an ex-homeless people and ex-Prisoner mentor before I was a counsellor, the very thought of abandoning people when they are most in need is alien to me and something I will never do.

So I have happily remained in Dante's and Katie's life since that court date in the summer of 2014. I care about his girlfriend and their beautiful daughter just as much as I do Dante now. He has never been back to Prison, just as I knew he wouldn't. He works extremely hard to support his family. I'm invited to his daughter's birthday party every year and without fail, every time I speak to him or his girlfriend, the conversation always ends with, 'We appreciate you.'

Client two, my first visit to the Seg and Exit Signs

Having started with Dante in July 2013, by the end of August I was referred my second client, Keiran. Lord alone knows how he ended up in Aylesbury because he hailed from Manchester. I'm guessing because Aylesbury was a category A Young Offender Institute at the time and Keiran was one of the many clients I saw who hadn't actually committed 'anything terribly serious', but had committed 'nothing terribly serious' numerous times.

I had picked up the referral from the pigeonholes, but when I first went to meet him on F Wing – he wasn't there. I was told instead he was in the Segregation Unit. More commonly known as 'the Seg' or 'the Block'. So, this was a new challenge. Where in God's name was the Segregation Unit? There was nobody around to ask so I trudged off across the Association area – in a school this would've been called the playground. Not a clue where I was going, but I was determined to find him.

The one thing you won't find in a Prison is signs. I'd had a little titter to myself one day when I was trying find my way out of the Prison, looking for exit signs. I then realised the one thing you won't find in any Prison – an EXIT sign! Me, like a plank, had been looking for them.

Not only were there no exit signs, but there were no signs to pretty much anywhere else until you actually arrived and saw a big sign saying 'A Wing', 'B Wing' etc. So it was a question of asking kind-looking Officers where the Segregation Unit was and finding my own way.

Once I arrived, it was quite an intimidating building. Definitely different to the rest of the Prison – more security measures and very austere looking. Also more gates than usual to get through; unlocking two gates and then moving a foot to the other side and locking the same two gates, then again, then again, until finally I found the Seg and the general office.

Here I found three quite jolly and friendly male Officers, who informed me that my new client, Keiran, was indeed with them, but did I want to see him? I thought this was a bit of a strange question but went with it. 'Isn't it more relevant whether or not he wants to see me?' The last thing I was planning on doing was forcing myself on a young offender who wasn't in the mood – especially when most people are in the Seg because they've kicked off, punched somebody, been caught with a weapon or were having serious self-harm or suicidal tendencies.

Five minutes later, one of the Officers was back confirming that Keiran did want to see me. I was taken through into a side office, just off the general office, where I was informed adjudications usually took place, and told I could see him in there. The reason for this became apparent later. They weren't used to having counsellors turn up on the Seg. It wasn't the first time I would see a client in a very strange environment at Aylesbury but, as this was only client number two, I just did as I was told.

It was the first I had heard of adjudications taking place inside a Prison, but apparently things could get even worse for you after you'd been sentenced in court. You could then get yourself into trouble in Prison and find yourself up in front of another 'Judge'. But this time it would be the Governor of the Prison! These adjudications most often meant you were given extra days, sometimes months, to add on to your sentence. If whatever you had done wasn't considered serious enough to involve the Police it was felt that your misdemeanour could be dealt with internally. Serious misdemeanours did involve the Police coming into the Prison. This was quite an intimidating and formal room to have your first session with a new counselling client in.

Keiran was twenty-one, tall, slim and fair, and if any young girl had met him in a pub, and not known his history, she would've thought he was quite a catch. He certainly met me with a disarming smile.

Rapport was quick to build. I formed the impression Keiran was just grateful to have somebody to talk to. So sitting in this very strange room, propped up against a small Judge's bench, I started to find out all about him.

Only a couple of months into my Prison counselling career, I already found myself agreeing with the Head of Counselling at HMP The Mount. Person-centred counselling did not cut it with these boys. Being myself, treating them like normal human beings and having a conversation worked an awful lot better. Very soon Keiran was telling me his life story.

Worryingly, one of the first things he told me was that he wanted to do one major 'anger-releasing' act to get fifteen years behind bars. This wasn't what I was expecting. When I enquired why, he said it would make him feel much better and he really wanted to do it.

Still attempting counselling mode, I asked him if it was because he felt he deserved punishing and he said absolutely not. He couldn't explain why, but he still strongly felt the need to do it. We moved on from that quite swiftly as I wasn't quite sure where to go with it. But I knew we had to come back to it at some point.

Keiran had what I later came to realise was a very typical background for so many of these young boys in Prison. We first talked about his mum, who he told me was on a cocktail of both legal and illegal drugs. He described her as 'a headcase' and 'mad', but insisted he did like her!

He told me how he had been bullied in school between the ages of five and seven and had gone into care aged thirteen. This was after he had seen his father injecting heroin and walking round the house with needles hanging out of his arms. He'd watched his parents get arrested. Both his parents had spent time in Prison.

Keiran told me how his father had taken him out 'thieving', how he enjoyed going along for the ride, and loved the excitement and the buzz he got from it.

His mother then took on a new man, who became his stepfather. Keiran was very scared of this man as was his mother. When he was eleven his mum had asked him to stab his stepfather. Thankfully, Keiran had declined.

He had also experienced the horror of watching his stepfather rape his mother.

Keiran told me that violence was normal in his household and his main anxiety when he was younger was his brothers being taken away from the family home. He saw being in Prison now as a 'break from reality'.

Good grief. When that was your reality who could blame him?

Now his main issue was paranoia. Severe paranoia. And this is why he had insisted on going to the Seg. Keiran was absolutely convinced that everybody was out to get him. He told me that when he had been out socialising, living in Manchester, if he was sitting in a lounge with a group of friends and one of them received a text message on their phone he would immediately run up the stairs, go into the bathroom, escape through a window and throw himself down the drainpipe. He assumed that when anybody received a message it was telling them that somebody was about to attack him.

He seemed to have cripplingly low self-esteem and two or three sessions in, when I told him how I loved his honesty, how open he was and how he was talkative and entertaining, I literally saw him bloom in front of my eyes. It struck me then that maybe nobody had ever told him how likeable he was. When we finished that session, he shook my hand. But he didn't so much shake it as hold onto it. It was almost like he was sucking the positivity out of me. He clung onto my hand and I felt the warmth and strength flow between us. I was really beginning to like this boy and I so felt for him with this traumatic past.

We talked about his current issues, which were all based around anxiety and paranoia, how his sleep 'was all over the place' and he had had terrible IBS for years. At the time I didn't know what all of these were indicators of. That knowledge would come in the future, but I remember him vividly telling me all this.

At college, I asked my Tutor – when you are dealing with a client with this sort of background, severe anxiety, extreme paranoia, low self-esteem and about as much trauma from childhood as it was possible to have – where on earth did you start?

My Tutor, who I had, and do still have, immense respect for, thought about it for a few moments and then gave me the best piece of advice I was ever given in all my years counselling Prisoners. 'Always be on their side, Sarah. Let them know that whatever they tell you, you are always, always on their side.'

For one of our sessions Keiran refused to come out of his cell because his arch-enemy, a sex offender, was out on Association. I had to wait over two hours to see him, but I waited. He talked a lot that day about being punished for not agreeing to move off the Seg. He was just too paranoid to move.

During later sessions, in October, I learnt just how much cannabis he had taken and after a lot of research realised that his paranoia had most probably come from the excessive amounts of weed he had smoked. Up until that point I had never heard the expression 'drug induced psychosis'. We talked about doing some CBT around this and he was keen. He desperately wanted to conquer his paranoia.

Keiran was opening up to me more and more. He told me that I knew more about him than anybody else did. When I assured him I had recommended a mental health assessment in the Prison he was pleased, I think, that somebody was bothered about him. The paperclip numpty told me that it was likely he had a 'personality disorder'. That meant nothing to me at the time, and I had no idea how much I would come to despise that diagnosis in future.

Keiran's only fly in the ointment now was his mother, who had flogged his phone to pay for drugs. He was livid, despite her saying she would replace it, because he had lost every contact and every friend he had ever had. Now, he wasn't being quite as complimentary about her and was calling her a 'scumbag junkie'. I was hanging all my hopes on this mental health assessment. This was in the halcyon days when I had complete faith in Prison mental health services, but on 19 November everything came crashing down.

Ghosting, consonants and vowels

I arrived at the Prison on Tuesday, 19 November ready for session 8 with Keiran, only be to be told by a laughing Officer, 'That won't be happening today, Miss, he's gone.'

Gone? I was completely thrown. This Officer just casually threw at me that Keiran had been moved that morning and carried on chatting to his mate, as my world collapsed.

I was in absolute shock. I literally didn't know what to do with myself. So many thoughts were racing through my brain. First of all, I was worried about him. I knew he hadn't wanted to move and he was only slightly less paranoid since he had been in the Segregation Unit at Aylesbury.

Keiran had had absolutely no idea that they were going to move him or we would have talked about it. I also knew he had not requested a move. He had only told me the week before that for the first time since he'd been inside he felt he could talk to somebody, somebody actually wanted to help him, and that his life could potentially improve now.

This would've come as a terrible shock to Keiran, and I knew he would be petrified if they just put him on a Wing and didn't immediately put him in the Segregation Unit. His paranoia would be in overdrive.

Secondly, I felt cheated. We had been doing some really good work. We were just about to start CBT on his paranoia. He'd been referred for a mental health assessment, which I felt he desperately needed, and then, just like that, he had been what I now know is called 'ghosted' – the equivalent of being whipped away in the night with absolutely no notice.

This was the first time it had happened to me and I wasn't prepared for it. In counselling training we talked about endings and they weren't like this! It wasn't a client just evaporating and neither of you having any control over it.

I stood, rooted to the spot on the Wing, not knowing what to do. I did have the presence of mind to think I must somehow find out where he had gone. And quick. People move around Prison all the time and if I didn't find out now, I probably never would. I knew this probably wasn't Prison protocol but I cared about this boy and I wasn't prepared to just let him evaporate.

I also had this horrible feeling that he might have thought I had something to do with this, and I had purposefully abandoned him. Chucked him aside. Like he didn't matter.

I waited for a gap in the conversation between the two chatting Officers and then very nonchalantly said, 'Oh, does anybody know where he's gone?', absolutely cacking myself they would say that they didn't know, or it was none of my business, or that it was confidential.

They had a bit of a chat between themselves trying to remember, and then one of them gave me some consonants and vowels that made absolutely no sense to me! It was like he was talking a foreign language.

But I hung onto those consonants and vowels until I could get out of the Prison and start Googling any Prison that sounded vaguely similar – and it turned out to be HMP Glen Parva. I had never even heard of the place before, but according to Google it was in Leicester.

The relief I felt when I knew where Keiran was was immense and there was no question of what I was going to do next. I had absolutely no intention of abandoning this boy so I went straight to a post office, bought a card and some paper, and sat and wrote to him there and then.

I wanted him to know that I was still there for him: if he wanted to write to me he could, if he wanted me to visit I would, and I was still really keen to support him in any way I possibly could. I had no idea if he would get the letter and no idea if he would reply but on 2 December a reply plopped on to my doormat.

The relief of Keiran knowing I just hadn't abandoned him was huge. He said he would love it if I could visit, so although I was now based in Dorset I made plans to go up to Leicester as soon as I could. It meant an overnight stay and, for the first time ever in my life, I became a visitor going into a Prison.

Seeing him in the Visit Hall was absolutely amazing and I know I did the right thing. He said it meant the world to him that I hadn't just forgotten him. We talked solidly for two hours and I was so happy to hear that although the move had shocked him he felt he was now in a good Prison, and in a much better place mentally than he had been before.

That was the last time I saw Keiran but we did have some letter contact and now he is one of the very few boys I am not still in touch with. I realised there and then that I was utterly crap at endings. I guess all those years as a mentor put me in a very different position to most counsellors. I wasn't used to abandoning people when they needed support the most and I just couldn't do it.

So he was the second after Dante, but there would be dozens of others I would support on the outside and I make absolutely no apology for it. Neither to the Prison service nor the counselling world. I was doing what I was doing because I cared and in my mind caring can never be wrong.

Witches, tea and biscuits

All counsellors have to have supervision when they are seeing clients, both when they are a trainee and once qualified. I'd not been given any choice. The Prison told me exactly who my supervisor was and I arranged an appointment to see this lady in a village the other side of Aylesbury.

It was nearly an hour away from where I was living, but on the first day I turned up in some godforsaken village I had never even heard of and rang on the bungalow doorbell. It looked like the sort of place a witch might live. Quite scary.

I was met by a very large, unfriendly woman who hurriedly ushered me through into her lounge. No offer of a cup of tea or even a glass of water, never mind using the loo after an hours' journey.

She then talked AT me for an hour! Literally, solidly. Didn't stop. Didn't ask me one question and just lectured me for an hour. She was the epitome of somebody who liked the sound of their own voice far too much.

I couldn't quite believe it, but in the car going home I reasoned, 'Well maybe that's what happens the first time and things will be different from session two.' So I paid more money and booked in to see her again.

When exactly the same thing happened the next time and I hadn't had a chance to talk about my own clients for even thirty seconds, which is, after all, the purpose of supervision, I managed to swerve it deftly when she bellowed, 'What date is good for you for next time?'

knowing there was no way I was putting myself through this ever again. I muttered something about having forgotten my diary and made a bolt for the door.

I really didn't care what the Prison thought at this point. I was much more concerned about what my college Tutor thought. I knew I had to have supervision as part of my course and I knew it made sense for it to be with somebody who understood the Prison system. It didn't take long for me to find the perfect person.

Robin had worked at the same Prison for twenty years as a counsellor and had only just left. His reason being, 'They changed all the systems and wanted me to fill in some bloody paperwork and I was buggered if I was doing that having worked there for twenty years.' This was far more my sort of person. I've always liked anybody who tells authority where they can shove their red tape and bureaucracy, and has a sense of humour, so Robin became my counselling supervisor for the next eighteen months.

There was nothing he didn't know about Aylesbury Prison. He had seen it, lived it, ate and slept it for twenty years and, as he was nearing retirement age anyway, he had left – literally refusing to fill in any of their newfangled paperwork. Knowing how inefficient the paperclip loon was with administration, I didn't blame him.

I had some wonderful sessions with Robin and we had many jolly afternoons over cups of tea, talking about all his old clients at the Prison and mine at the same time.

So that was me all legal and above board, blissfully seeing my Young Offender clients and getting the right kind of supervision over tea and biscuits once a month. And I did get to use his toilet.

Dodgy parenting and my first 'diagnosed as a child' ADHD client

On 3 December 2013 I met my third client. They were coming in thick and fast now. Word was getting round that I wasn't your typical drippy 'how does that make you feel' sort of counsellor, and in a relatively small Prison I was told that some potential clients were opting to wait to see me, which was very flattering seeing as though I didn't have much of a clue as to what I was doing. But I did care and I cared deeply.

The referral sheet told me that Thomas was on B Wing and had been referred by a staff member on the drugs team. It said he had witnessed domestic violence between his parents and was now suffering with low self-esteem.

The room they had allocated us was on the end of his Wing. It wasn't a thoroughfare Wing-to-Wing area, which was a good start. The fact we wouldn't have people constantly interrupting us was a blessing. However, the first session wasn't without its own issues. The one and only light bulb had blown, meaning there was absolutely no light in the room on an already dark and dingy Wing. Hardly ideal, especially for a first session! I had never met Thomas before so I had no idea what he looked like.

He was waiting for me when I arrived, but I could hardly see his face. He was just an outline sitting across the room. Nobody had prepared me for this at college.

Because his name was Thomas my opening words were, 'What do you like to be called, Tom or Tommy.' I was met with a very firm, 'Thomas.' It was difficult to gauge his mood in the dark. They say you always make these mistakes once and never again. I have never assumed anybody likes to be called anything other than their full name ever since!

However, he soon warmed up and once he started talking, he didn't stop. He told me how he was twenty-one now and was sick of being in Prison. All he wanted was to wake up in the morning and to be able to walk to a local shop and buy a pint of milk. That's not too much to ask I thought, bearing in mind he was due out within the next six months.

Thomas then proceeded to tell me how he had been born in Brixton to an eighteen-year-old mother who, as a child, he adored. He had never known who his father was and had had his mum all to himself as a youngster. I questioned some of her parenting techniques when Thomas told me she would encourage him to throw glass ashtrays at people in pubs to see what reaction they would get – when he was five years old!

And when he was even younger, aged three, and playing in their flat's playground area, he said how he had run home crying to his mum and told her that some children had been nasty to him. He was given no sympathy from his mother and instead she insisted he go straight back out and 'beat them up properly or she would batter him even worse'. He was three!

Everything changed when he was eight years old and his mum met the man who was to become his stepfather. Thomas didn't like him and they clashed from the start. When Thomas was ten they all moved to Watford, in Hertfordshire. His mum and stepfather had gone on to have two little girls who were now eight and five. Thomas always blamed his stepfather for taking his mum away from him. But he did love and care for his two younger sisters.

Thomas had been diagnosed with ADHD at the age of nine, after he had started to get into trouble with the Police from the age of eight. By the time he was eleven his mum had had enough and wanted to put him into care. His mother's mother, his beloved nan, said there was absolutely no way he was going into care and she would take him in. Which she did. Although she was his mum's mother, she had never liked how her daughter had encouraged him to be violent and was more than happy to have Thomas live with her.

Thomas was very open with me about why he was in Prison. It was for thieving, robbery and burglary. His main aim with counselling was to find out why he did what he did and to stop his constant offending.

By session 2, he was telling me how he had always been violent as a child. 'No wonder, with a mother who encouraged you to throw ashtrays at people,' I thought, but didn't say.

Now I could actually see him I could see that he was quite slight. Probably about 5 feet 8 inches tall with brown hair, quite pale skinned and wiry rather than stocky.

Thomas told me he was the archetypal ADHD kid, 'a little shit' in his words, and he used to chuck chairs at teachers at school. He'd also been involved in violence in Prison and was constantly getting into fights and adding extra days to his sentence.

It took me a while to warm to Thomas, but by session 3 I was starting to feel for him. Although his nan had adored him, and he didn't have a bad word to say about her, she worked in an old people's home and didn't get home until 10:30 p.m. – and she worked six days a week. So after school, Thomas was very much left to his own devices. This is always fatal for ADHD kids, because they so often fall into exactly what he had fallen into. Mixing with older teenagers who were allowed out later and who involved him in petty crime from a very young age.

Thomas told me something that made me feel so sad. He said his overriding feelings were of 'rejection' by his mother and 'neglect' by his nan. His mother had just started to come to see him once a month in the Prison, but he said it was 'too little too late' and his nan agreed with him. During the April his mum visited and they ended up having a massive row when Thomas said if he ever saw his stepfather again, he would punch him. Probably not what his mother was hoping to hear.

Thomas' nan was Romany, with her family originally from Romania, and Thomas was born and raised a Catholic. This explained the beads around his neck, which I had never been able to fathom – they were rosary beads.

Thomas told me all about his horrendous sleep problems. During session 4 he told me that the previous two nights he hadn't slept a wink. He had asked to see Health Care, which I was glad about.

By session 5 Thomas told me that he had been asking for a move out of the Prison. He wanted to move to an adult male Prison rather than the Young Offender Institute he was in, and he also wanted to move down to a category C, but Aylesbury had just moved him onto a different Wing. He was now on C Wing. But now he was seeing me he had decided he would rather stay.

I was glad. I really wanted to help this boy. We started with some CBT exercises, which he enjoyed doing and proudly brought his homework to the next session every week. The CBT was all around reducing anger and violence and choosing different responses. I genuinely felt this boy had already moved on in his head and I was just cementing what he had already decided, which was that he didn't want to go back to Prison.

By session 8 Thomas was in the Seg. He was very cheesed off and yet again I had to see him in the dark because the lights weren't working. He looked absolutely dreadful, white as a sheet, said he was not sleeping and was freezing cold because his windows wouldn't shut. I asked the paperclip numpty about this, who said he was 'probably lying' and to 'ignore him'. That was helpful.

He wasn't getting much encouragement from the Officers in Aylesbury either. In his opinion the Officers talked to them like shit and called them criminals, telling them regularly they, 'are a waste of space', 'won't amount to anything' and 'would be in and out of Prison all their lives'. Crikey. If this was true, my work raising their self-esteem was going to be a lot tougher than it had been at HMP The Mount, where the Officers spoke to everybody with respect and they received the same respect back.

Thomas told me about his Parole terms. When he was released, he would apparently have to ring Probation up at 10 a.m., 12 noon, 3 p.m. and 5 p.m. Monday to Friday for the next twenty months. I couldn't believe this. Who on earth could keep that up? Let alone somebody with ADHD, who would have a poor memory and be disorganised. But apparently, if he breached this it meant he would go back inside for another twenty months.

It was roundabout then that I first heard the term so many of the Prison Officers use, 'They set them up to fail.' Surely this was a classic example of just that?

I knew I would struggle myself to remember to phone somebody four times a day at an exact time, five days a week. It seemed ridiculous and it still does.

In session 9, Thomas suddenly whipped up his T-shirt to show me where he had been stabbed, three separate times, in the stomach. He told me he had been stabbed twice in the groin too but luckily didn't drop his trousers to show me the scars. Thank the Lord.

The big news that week was that he had managed not to punch an Officer who had interrupted his phone call with his five-year-old sister after thirty seconds, when Thomas had been told he was allowed ten minutes to speak to her. We had been doing a lot of work on how to reduce his violence and this time he actually walked away rather than react, which made me so proud of him. He had then gone back to see the Officer later when he had calmed down and explained how the ten minutes had turned into thirty seconds and he had felt terribly guilty for only speaking to his little sister for that short a time. This was a big step in the right direction for

Thomas and I could tell he was proud of himself. Normally he would've punched first and thought later. I made it very clear how huge this was and how it was the start of changing how he reacted to all situations in future.

He talked about his girlfriend Milly, who he had been seeing for two years. Although he was twenty-one she was only eighteen and wanted to get married as soon as he was released. Thomas thought this was a very stupid idea and had no plans doing it. Despite the violence, he showed real maturity at times.

In session 11 Thomas' main concern was his stepfather now talking about moving the family to Devon. This had Thomas very worried because he was still close to his mum and wanted to stay close to his sisters. Thankfully it came to nothing.

During session 12 he told me he had been moved to E Wing, which had totally cheesed him off. Apparently it was the biggest Wing and in his words, 'full of kids and incredibly noisy'. He wasn't getting anywhere nearer to an adult jail – instead he was doing a circuit round most of the Wings at Aylesbury.

We were now doing regular CBT work on reducing his violence and Thomas was making great steps every week. He even told me that when he started to get angry, he now sat down in his cell and read his previous CBT assignments and it always stopped him from taking action. This made me chuffed.

On my way out of the Prison after a Thomas session, I was told, ominously, that I 'needed to see Security' before I left that day. Blooming heck. This was a first. I had no idea if this was just to give me a new belt, or key pouch, or anything more sinister.

I entered the Security Office and was met by two Officers in massive security jackets, who started asking me odd cryptic questions. I couldn't work out what they were on about. I was clueless. It turned out that I had not locked one gate on one Wing. They were trying to work out if I'd done it on purpose. Because I'd locked the other one, and there were always two gates bang next to each other, I was let off but told if I did it again I'd be out. The scary thing was I had no memory of doing it. None at all. Or obviously I wouldn't have done it. The explanation for forgetfulness would come in my life – just not yet.

In session 13, Thomas was very happy because his mum had been in to visit him. Apparently this was a rarity, but he absolutely loved it when she made the effort.

Session 14 he was still doing well with the CBT and we decided together to make a note of all the things he had been arrested for in the past, so we could work out different ways of dealing with each and every one.

Dear God. When I started that exercise, I thought we might be filling up half a page of A4. But no, we filled up two and a half sides of A4 with the biggest array of arrests I'd ever seen from any client.

Talk about prolific! Everything from arson, stealing cars, muggings, robbery, burglary, theft, affray, the list just went on and on. Actual bodily harm (ABH), Grievous bodily harm (GBH), attempted murder, dozens of attacks on Police Officers and Prison Officers.

Quite how he had managed to fit this lot into twenty-one years I didn't know. But I hid my shock as the list grew and grew.

At the end of it, I asked him which of these was the most likely he would return to and he told me 'robbery and car crimes'. For him, these were the easiest two to drop back into. I thought this showed good insight but after reading that list I realised what a humongous change in behaviour I was asking him to make.

Thomas told me how I would be getting a new client soon and to make sure I saw him rather than anybody else; it was his best friend, not only in Prison but in life. They had met as they were both Catholic and went to the Catholic service once a week in the Prison.

Week nineteen, things weren't going so great. Thomas had punched somebody in his cell and was feeling rough, with a really bad cough.

By session 22 he was making plans to get out very soon. Probation had even been and checked where he was going to be living. It looked like it was off with the girlfriend as they'd had a massive row and by session 23, on 27 May, he was full of excitement about getting out, changing his life and starting afresh.

And I was looking forward to supporting him with that during those final weeks before release.

A nasty shock and losing faith in professionals

When you are a Trainee Counsellor, to qualify, you need to complete 100 hours of face-to-face therapy. At the point you have completed fifty hours you are given a form, which has to be completed by your 'placement supervisor'. It's the standard sort of appraisal questions and I had absolutely no qualms when I dropped mine in to my contact at the Prison. Yet again, not in the office, so I just left it on the desk with a polite note asking if it could be completed and sent to my Tutor in the stamped and addressed envelope I had provided.

The boys had their own explanation as to why the numpty was never in the office. Apparently, they were supposed to split their time between Aylesbury and another Prison. More than one boy told me that they could never be got hold of at either Prison, and many were quite sure Numpty was sat at home with their feet up in front of the telly with the handy excuse that they were actually at the other Prison.

I knew things had gone well with all of my clients. I hadn't missed any session times at all and had never been late. In fact, I had been extremely flexible when session times had had to change due to Prison lockdowns, being on 'Patrol State', which meant only three Officers were on a Wing and nobody could go on or off it, usually because some kind of incident had taken place. I had bent over backwards to see my boys and I knew they appreciated it.

I had had pretty much nothing to do with the numpty since I started at the Prison, and was much more familiar with the Officers on the Wings of the boys I was seeing.

A couple of weeks later, at college, my Tutor sent everybody out into breakout groups and beckoned me to go with her outside. We sat in the College Gardens, where she showed me the Prison's completed paperwork and I was absolutely shocked to the core. Nothing could have prepared me for what I read.

Bearing in mind I had not missed one session in the six months there, Numpty had said that my attendance was 'poor' and my timekeeping 'poor'!

They had had nothing to do with my paperwork, all my session notes went to my Tutor and I had been on time with every single assignment, yet they had marked my administrative skills as 'poor'. Not one case study, weekly journal, exercise or anything I'd written had ever been seen by anybody in the Prison – just my Tutor. How could they blatantly lie?

My Tutor had known that I had found it difficult to warm to this character, but neither of us had expected them to outrightly lie on official college awarding body qualification paperwork. I can't remember if I cried. I probably did, but as always I had my wonderful Tutor backing me up.

She had to send the report in to the awarding body – we didn't have a choice because I had done all my fifty hours at the one placement. If the hours had been split between two placements, like many students had done, we could've juggled the figures but there was no getting away from the fact that I had given fifty hours to that one Prison and I had one report saying I was crap!

I just didn't know what to do or where to turn. I was totally in shock that a supposed 'professional' could blatantly lie and think they could get away with it. But my Tutor, as always, had my back. She wrote a huge contradictory report that went with the one full of lies, explaining the truth, which was I had attended every session, never been late, stayed late to see boys if necessary and had never been behind once with any of my administration, which was currently up-to-date and always had been.

Thankfully the awarding body accepted this report and not the fabricated one the lying numpty had put together.

I have had ten years to think why this person did this to me and I can only put it down to one thing. I think they had genuinely muddled me up with somebody else! Because their report bore no relation to the truth.

They honestly didn't have any other reason to not like me because I hadn't seen them more than twice the whole time I'd been counselling there and in the very occasional email contact I'd been polite and professional, but if I thought their dastardly work was done, boy was I wrong. They weren't done yet.

Chelsea, porn and
frying pans

One of my standard lines to my clients was that, 'Nothing you can say will shock me.' It was okay to tell me anything they wanted and I would not be horrified. After I met Thomas' best mate, Barney, who became my client number four, I stopped saying that. Because a lot of what he told me did really shock me! The very first thing he said to me was he had only agreed to see me because Thomas had insisted I wasn't a twat! High praise indeed.

I was to see Barney back on A Wing where I had started with Dante, but luckily not in the room with the thoroughfare through it. This time they had found a proper room I could see Barney in. Heaven be praised.

I first met Barney on 24 February 2014. He was twenty-one, had baby blond hair and a bit of a beard. He told me straight away that he was in Prison for carrying firearms and class A drugs with intent to sell. This wasn't what shocked me. Standard stuff in Prisons.

He had received a seven-and-a-half-year sentence and had to serve three and three-quarter years inside and the rest on licence. This meant he wasn't due out until October 2016, which seemed an awful long way off from March 2014. This was the longest-sentenced client I had yet to work with.

Up until then, it had all been short-term sentences and people due for release. But sitting in front of somebody aged twenty-one, who had another two and a half years to waste his life away behind bars seemed sad, no matter what he had done.

In the first session I found out Barney's mum had been an alcoholic and had died when he was sixteen. His dad was still alive but Barney considered him a 'lowlife thug' and he had actually stabbed his own father three times. He hated his father, who was apparently a drug dealer and a drug addict.

His father was also a diagnosed sociopath who would often rock up to the Prison rolling drunk, make a show of himself in the waiting room, chat up all the female Prison Officers in the Visit Hall and get thrown out early for being inebriated and aggressive. Barney was hugely ashamed of his father and didn't want him to come and visit him, ever again.

Barney was a real London boy and had been born and brought up in Pimlico. He told me how his nan had caught him in a local park once with a gun and had taken him home and hit him over the head with a frying pan. He told me they still had the frying pan and it was still in use!

I said I had a lot of admiration for his nan, dragging him home from the park for messing with guns and smacking him over the head with a frying pan. He retorted, 'Well don't admire her too much because she's been in Prison as well.' Honest to God what hope do these boys have when half their family have been in Prison? Bad enough that your parents might have been to Prison, but your nan? My nan made the best coffee cake and shortbread ever and was constantly in the kitchen. The thought of a nan being in Prison was totally alien to me.

Barney was completely against counselling, because his father had had it and Barney believed it had made him weak. He had only agreed to see me because Thomas had insisted it would do him good. And that I wasn't a twat. But the one thing he didn't want was actual counselling.

I assured him this was fine, and we could use the hour exactly as he wanted. Even from session 1 I knew this boy desperately did need counselling but I wasn't going to put him off by insisting on structured sessions. I said we could talk about absolutely anything he wanted to and immediately regretted it when he said he would like to talk about porn.

Luckily, we were coming to the end of that session and it gave me a week to think how I could swerve that the following one!

In the next session Barney started to tell me a bit about himself, which included the fact that he had eleven GCSEs and one AS-level in History. I had had the feeling he was bright. He also told me he'd been a chef for two and a half years at top London hotels and even did the catering for Kate Middleton's hen night (Kate Middleton being married to Prince William, and future Queen of England). He'd only become a chef because his father was a chef and he said he'd never really known what he wanted to do. And had very little guidance with that I imagined coming from this sort of family.

Barney told me he was one of nine children. His dad's first born, but the only child to come from the same mum and dad. So he had half-siblings on both sides but I had the impression he felt quite isolated not having any full blood brothers or sisters, a deceased mum and a father he despised.

By session 3 he was telling me how he was a massive Chelsea Football Club fan and how him, his dad and his dad's brother, Uncle Keith, used to go to the football on a Saturday afternoon primarily to beat people up. They were well known for it at QPR and Fulham and were now all on a lifetime ban from all three football clubs. He seemed proud of the fact that his dad and Uncle Keith were considered to be the most feared men in Pimlico.

All I could think of was what a background? And how it was a foregone conclusion this boy was going to end up in Prison.

He had joined in the beating-up of anybody who didn't support Chelsea but said, tellingly, that he 'wasn't happy as a chef or as a criminal'. I distinctly got the impression he hadn't been happy ever since his mother had died. He told me how his mum used to call him Bubble and now he had absolutely no idea who he was, what he wanted or how to be happy.

He believed he was an alcoholic and attended AA meetings in the Prison.

His Chef career had taken him to a very well-known five-star London hotel. He and his boss used to take cocaine, but never on the same day. That was the arrangement. So at least one of them was compos mentis and able to function properly. However, there was one day where they got it wrong and both turned up at work having taken cocaine. It ended with a fight when they hit each other over the head with skillets. What is it with this boy and frying pans? Anyway, that was the end of his job at the hotel. They were both sacked the same day.

By session 4 Barney was still wanting to talk about porn, so I threw caution to the wind and told him that I had always wanted to run a legal brothel. But I wanted my brothel to be different. I wanted it to be run like a beautiful hotel with girls who were well looked after, received free counselling and the best private Health Care there was on offer. I also wanted the clients to be able to have sumptuous lunches, luxury afternoon teas and exquisite dinners, and for the whole thing to be run very professionally. I've never done this of course, but I've always thought it was a good business idea. I'd seen it work on a similar basis in different countries on my travels where it was legal. But nowhere near as high-class and as exclusive as I thought it could be done.

This got Barney chatting and I was pretty sure he no longer saw me as a potential twat. It was enough for us to spend the next few sessions deciding on how we would set up our brothel, how he would do the catering and I would do all the counselling and looking after the ladies' AND gentlemen's mental health and physical wellbeing. Our brothel was going to be different because we were going to cater for ladies as well as gentlemen.

We were doing sod all counselling but we were building very good rapport!

He talked about how he had become a Catholic to feel closer to his nan, who had now passed away but had been a staunch Catholic when she was alive. But he'd now been banned from the chapel, along with Thomas, for doing something daft. They were obviously very close friends. God-fearing Catholic boys, the both of them.

I started to hear more about Barney's mum. She had had a tough life. Abused sexually as a child by her uncle, she moved Barney around the country, constantly, dodging paying rent and kept changing his name. Up until the age of ten Barney thought his name was Tucker.

His mum had been a prolific self-harmer, had even set fire to herself, and by the time Barney was nine she had made the decision to put him in care. I think she had carted him round the country so much she was beginning to feel guilty.

In session 5 he told me he had been 20 stone at one point, which was staggering as he only looked about 12 stone at the time. He then proceeded to whip his T-shirt up to show me his stretchmarks and it was true, he did have a lot of stretch marks so he obviously had been much bigger.

Barney managed to swing the conversation back to porn and asked me if I knew about dwarf porn. No, I absolutely did not. He warned me if I Googled it I would never see small people in the same light again.

Barney was absolutely determined not to go back to Prison and said he would rather kill himself first.

By session 6 I had worked out that he was actually okay about talking about himself, but only when he didn't realise he was, so I had to word things very carefully – but more came pouring out of him.

He told me the only time he ever felt close to his dad was when they were in fights, because they could read each other's minds. But realistically, he had only ever had respect for Uncle Keith, his nan and his mum.

He then brought the conversation back to sex by asking me did I know that masturbation was banned in the Prison? The thought had never entered my mind, but apparently if anyone is caught masturbating they can receive an adjudication. Ditto if somebody should catch you naked in your cell, you would get an adjudication – including if you threw the sheets off yourself at night because you were hot. This was all news to me.

By session 7 Barney had agreed to start some CBT. I knew he wanted help to change, but he was very resistant to it at first. He was still talking a lot about violence, killing people, shooting people, hurting people and I must've said at some point that I just didn't know where to go with that, because I remember him distinctly saying, 'Surely it's beneficial just talking?' And I of course agreed.

I was bringing this boy up in supervision a lot because the violence and anger seemed to be ingrained, yet he said he wasn't happy when he was a criminal.

He had filled in an initial 'happiness questionnaire' but told me he had chucked it into the corner of his cell. I asked if I could see it and we agreed we would go through it the next week. He said it left him feeling 'oppressed and depressed' and he didn't like the feelings. I said, 'Ah-ha, at last! Some feelings?' We both laughed about this as he was constantly insisting he didn't have any.

He managed to get the conversation back onto porn towards the end. Of course.

The next session was a classic for my counselling at Aylesbury. My room with Barney had been booked by one of the other counsellors as I had totally forgotten that this was a room that I needed to book in advance. I was supposed to tell them I needed it again and I had forgotten. We had to have our session sitting in the corner of the Wing by the cleaning cupboard. Having pinched two chairs out of the janitor's cupboard! We then walked up to Barney's cell, which was on the third floor, and chatted for another twenty minutes hanging over the banister. I could tell he didn't want me to leave.

On 6 May, our session 10, Barney actually became angry. My supervisor told me this was good. Often the best sessions come after a client loses their temper. We had been going through his CBT paperwork and when I pointed out there was some inconsistency in the answers he wasn't happy. I think he took it as criticism, which it wasn't. I was angry at myself for not wording it better. However, the bigger news that week was that he admitted he spent half his time in his cell trying not to cry. This, for somebody who insisted they had no emotions, was a big admission.

I'd had an idea of a book by Noel 'Razor' Smith, an armed robber turned good, that I thought might help Barney. I said I would drop it in for him, and the next day I did.

We were at the very beginning of Barney opening up to me, which made what happened in June even more devastating.

But before that, I had another two clients to see. One was also connected to Thomas but for a very different reason. They both came from the same Hertfordshire town, had had numerous altercations and physical fights and absolutely loathed each other. And then they ended up in the same Prison.

Penge, football, guns and telly

Before I was to meet Thomas's arch-enemy, I was given another client who I only ended up seeing for eight sessions. Again, not my choice but more on that soon!

I was told his name and I would find him yet again on A Wing. He had a very unusual surname, double-barrelled, with one half sounding English and one very Irish. But his first name was Junior, so that was easy enough.

We met in yet another office on A Wing and this really was an office. It had a desk and chairs and other seats and it was actually clean. This was the first room I had ever used in Aylesbury that was faintly clean and tidy.

I soon found out that Junior was due to be released within weeks. He was twenty-one, tall, slim, good-looking and, for those old enough, reminded me very much of the singer Terence Trent D'Arby.

In session 1 he told me he was the youngest of three; his older sister was thirty and a drug addict. He didn't have much good to say about her. He did, however, have a brother who at twenty-two was only just older than him and Junior had a much higher opinion of him.

His parents were divorced and he got on a lot better with his father than he did his mother, who he said, 'does nothing but nag'. He was a Liverpool FC supporter so we had that in common from the start (I was born in Liverpool) and he told me he was inside for one gun crime, but insisted he had been set up, and he was actually a successful drug dealer – but hadn't been caught for that!

Junior had apparently received a six-year sentence, of which he had to serve three inside Prison. And he still had eighteen months to go.

He was a bit slow to warm up, but I always told my clients that session 1 was just an exploratory session to see if they thought I could help them, and by the end of it he was absolutely adamant that he would like to see me every week. So we put plans in place to meet the next Tuesday.

On session 2 he was raring to go. When I asked him what he actually wanted from counselling his exact words were, 'Just someone to talk to really, and even after one week I can talk to you better than anyone out there,' nodding his head towards the Wing.

We soon returned to the subject of football and apparently he had been a very good player as a teenager. Junior had been an apprentice at Fulham Football Club but was given red cards in his first two games. One was for a bad tackle and one was because he punched somebody.

Junior told me that his mum was black and his dad white. He described his mother as being very controlling, diabetic, had had a heart attack, and carried an oxygen pack on her back.

The family came from Penge in South London, which is somewhere I have never been so he spent quite a long time telling me about it. His dad lived five minutes away. He got on really well with him and he felt his dad understood him, whereas his mum just nagged him to death. I had sympathy for the mum. She had obviously seen where Junior's actions were heading and hadn't managed to keep him out of Prison.

By session 3, he was telling me he was loving the counselling. But it was not counselling! It was just a lot of talking, and he laughed a lot. He said he just wanted a grown-up chat, which he couldn't get anywhere else so he liked having it with me once a week.

Scarily, but I was getting used to this, Junior told me he saw his first gun at the age of ten. And even more scarily, when he was thirteen and his brother was fifteen, they bought their first gun. I could quite see why the mum was a nag bag. She had her work cut out with these three kids.

By session 4 Junior was telling me he had been in stage school from the age of three to eight. I hadn't seen that coming! He ran off a list of TV shows he had been in as a child – one of them a hugely successful, well-known series that was on television for many years. He had played a baby and then a little boy in this series. It wasn't one I had ever watched, but I wasn't surprised because he did have a very aesthetically pleasing face and was probably a photogenic child.

We then returned to the guns, which Junior insisted were just part of his life and also part of 'living in Penge' life. I didn't quite know how I was going to convince this boy that having a gun wasn't normal when it would appear that in his life it was.

In session 5 we hit a bit of trouble. His girlfriend had told him she had slept with somebody else. He showed me a photograph of her. An absolutely stunning twenty-year-old girl. Apparently, she cried on the phone to him all week and then came to visit him and cried again. He didn't understand why she was so upset. 'I've told her it's ok,' was his reasoning.

I tried to explain it from her point of view. That she probably felt horrendously guilty, wished it hadn't happened, wouldn't know if he was going to change his mind and dump her for it, despite what he was saying now, and could be terribly upset by any or all of that. He thought because he told her it was okay she shouldn't be upset. I had to do a lot of explaining of women's emotions in that session.

As normal, Junior and I were sitting on one seat each with our legs up on a chair. At one point an Officer came barging into the room and shouted at him to get his feet off the seats. Both of us had hurriedly removed our feet as soon as we saw him approaching, but the Officer had definitely seen me have my legs up as well.

When the Officer left I said, 'That wasn't fair at all. I had my legs up just as much as you. He should've told me off as much as he did you.'

Then Junior said these exact words, which have stayed with me ever since – 'That's the trouble,' he said, 'they think you're one of them and you're not – you're one of us.'

It's not every day you get likened to a black, gun-toting drug dealer from Penge, but it meant more to me than anybody would've realised. I so didn't see myself as any different to these boys and I loved the fact that they saw me as one of them.

By session 6 things had improved with the girlfriend. They had spoken on the phone every day and he was seeing her the following Monday. However, there was another shocking revelation when he told me that he was pretty sure his mother was a drug dealer when she was younger, and she most definitely sold guns when he was a kid!

Again, I was speechless but tried not to show it. What hope do these boys have when they have been brought up by drug-dealing, gun-dealing parents?

Junior also talked about his sister kindly for a change. He said she was his favourite till she left home at sixteen for three years, but when she came back home she was heavily into drugs.

We talked about what he would be doing when he left Prison. He was quite keen to get back into acting and thought that lived experience of the criminal justice system would help him play characters with criminal records. But he was also not sure whether he would go back to his previous criminal activities. Primarily because he lived in Penge!

Yet again, I dug out one of my copies of Noel 'Razor' Smith's books about how he had been an armed robber and then turned his life around. I was buying copies of this book quite frequently on Amazon. Every time I gave one out it never came back. But I didn't mind because it was such a good book and a brilliant example of how crime doesn't pay. You just waste your life behind bars till you realise there is another life to be had. Junior told me that week that he also quite fancied being a football coach and was already qualified to level one.

My final session with Junior, although we didn't know it at the time, was on 27 May 2014. He'd had bad stomach pain and although he'd been to Health Care five times all they had given him was Gaviscon for trapped wind. I had spoken to a medic friend of mine on the outside who said it sounded much more like a potential ulcer. So Junior and I decided that between us, with our acting skills, we would plan a scenario where he would need to be taken to Health Care and be investigated properly.

Sadly, we never got round to that, as there was just about to be one hell of another kind of drama of a very different kind.

Thomas' arch-enemy, a decent Wing and the good idea

The day had arrived for me to meet the person Thomas hated most in the world! I was fascinated to know who could bring out such strong emotions in him.

I was told to meet Aidan on G Wing, which was a new one to me. It was on the other side of the playground, sorry Association area, to Wings A, B, C and D, where I had mostly hung out.

This was quite a trek from the entrance to the Prison but I thought it was by far the nicest Wing I ever went on at Aylesbury. It was calm, quiet, looked newer than the others, was nicely painted and had a lot of space. The cells were bigger, the table tennis, telephones and recreation area was big and spacious, and the Officers were also extremely friendly and chatty on this Wing. It definitely seemed to be a very different part of the Prison.

When I first saw Aidan I was struck by how tall he was. He must've been well over 6 feet and extremely thin. From the moment I met him he was incredibly polite, grateful and thanked me over and over for coming to see him.

He told me that he had found us a good room where we could talk, and he absolutely had. It was upstairs, away from everybody else on the Wing, in a large room that had huge windows overlooking the rugby pitch at the back of the Prison, with quite a lot of video equipment that I was told was used for Parole hearings and court appearances.

As we had the whole huge room to ourselves, we chose two comfy seats near one of the big windows and started to talk.

It was very clear from the off that this boy hated himself. He told me that he was twenty-one and this was his twelfth sentence.

He also told me that he was the youngest child of five and the only one of the five who had been put into the care system. At the age of six. Just after he had been diagnosed with ADHD. I could see straightaway that this was a huge part of the problem. Fancy having two older brothers and two older sisters and you being the only one put into care! What does that do for your self-esteem right from the get-go?

Aidan could talk, and the first session was pretty much a monologue but I was happy to listen. He told me how he loved raving, music, party drugs and cocaine.

He had recently taken an overdose, which I had been warned about, but said it was purely because he hated Aylesbury Prison and was desperate to get out.

He also told me that he had two children, by two different 'baby mothers' – not a term I had heard until I started working in the Prisons. He was father to a four-year-old boy and a two-year-old boy.

Aidan told me he came from the same town as Thomas, but immediately said he didn't want to talk about him because he 'was a waste of space'. I found out that the grief between these two was primarily over a dog. One had sold a dog to the other, the dog was found to be badly kept, with rotting teeth, and the other one refused to pay for the dog. I truly cannot remember which one sold the dog and which one bought the dog but the issue had all started over this dog and had only become worse over the years! Now they were sworn enemies and everybody in the Prison knew it.

In that very first session Aidan seemed to have already given up on himself. He didn't think he would ever be able to stop doing what he had done, offending-wise, and couldn't see how he would be able to change his behaviour. He even said if he was released from Aylesbury he knew he would be back inside within minutes. He was in Prison for burglary and robbery. He didn't think he would be able to stop that when he was out and this was obviously the cause of a lot of his self-hatred. I, however, warmed to him instantly and was determined to help him.

For a twenty-one-year-old, I found Aidan incredibly mature. He was almost like an old man in a young man's body. Maybe that's what being sentenced twelve times before the age of twenty-one does to you. He told me the last time he was released he was only out for sixteen hours before being recalled to Prison. There was going to be a lot to this boy and I couldn't wait to find out more about him.

Aidan told me he loved his mum and she came to see him regularly in the Prison, which I was very pleased to hear. He said he was done with women. Both the mothers of his sons were mad as a box of frogs and he couldn't be doing with women at the moment.

By session 2 he was telling me the most incredible stories about how, when he was in care, he had done nothing but try and get home to his mum.

Social Services had obviously had a nightmare with him. He had to have two Social Workers with him at all times, because he was known for absconding. He constantly ran home to his mother's house, and the heartbreaking thing about that was he knew as soon as his mum saw him she would ring up Social Services and get him taken back. So instead, he used to run up to her house, knock on the front door and then rush across the road and hide in the bushes to catch sight of her when she came outside, just so he could see his mum. This nearly had me in tears.

His 'absconding from care' stories were unbelievable but obviously true. He had so many of them and went into great detail about each one. This boy was more clever than he realised. He told me one time he was in a cinema with one Social Worker on either side of him and he managed to slither down his seat, slide under a few rows of seats and then shoot out of the exit – unseen!

He was expert at getting on trains home without paying, by waiting for a family who had quite a few children. He would mingle with the kids to get through the gate. And then when he was on the train, he would curl up underneath the seats so the inspectors didn't see him.

Because he always ran back to his mum in Hertfordshire, Social Services took him further and further away. They took him to Wales but he still managed to get back home and he ended up in Scotland in the middle of a field in a tent, with two Social

Workers, and miles away from anywhere. Then in the middle of the night he wriggled out of the tent and managed to get back down to Hertfordshire to see his mum again.

By session 3 Aidan was telling me he was very surprised he had kept up seeing me because he didn't usually stick to anything. He told me he really wanted to be 'the nice guy', like he felt he was when he was talking to me, but then he would go and do something awful like robbing his nan or mum's purse and he would feel that self-hatred again.

When I arrived for session 4 there was a lockdown on G Wing and I was told I couldn't see Aidan. I asked an Officer if I could talk to him through the door and I was told yes I could, so I stood at his door for ages talking to him. Aidan kept on asking the Officers if he could come out and eventually they said yes.

His big worry that week was that one of his baby mothers was having his son taken off her and Social Services were coming to see him at the Prison to bring the papers to sign his son over. He wasn't happy about that and was worried it would mean he wouldn't see his son again.

When I arrived for session 5, I found out there had been a massive cock-up and Aidan had been told that I wasn't coming to see him anymore. I can only imagine the paperclip numpty with their crap admin had informed the wrong client.

Aidan had put his fist through his cell wall because he was so angry and upset. So when I turned up as normal he showed me his bloody and bruised hand and was over the moon that I was there. He told me that he had been trying to move to a category C Prison, but there was no way he wanted to go now he was seeing me because he finally felt somebody understood him.

Also, he had requested his 'care history' be sent to him by Social Services and three big boxes had arrived. He wanted me to go through these with him, which I agreed to do in future sessions.

We went a lot deeper in session 6. Aidan said he felt a lot calmer and more settled knowing that I was going to turn up every week, because everybody else in his life had let him down. He saw himself as very weak and easily led, and although he knew it was wrong, if he saw money sitting around, he absolutely knew he would pinch it. He felt he had no strength, no inner core, no moral compass. He knew what all of those things were and he knew right from wrong, but he didn't know how to be the man he wanted to be.

He also talked of how his baby mothers had only loved him when he was the bad boy. They liked it when he had money and he knew that if he got back with either of them he would fall back into his bad ways. He reiterated again that he had withdrawn his application to move to HMP The Mount as he enjoyed our sessions so much. I'm just glad he thought they were helping.

Aidan had done a lot of thinking and decided that he did not want to go back to his hometown, because he knew he would be drawn back into all his old ways. However, he didn't want to be that far away because he still wanted to visit his mum, brothers and sisters – some of whom now had children so he was an uncle. But he wanted to be within travelling distance of his two sons, who he was still very hopeful he would be able to see.

Because I knew his area extremely well I said, 'In that case you're really looking at this one particular town,' and he said, 'absolutely – that is smack in the middle of the two and where I want to live, as I think it's the only way of me keeping out of trouble, being able to see my mum and being able to see my children.'

I then had what I thought was the best idea ever and shared it with him. I knew of a charity based in that town who helped house people who were either ex-homeless, ex-Prison or ex-addicts. I had a friend who had used their services for her son, so I knew exactly what this organisation offered.

They installed you in a supported-living flat for two years, gave you a mentor and an accountant, to give you any guidance you needed with budgeting and sorting out previous debts and to help you get your benefits organised. If you had addiction issues you received intensive free addiction therapy, you also had access to a free counsellor and, perhaps best of all, if you stayed the course, at the end of the two years you were automatically elevated to the top of the local council housing list and guaranteed a permanent place to live.

When I told Aidan all about this he was so excited, because he knew he needed support on the outside and couldn't believe his luck that there was an organisation offering this level of support in the exact town he wanted to live in. I promised him I would look into it and come back the next week with as much information as I could.

How could something so right turn in to something so wrong? I was about to find out.

One nervous boy
and two lovely ladies

Session 7 with Aidan and he was in a buoyant mood. I had, as promised, looked up the Housing and Ex-Prisoner Support Charity and brought in the telephone number for him.

I was well aware that in counselling you're not supposed to do everything for your client, so all I had literally brought into the Prison was the telephone number. There was no point bringing in an email address or website details because Aidan didn't have access to the internet. He was more than grateful and was just terrified that he would lose the number! We picked a place for him to put the phone number so he wouldn't lose it.

He also had news for me that week.

He told me, very proudly, that just that morning he had learnt to spell his middle name. It was Joseph and he could now, finally, aged twenty-one, spell it.

He was very excited about the prospect of support when he was released from Prison and I tried hard to not get his hopes built up too high. I explained that they only had approximately twenty-two of these flats, and there were no guarantees, but it was definitely worth investigating.

The following week, when I arrived for session 8, he told me very excitedly that he had called the charity and had a really good conversation with them. He told me how nice they had been, and how kind, and he had given them all his details so they could contact him directly at the Prison and make an appointment to come in and see him

When I arrived the next week to see him at our normal time he was waiting for me at the entrance to his Wing. He was looking very excitable, and as soon as I opened the two gates to get to him, he started to shout, 'It's today, it's today! They're coming today.'

This was quicker than I had expected but I was thrilled for him. The charity were due in half an hour. Standing right beside Aidan was one of those lovely Officers. They were definitely more chatty on this Wing. And respectful to the boys. Aidan had obviously told him who was coming and the Officer said to me, 'This is really good news isn't it?' And I said, 'Yes, hopefully.'

The Officer asked, 'Are you going to take him over?'

I hadn't envisaged this was even going to be an option, so said, 'Am I allowed?' knowing that Aidan would be going to meet them in the Visit Hall.

The Officer replied, 'You've got keys haven't you?'

I showed him my belt with my keys, 'Yep.'

He smiled and said, 'Of course you can take him. Just make sure you bring him back.'

As we still had thirty minutes to go, Aidan and I had a sit down and a little chat and I calmed him down. I assured him that he really only had to be himself. He was such a lovely person – so kind, so considerate, so humble – so I said, 'Please just be yourself and don't try and put on any sort of act. You don't need to. You are absolutely lovely and they are going to love you.'

After telling the Officer we were off, he wished Aidan good luck and we set off for the Visit Hall, which was a good ten minutes' walk. We arrived before the visitors but very soon two ladies arrived called Helen and Karis. I made sure that Aidan sat opposite them and I sat just away to one side.

I introduced myself, of course, but told the ladies that they were there to speak to Aidan and to just ignore me because he was perfectly capable of speaking for himself. Which he did. I could not have been more proud of that boy that day. The ladies were absolutely lovely to him and he spoke from the heart about how he knew he had it in him to be a good person, but equally he knew he needed support on the outside. He was chatty and warm and personable and so were they. Very unusually for me, I did manage to keep my mouth shut for nearly two hours and there were just a couple of times when Aidan looked at me with a big beaming smile. He could tell it was going well and so could I.

At the end of the visit, the ladies shook hands with Aidan, he thanked them so much for coming and as they left the Visit Hall one way, I took Aidan back to his Wing. As soon as I was on the Wing, I saw the same Officer who'd seen us off, who asked me how it had gone? I told him 'exceedingly well' and that I had brought Aidan back, and there he was.

Now all we had to do was wait to hear from the charity. I left the Prison that day without a care in the world and hugely hopeful that Aidan had just found the support he desperately needed on the outside.

Sad pasts
and happy futures

I went in the next week to see Aidan, as usual, and he wanted to dissect the meeting from the week before. As I suspected he didn't think he had done well enough but I assured him it could not have gone any better. He had completely won those two ladies over and I was feeling very positive about the whole thing.

With perfect timing, I had had an email from them just before I went into the Prison saying that 'it was looking extremely good', 'he meets the local connection criteria' and 'they hoped to be in touch very soon'. I told Aidan it doesn't get better than that and now we just had to forget about it and carry on as normal.

Aidan told me that he'd received the first box of his care records from Social Services and the biggest shock to him, so far, was seeing written down that him going into care was his mother's 'fault', when he had always blamed himself.

He said he'd only looked at a very small portion of it because it was very upsetting, but had seen entries saying his mum collected him from school and took him to the pub till 11 p.m.

This had really confused him because he adored his mother but he kept saying, 'I've always blamed myself for all of this.'

He literally broke my heart, this boy. He wanted me to go through all these boxes with him and to take paperwork home to read. I told him I would, but I was going to have to bring in a very big box, or a ginormous bag, to get it all home with me!

He told me that he had heard on the wind he was likely to get moved to another Prison, but he would stay in touch if that happened.

Sure enough, the next week when I went to visit him he had been moved to HMP Bullingdon.

I didn't have a breakdown over it this time because I knew Aidan was due out soon and was hopefully going to be looked after by this fabulous charity. And be housed about twenty minutes down the road from me.

Joyously, within a fortnight I received an email from the charity to say that they would definitely be offering Aidan accommodation and support as soon as he was released. I was absolutely thrilled to bits for him. I was staggered that everything he wanted and needed had fallen into place and just so pleased that he was going to get such intensive support from an organisation who really understood young people like Aidan.

This couldn't be
happening. Could it?

I remember vividly where I was the night I received the email. I was at the Wycombe Swan Theatre in High Wycombe with a friend and her mum. I happened to check my emails on my phone and my blood ran cold.

I had at the very least an anxiety attack, if not a panic attack. The friend I was with was a much more highly qualified counsellor than me and kept saying, 'What on earth's wrong?' All I could get out was, 'I've had an email from the Prison.'

She was very blasé and said, 'Oh, screw them. You're far too good for them anyway.' But I was in deep shock and absolutely horrified.

The numpty had resurfaced. And had sent me a very short, abrupt and, frankly terrifying, message.

It said they had heard 'very concerning things' about my 'activities in the Prison' and demanded that I go to meet them at 2 p.m. on Tuesday, 3 June and I was to bring my supervisor with me.

What they didn't know was that Monday, 2 June was my birthday, so they had just ruined that, never mind my night out with my mate and the entire weekend to boot.

I was so embarrassed having to tell my supervisor that he had been called to this meeting and I explained the circumstances. Or what I assumed were the circumstances.

I guessed my 'activities in the Prison' were taking Aidan to the Visit Hall. My supervisor was, as always, wonderful and told me that he would be there with me on Tuesday and we would sort it.

Tuesday rolled around and I was due to see my clients after this meeting at 2 p.m. All I can tell you now is that what happened next was one of the most traumatic and painful hours of my life.

Coldly, the numpty started by saying, 'I want to make it very clear at the beginning of this meeting that it is my intention to remove your keys and your belt and you will be escorted out of the Prison.'

This was my worst nightmare. I had fought so hard to get into the Prison system and by just trying to help somebody I was going to get thrown out? At this point I still didn't know what I had actually done.

I sat there dazed and speechless, which really isn't like me. This just couldn't be happening.

My supervisor, however, went into battle. He insisted, in no uncertain terms, that I had done nothing wrong, that they always encouraged multi-agency working, that I had bent over backwards to help boys in that Prison and I hadn't done anything that risked anybody or hurt anybody.

Numpty however was enjoying every moment. For whatever reason I'd never been liked by them and now they were going to have their day. At one point I was asked about the clients I was seeing and what position I was in with all of them.

I remember saying that Thomas was due to get out any minute, all ready to buy his pint of milk, and Aidan had just been moved so they were fine, but the one I was concerned about was Barney. At which point I burst into tears. Again.

I was due to see Barney that afternoon and I knew he would be hurt that I hadn't turned up. I was informed that I could write a formal letter telling them that I was leaving but I couldn't put any explanation in it as to why.

All I can remember doing is sobbing and sobbing and sobbing, and hearing my supervisor shouting louder and louder – until it became a shouting match between Numpty and my supervisor, while I just sat and wept.

Anybody who knows me now will tell you what a fighter I am, but I had no fight in me that day. I knew I would never win over this unfeeling human and I was angry at myself for 'going outside the bounds of counselling' as they kept throwing at me. I call it 'helping people' but, no, to them I had committed a mortal sin. I'd only done what the Officer had told me I could, for goodness' sake.

I was duly stripped of my Prison belt and my keys, and we were shown out of the Prison. All I could think of was Barney sitting in his cell waiting for me, thinking, 'Oh well there's another person who's let me down.'

I cried all the way home and I didn't stop crying for about two days. I didn't stop feeling bad about it for months. And to be honest, writing this eleven years later, it is still bringing up painful memories.

There was no way I needed to be treated like that. I could've been gently told that it wasn't appropriate to go to the Visit Hall with a Prisoner, even with an Officer suggesting and approving it, and not to do it again. I'm quite sure that that's what would've happened at HMP The Mount. But no, Aylesbury had been unforgiving and heartless. And to my mind, most definitely NOT putting their clients first, which I have always thought paramount.

I spent weeks thinking I had just wrecked my entire vocation. But as I was now living pretty much full-time in my Dorset flat there was still just enough fight left in me to try and get into a Prison in the West Country. I had my eye on HMP Portland, which I knew was a Young Offender Institute, but I had absolutely no idea if this slinging out from Aylesbury would follow me. I wouldn't put anything past them. After all, they had lied on my official counselling qualification paperwork. If they could get that so wrong, what else could they get wrong?

But I now had an absolute passion for helping Prisoners and on top of that I still had nearly fifty hours of my counselling placement to go, so I just could not let this finish me. I had encountered the most uncaring human being I have ever met in the Prison system in the last twenty-five years and back then I was just so sorry that our paths had crossed.

From that day on my supervisor referred to Numpty as 'The Aylesbury Assassin' and never did a description fit anybody better.

As for me, I was down, but I was most definitely not out.

Then just when you think the numpty couldn't stoop any lower ...

Because my main concern was Aidan, within two days of being booted out I was in touch with the charitable housing association with the main aim of telling them I was no longer seeing Aidan and to please deal with him direct at the Prison. There was no need to copy me into emails anymore. Some of us were efficient with our admin and I knew this was important.

I thought I would ring the charity who were going to house Aidan and provide him with all this much-needed intensive support and housing. Both Aidan and I knew he needed this kind of wrap-around care to stay out of Prison and I just wanted to make sure that it actually happened.

When one of the two ladies, who had actually met me and Aidan in the Prison, answered the phone she was very warm, friendly and chatty. I explained that I was no longer Aidan's counsellor, but I would carry on supporting him on the outside as I was an experienced ex-Prisoner mentor, but definitely wouldn't be stepping on their toes as I appreciated they offered the complete support package for people leaving Prison.

Nothing could've prepared me for what she said next. 'I'm so sorry about this, but we've already heard from the Prison and they have put a stop to us offering Aidan accommodation and support.'

I was speechless. Which I'm not often. I think I said something along the lines of, 'Are you serious? Please don't let the Prison stop you helping that boy because he desperately needs it.'

But this lady had obviously had the fear of God put into her by the Prison and said, 'I'm so sorry. He is such a lovely boy and we so wanted to help him, but we just can't because we have been contacted and told that we are not allowed to have any further dealings with him.'

It was a relatively short phone call, because I was in shock. Would any professional be so short-sighted and petty that they would stop somebody receiving a complete support package, including accommodation, when he left the Prison, purely because I had had the smallest amount of involvement in introducing the charity to them? It would appear that they would, because nobody else to my knowledge had known anything about it.

I was incredulous. Absolutely incredulous. Did the Prison service want to help these boys stay out of Prison or not?

And if I tell you what happened next, you will see the damage that decision caused, and also the cost to us, the taxpayer.

Aidan was released just at the time I was in bed with flu. The sort of flu that knocks you off your feet and you can't even walk. He telephoned me and said he was out and he had to get to Probation that afternoon but had no idea how to get there and could I take him? I coughed and spluttered, 'Aidan, if I could get out of this bed, I would take you in a heartbeat but I can't even walk let alone drive. Is there anybody else you can ask?'

There apparently wasn't. Aidan had ADHD and learning difficulties. He had only learnt to spell his middle name while I was seeing him so reading road signs and train platform signs was just beyond him. Added to his lack of knowledge of the area he was stranded in, and clueless about how to use public transport, he did what he had done the last time he was released from Prison – went round to a mate's house, got drunk, swiped somebody's wallet to buy more alcohol and was back in Prison within thirty-six hours.

And this is where I tell you how much it cost us, as in taxpayers, because of a petty decision. Aidan was recalled to Prison for another eighteen months. That cost you and me approximately £75,000.

It also cost me in other ways, which I paid gladly. I went to visit Aidan in every Prison he was in. Including on an enclosed visit, which meant he had to be on one side of the glass and I had to be on the other. But for the entire eighteen months he was stuck back in Prison, rather than benefiting from the housing charity and their support. I visited him regularly. He also wrote to me constantly and I wrote back. I supported him through the whole eighteen months.

His mental health hit rock bottom during this time. He knew that if he had been getting the support the charity had offered he wouldn't be sitting in a Prison, yet again. Can you imagine how much he hated himself then?

I've been on this planet for over 60 years now and I truly think that taking away that boy's opportunity for a new life was the most shocking and disgraceful decision I have ever seen made by anybody.

Bruised, wounded pride
and mad vicars

I was in a right predicament. I still had nearly 50 hours of my 100 hours placement to do and I was Prison-less. A Prison Counsellor without a Prison! I still had the determination to get into a Prison, despite off-the-scale levels of anxiety, because I didn't know whether my Aylesbury-exit scenario would follow me.

But getting into Prisons took time and I needed hours quickly for my qualification, so I decided to turn to the two things I knew best – the homeless charities and ex-Prisoner charities. But not in London this time, instead in Poole in Dorset where I was temporarily based.

The traumatic situation at Aylesbury took a very long time to get over. I had given my all to those boys, and adored all six of them, and then to be slung out the door like that? It was shocking and horrendously painful at the time. As the years have gone by I still think it was totally unnecessary. Everybody makes mistakes and all I needed to be told was that it wasn't acceptable and not to do it again. There was no need to make such a drama out of it and cut me off from my clients, because that hurt them and they should've come first.

In later conversations with my supervisor he hadn't even realised that I'd been given permission to take Aidan off the Wing. He thought I had just taken him!

I assured him I would NEVER have dreamt of doing anything like that and every single thing I ever did at Aylesbury, I ALWAYS asked an Officer first if it was okay. For example, the time Barney and I needed to have our session in the Wing corner by the cleaning cupboard. I didn't just do things like that. I always asked an Officer if it was okay or not.

I had learnt in my training that the Officers were the Gods who ran the Wings and I was to do nothing without their permission. And I never did! Yet I was still treated like I had committed the crime of the century.

And on this particular occasion I hadn't even suggested it. I had been told that it was okay to take Aidan off the Wing. Saved the Officer a job I imagined.

My supervisor said if he had known that he would've gone for the jugular even stronger than he did.

With a very nasty taste left in my mouth, and feeling battered and bruised, I started the search for new placements in Dorset. Very soon I found out there were two charities I could apply to – one that focused on the homeless and one that focused on ex-Prisoners. Bang on perfect for me.

The Footprints Project was a charity based in Dorset (and I believe now in Somerset and Hampshire), and they focused on mentoring ex-Prisoners. I started there. I played a bit of telephone tennis with what turned out to be a mad vicar but eventually found myself in a church being interviewed by one of the nicest people in the world. This vicar had several roles with The Footprints Project, but one of them was utilising the skills of mostly homeless people, and a lot of ex-Prisoners, to paint and repair his huge and crumbling church!

He had the biggest smile and the biggest teeth and reminded me of a television vicar. But I could see straight away he was the kindest man as he even let some of his homeless people sleep in, under and around his church, rather than see them on the streets.

We had a brilliant meeting. I always find I do with people who CARE – the direct opposite of the first one I had had with the paperclip numpty.

Mark, as I found out the vicar's name was, told me there were always a lot of homeless people and ex-Prisoners in and around the church, decorating it, doing plastering, roofing, plumbing and electrics, and he would help them pass NVQs in these subjects to strengthen their job prospects. He thought a lot of them would welcome counselling. He then showed me to a tiny kitchen and said, 'Do make yourself a cup of tea. I just need to make one phone call and then I will take you on a tour of the church.'

In the kitchen was a man in a very brightly coloured jumper. I immediately said, 'Hello, I'm Sarah,' and he said, 'Hi, I'm Andy,' and we had a chat while I waited for the kettle to boil, having offered to make him a cup of tea as well.

We talked for a good fifteen to twenty minutes about who he was and what he was doing at the church, and I found out afterwards that the vicar left me with him 'sort of on purpose' when he saw Andy was in the kitchen, to see how I related to his clients. He told me I had passed with flying colours and Andy loved me. And was grateful for the tea!

Then Mark took me on a tour of the church, which was absolutely massive, to find a suitable spot for me to use for counselling. This was one of those churches that has community rooms attached to it and they went back literally miles. I've never seen such a big church in my life. There was one huge room where a children's nursery ran Monday to Friday and then about thirty other community rooms used by Slimming World and numerous other organisations. No wonder the poor man needed people to help with the upkeep.

For my counselling we decided on the vestry! There were two huge old sofas opposite each other and it was a relatively small room. Importantly, it was quiet and confidential because nobody used the main church in the midweek afternoons when I was going to be in, so there would be no congregation at that time.

Everything was set for me to start, and Mark was very excited about being able to offer free counselling to his clients.

Meanwhile, a mile away, but still in Poole, was the homeless charity Routes to Roots. I've volunteered for probably twenty charities in my time and I still think that is the best name for any homeless charity ever!

I was invited in for an interview, where I met yet another lovely person. The lady in charge was Gabi. When I told her about all my homeless experience with Crisis, *The Big Issue*, The London Connection, No Second Night Out, The Prince's Trust and The Depaul Trust she was incredibly welcoming and thrilled that I was prepared to offer free counselling to some of her clients.

So within six weeks of leaving the Prison in June, I had found two placements with MY client groups and I was ready to start racking up those hours again.

Next came the task of getting back into a Prison. If I thought it had been hard the first and second two times,

I had no idea what was to come next! If I had known, it wouldn't have put me off because what was coming was fantastic. But it took months and it certainly wasn't easy.

My first Footprints client and my first visit to Poole Hospital

Mark was doing his best to find me clients and the first one stayed with me for many months while I was beavering away trying to infiltrate the Prison system in Dorset.

Like a lot of people in Poole, Matthew wasn't from the South Coast but had found his way down there from Cambridgeshire. He was forty, homeless, one of the men who were taking up the vicar's offer of accommodation underneath the church, and had terrible addictions to just about every drug going.

He was diagnosed as a paranoid schizophrenic and used to hear voices. Matthew was an absolutely lovely character who I became very fond of as we battled together to reduce his addictions.

When he couldn't recall something I was asking him about his past, his most repeated line was, 'You've got to remember, Sarah – I've taken an awful lot of drugs.' I loved his honesty.

He did, however, have quite serious psychosis and heard a lot of different voices in his head telling him to do things. The worst time was when he had just been housed in a hostel, and on the very same day heard voices telling him that he was going to be attacked by the residents and buried alive.

Because being buried alive was his biggest fear he decided instead to chop his own head off and kill himself before they did it. I only found out about this via a frantic phone call from the vicar to say that Matthew was in Poole Hospital and was I around to go because he was already out with another client?

I leapt in my car and drove to the hospital, and found Matthew outside having a fag in his hospital gown with his backside on full view to the world. Fag finished, we went inside. I bought him a cup of tea and a cake and we had a chat. He told me, over apple pies and two mugs of tea, what had happened.

He had moved into the new hostel absolutely fine earlier on that day, but when he had gone into the common room he was quite convinced people were talking about him and that they were going to bury him alive. This being his biggest paranoia, he had gone back to his room, grabbing a knife from the kitchen on the way, and then sliced from the bottom of his hairline on the left to the bottom of his hairline on the right, round the front of his throat. He had literally nearly decapitated himself.

He had then run from his room back to the common room and through reception, screaming at the top of his voice, 'You'll never get me, you'll never get me!' Within minutes, the Police did get him and he was swiftly removed.

By the time I arrived, he had been seen to at the hospital but very badly in my view. It looked like somebody had sewn great big tacking stitches round his neck. I then realised he had probably been there many times before, being prone to this sort of behaviour, so maybe they didn't spend too much time on him knowing it would happen again. Either that or these great big loose stitches were just to hold him together and he would get sewn up properly later.

After a good chinwag, and offering to get Matthew anything he needed, I left him in the hands of the nurses. The vicar had already texted me that Matthew had been immediately evicted from the hostel, not surprising as he had scattered blood all over their common room, but when he was released from the hospital he would have nowhere to go. Unless he went back under the church.

When I told Mark about the extent of the wound and how he had come dangerously close to decapitating himself, we both agreed there was absolutely no way, with a wound like that, he could carry on sleeping under the church, because of the risk of infection.

So Mark and I, between us, started talking to Bournemouth and Poole Housing and did our damnedest to get him accommodation. To say they weren't interested was an understatement. In the end they gave in and agreed to put him up in a B&B, which I took him to and installed him in.

He was then moved from B&B to B&B until something happened, which meant he automatically had to be housed. I didn't know this at the time but he was newly diagnosed with diabetes and, apparently, as insulin needs to be stored in a fridge, that shoots you to the top of the housing list.

The last time I saw Matthew it was just before Christmas and we went for a festive coffee underneath all the pretty lights in the suburb of Bournemouth he had been allocated supported housing in. He had been given a very nice one-bedroom flat. I was thrilled that he was now on the right medication, had conquered pretty much all his addictions and was in supported housing, which he desperately needed.

Mark was keeping me busy with new clients and then I started to see some for Gabi at the homeless charity as well. I was still itching to get back in a Prison and things were at last starting to move in that direction.

Mad vicars and tea parties

Mark and Gabi were well aware of the trauma I had experienced at Aylesbury, having my placement cut short unnecessarily, and both of them did their absolute best to find me clients.

Another one of Mark's was, to my delight, an ex-Prisoner. Steven was in his mid 30s and had spent most of his life in and out of Prison. He was a very good-looking black guy with dreadlocks, who didn't look his age and had a very low opinion of himself.

Like so many, he had become involved in the drug world in London and had come down to the coast to escape his old contacts. He loved the fact that I had worked in Prisons and I knew his world, and we talked at length about his time in different Prisons and how it had made him feel about his life. He definitely didn't want to go back.

He was, however, very firm with me that I had to get back into a Prison, 'Because you have to help all the little Stevens like me who are still in there.' Although he had turned his life around, he knew there were tens of thousands who hadn't yet. He was so lovely and supportive of me getting back into a Prison and every single week he would ask me, 'What's the latest? How are you doing getting back in?'

One of the most hysterical events of my life involved both Steven and Matthew, and of course the vicar. It was Matthew's birthday so the vicar and I decided to take them out for afternoon tea. We all turned up at a hotel in Bournemouth, Steven with his dreadlocks and Rastafarian clothes and Matthew with his very obviously slashed neck, bloodstained trainers, and dressed for a rave rather than afternoon tea.

We noticed some very strange looks as we walked in, but the vicar and I were adamant that these boys were as good as anybody else and deserved their afternoon tea. So we took our place at a table with a stunning sea view and had one of the most uproarious afternoon teas I've ever had in my life.

It wasn't long after this that the vicar took some of the boys and men to the Dorset County Show. I couldn't go on that occasion, but I remember I was invited. However, the vicar had taken four of his clients with him to the big annual county event.

At lunchtime he sat them all at a table while he went up to the counter to get their tea and sandwiches. When he arrived back some snooty woman sitting at the other end of the table snapped at him, 'I've really no desire to sit at a table with people like this.' I'm assuming they were looking a bit rough around the edges, as people living under churches tend to.

Mark the vicar, who had a very good sense of humour, said, 'Madam, you are right. I would not want my guests to sit at table with a person such as yourself, so would you kindly fuck off?' I so wish I had been there.

Gabi had found me a good few clients at Routes to Roots by now, and between the two of them they managed to get me up to the 100 hours needed for my counselling qualification. That's the sort of kindness I will never forget after the brutality at Aylesbury.

But things were finally starting to move in the Dorset Prison world, so although I never abandoned any of these clients, I was busy the rest of the time trying desperately to get back behind bars.

Guys Marsh v Portland
and useless Solicitors

Having managed to get myself into two Prisons now, you would think I would know the routine. Sadly, there is no routine. This is just one of the things that is frustrating and time-consuming about the Prison service and I'll be going into that in a lot more detail later on, but for now, believe me, the inconsistencies are breathtaking. So I had to start again from scratch.

Everybody was very helpful and told me I could try this person or try that person. I did all the normal stuff like sending my CV and letters into the Prisons, but nothing was coming back.

Prisons chop and change their categories more often than some people change their underwear but at that particular point, in summer 2014, my research had taken me as far as knowing there were currently three Prisons in Dorset. There was HMP YOI Portland, which had been purely a Young Offender Institute, but now also held adult males. That was right over in West Dorset on an island, not far from Weymouth. HMP Guys Marsh was in North Dorset and quite a long way away from me. Then there was The Verne. This was the one that changed category more than any of the others, but when I was there it was an Immigration Removal Centre, so it wasn't of great interest to me. It just reminded me of Dante every time I saw the sign.

HMP Guys Marsh did interest me because it was a category C Male Prison, exactly the same as HMP The Mount. But my head had been turned by those Young

Offenders! So, really, I had my eye on Portland right from the beginning.

I knew I couldn't be picky, so I had to just throw everything at anybody who would listen. Along the way I picked up a random solicitor. Somebody introduced us. She was an Indian lady who had been a solicitor for many years, but swapped sides and decided she wanted to help offenders instead. She was two-thirds of the way through her counselling training and looking for a placement.

I quite liked the idea at the beginning and thought having a solicitor with me, and us offering our services as a team, wouldn't be a bad thing. Also, she hadn't done namby-pamby person-centred counselling. In fact she was doing the polar opposite – very heavy psychoanalytical counselling, and far more the sort of stuff that would be of use in a Prison. I also thought us having a range of counselling modalities wasn't a bad thing to be offering any of these Prisons. So we teamed up and presented ourselves as a pair.

We managed to get a meeting with the Head of Dorset Mental Health Care in some godforsaken, off the beaten track location in the depths of rural Dorset.

This was very exciting, and we thought it would lead somewhere, but it turned into something and nothing. The people we spoke to thought it was a great idea to have counselling in the Prisons but were obviously not the decision makers. They, however, give us permission to counsel in any Prisons in Dorset, which was a step forward. But still didn't get us through the door of any Prison!

One lead I had did turn into something. I was told Barnardo's ran the Family Days at HMP Guys Marsh, and possibly other services too, so I applied to Barnardo's. I had an interview and was accepted. It seemed like they did offer quite a few services in the Prison that a counsellor would be useful for. I felt I was getting somewhere. Not quite where I wanted to be, but somewhere.

While Barnardo's was sending off for a DBS check for me I had an email from a Senior Prison Officer called Graham, at HMP Guys Marsh, inviting us in for a meeting. This was very exciting!

When we arrived, the first thing I noticed was how beautifully the Prison was kept. Even from the outside you could see the gardens, lawns, flowerbeds and grounds looked bright and colourful, and were obviously very well looked after. Even the Prison Wings looked like Swiss chalets. 'I bet this is where they send newspaper journalists and photographers to take pictures when they call Prisons holiday camps,' was my first thought.

On meeting Graham he gave me a huge hug and a big warm smile. Instantly, I thought, 'My God, at Aylesbury that would've got you the sack.' Maybe things were going to be different in Dorset. Graham could not have been nicer. He had even done levels one and two counselling himself and was all for having counselling in the Prison. The meeting went extremely well. Such a lovely man. And he said he would be in touch to progress things soon.

Then out of the blue we had an email from HMP YOI Portland inviting us in for a meeting. OMG. I was so happy. I remember that day so well. Driving from Poole over to Weymouth, across the Chesil Beach Causeway and up onto the Isle of Portland. The views were absolutely stunning. My mum had always been a fan of Dorset and in particular Chesil Beach and now I could see why.

Me and the solicitor were met at the gate and taken through to the Admin block, which wasn't actually too far from reception, meaning not too many gates to get through – straight into a meeting with approximately eight people: me, the solicitor, five unknown staff from the Prison and the Head Governor, James.

This was my moment to sell myself and I was only slightly pissed off that the solicitor hadn't made any effort whatsoever with her appearance, and had badly bitten half-painted red nails, which was all I could see in the room. 'How unprofessional,' was all I could think. Didn't she know how important it was to make a good impression?

I didn't have a clue who all the other people in the meeting were, but I knew very well who the Governor was. I liked him instantly. He was very young, only looked mid 30s, and was highly delighted at the thought of having counselling in his Prison. I formed the impression he hadn't been at the Prison long and was trying to make positive changes.

He told us that there had been a counselling service but it had collapsed some while ago and nobody seemed to know the reason for that, but he was very passionate about there being a counselling service in the Prison again.

What impressed me most about James was how well he knew the boys and men in his Prison. I kept hearing him talking to the person who was sitting to his right, 'This will be perfect for the boy on Nelson who is self-harming, Kenny,' and then five minutes later he would turn again and say, 'And it will be absolutely brilliant for Pete, who is anxious about being released.' I thought, 'Wow – this man actually knows the names of some of the people in his Prison and, not only that, he knows the ones who would benefit from counselling.' I knew from that moment he was somebody who cared. Caring is so hugely important to me.

I felt the meeting went brilliantly, especially when the Governor said, 'Have you been talking to any other Prison about doing this anywhere else?' And I answered, 'Yes, Guys Marsh.'

Straightaway, he said, 'Right, forget them. You're coming here. We can get you started straight away.'

This was music to my ears. I had always had a gut feeling I would do something at Portland Prison. Don't ask me why, but every time I had seen it on a map of Prisons, I just knew it was 'my' Prison. Much as I liked Graham and HMP Guys Marsh, the draw of Young Offenders was very strong now.

And once I had been inside I knew for certain. HMP YOI Portland was on the most beautiful coast, with a stunning drive for me from Poole through Weymouth on to Portland, with a Governor who cared about his Prisoners, most of whom were Young Offenders but with a few adult males for good measure. I was in! I was bursting with happiness. I was excited and desperate to meet new Young Offenders who I could hopefully help.

The solicitor proved to be a waste of space. After that meeting she told me she wouldn't be able to take this on because she had too much on her plate with her college course, supervision twice a week, clients twice a week, and it was all too much. Blah blah. So she buggered off, but I didn't care. I was IN and I knew I could do it on my own. She hadn't contributed much to the meeting anyway. I had begun to think she was quite lacklustre, whereas I was brimming full of passion.

Unlike Aylesbury, where I was a junior counsellor to about four others, this was going to be MY baby and I was going to run it how I wanted to run it.

At this point I had been successfully self-employed for twenty-five years so setting something up from scratch didn't concern me. Running something on my own didn't faze me. I knew how Prisons worked and I knew how to organise a new service, so from that day on I did nothing but focus on HMP YOI Portland. Happy, happy days.

Posters, cell drops and my own counselling room

It had felt like an age, but it was actually only in June that I had been unceremoniously slung out from Aylesbury, and I saw my first client in HMP Portland on 19 November – so it was only five months, but it felt like forever. I had missed working with those Young Offenders so much. Mark and Gabi between them had kept me busy and I'd achieved my 100 counselling hours. Unlike last time when the paperclip loon had either lied on my six-month 50 hours report or, if we give them the benefit of the doubt, completely muddled me up with someone else, both Mark and Gabi gave me glowing testimonials for my 100 hours report. I could've wept after the drama of last time. Kind, caring people both of them.

I also passed my Level 4 Counselling qualification and was a fully fledged qualified counsellor by November 2014. I hadn't wanted to stop studying though and had already started on a CBT Level 5 qualification in the September, which I was absolutely loving.

So, by the time I started at HMP Portland, I was a qualified counsellor. There was to be no training here like I had had at Aylesbury. I walked straight into the Security Department, was handed a belt, keys, ID and a car park pass, and sent on my way! I'm guessing they realised I'd had all this training before, having now worked in two Prisons.

I was literally starting from scratch with this service so the first thing I did was design a poster, informing people that counselling was now available at HMP Portland.

I paid for this poster myself. I had it designed professionally, printed and laminated, and then walked miles round the Prison putting it up on every notice board I could possibly find. I made sure there were several in Chaplaincy, where Prisoners went when they were feeling distressed or even suicidal, and also where they were told of any bereavements. Plenty of posters went into Health Care. Some in Education. A few in the library. At each of these drop-offs I had a good chat with the member of staff in charge and explained that counselling was now available and would they please let anybody they thought needed it know? All of them were absolutely lovely and thrilled to hear that they could now refer people for counselling.

I also went round to every single Wing, including the Induction Wing where Prisoners spent their first night and were considered to be most vulnerable, and put posters on all the noticeboards.

I had been allocated an Administrator called Charley, who was helpful, kind and was to become a huge support. It was Charley who organised the initial 'cell drop'. We had decided we would put an application form for counselling underneath the cell door of every person in the Prison.

I had designed the form. It asked for the client's name, Prison number, age, Wing and cell number and the 'reason for referral', which could be written by them or somebody who was referring them. It made it clear that this question was not obligatory and could be kept confidential if preferred. Then it asked for their availability for counselling, i.e. when they were either not at work or education, and the date they were making the request.

Charley printed off hundreds of forms, which were literally put under the door of every single cell.

I then sat back and waited. Within a week we had twenty-seven completed referral forms requesting counselling and I drove over to the Prison to pick them up. I wanted to go through these at home, quietly and meticulously, as some of these could be from desperate people.

Having loved every second of working at Aylesbury, I decided immediately to counsel two afternoons at Portland. I needed to get cracking on helping these twenty-seven people and one afternoon a week wasn't going to do it. So from that November I started to go in every Wednesday and Thursday afternoon and crammed in as many clients as I could.

At Portland I even had my own counselling room. I can't begin to tell you how squalid it was BUT it was my own room! No more having to find rooms, or remembering to book rooms, or do counselling in corners of Wings or out in the yard, which had happened once at Aylesbury.

This old office had one tatty, ancient brown leather sofa, one even tattier armchair and an almost deceased desk, just about clinging onto a wall. And the carpet? I can't even begin to describe it. There was more stain than there was blue carpet.

The once magnolia walls were peeling with old rotten paint, there a very high ceiling smothered in cobwebs, and it had obviously sat empty for a very long time. But did I care? Absolutely not! I finally had my own counselling room and, while I still had to walk to every Wing to pick up each client and walk them back after the session, we actually had our own counselling space.

I was back and I had never been happier.

Cat phobias, knowledgeable counsellors and obstructive doctors

Now I was finally settled in a Prison where I belonged I had promised myself I would get some counselling of my own. I had had a very irritating cat phobia for twenty-five years, which I was desperate to get rid of.

It was severely affecting my life. Restricting where I could go on holiday and especially having an impact on eating at outside restaurants, which were a complete no-go area for me if there was the potential for a cat under the table. I was a nervous wreck unless I knew I was somewhere a cat could not get to me.

I know exactly where the cat phobia came from. It came when my stepmother moved to Cyprus after my dad died when I was twenty-three. Cats are everywhere in Cyprus and for some godforsaken reason seem to like me. I'd had two of them jump on my lap in restaurants before, and from this came the debilitating cat phobia. I was visiting my stepmother regularly and the cats became more and more of a problem.

So I had a Google and found a counsellor who specialised in phobias and was based in Poole as well.

On our third session, completely out of the blue, she said to me, 'Has anybody ever suggested that you're ADHD?'

I looked at her perplexed and answered honestly, 'No. Why?'

'Because I think you've got it. Go home and Google "adult ADHD" and see what you think,' she said.

I went home that night and did as I was told. I started to Google 'adult ADHD' and I didn't only have one lightbulb moment – I had about 200. How could I not have known this before? I was fifty-one years old. Nobody had ever once suggested that I might have ADHD, yet here I was reading everything about ME the more I Googled.

I was probably as ignorant as most people and had always thought ADHD was naughty boys at infant and junior school. I hadn't thought it went further than that. How wrong could I have been?

Everything I read that night blew my mind. I could fill a book with all the traits, but the ones that resonated with me hugely were high propensity to boredom, always thinking you are right, wanting everything your own way, having no patience, taking rejection very badly, compulsive eating, interrupting people, not liking authority, hating being told what to do … the list just went on and on and on.

The next time I saw the counsellor, I told her how much of it had resonated and she said, 'I knew it. Now we need to get you diagnosed – go and see your GP.'

I also asked her why, the week before, me telling her I had IBS had confirmed in her mind I had ADHD? 'Simple,' she replied, 'IBS can be connected to ADHD. The brain works too fast hence so does the digestive system.'

So I duly went to see my doctor, who told me that, 'There is no money in the NHS for adult ADHD.'

So I went to see another doctor at the same practice, who also told me, 'There is no money in the NHS for adult ADHD.' Word for word, exactly the same. I definitely felt this was a line they had been instructed to tell patients.

Hmm, this was getting very annoying. Now my counsellor was telling me more about ADHD I 100% knew I had it and I wasn't about to take no for an answer. Which of course is an ADHD trait! So I booked an appointment with an ADHD Specialist Psychiatrist in London. Forked out £350 for the appointment, and £70 on the train fare from Poole to London, only to be told by him that I couldn't have ADHD because I wasn't diagnosed as a child.

I went back to the counsellor and told her. Her exact words were, 'This is bollocks. You are ADHD – go somewhere else.'

By now I had joined some adult ADHD Facebook groups and there was one ADHD Psychiatrist who was repeatedly recommended, so I booked in with him. He was in Essex, which was a bit of a trek from Dorset, but I was determined. I thought I would prepare him by sending him a typed-up list of my newly found ADHD traits in the post. The night before the appointment he rang me up and said, 'Sarah, don't bother coming to see me – it's very obvious you're ADHD. Why isn't your doctor getting you diagnosed?'

I repeated the 'No money in the NHS for adult ADHD' line and this very kind Psychiatrist wrote to my GP and told him, quite strongly, that there was money in the NHS for adult ADHD and to get me referred. Within three months I was diagnosed and on ADHD medication.

The diagnosis and medication changed my life. Up until that point I had never been able to relax because I had what I now know is called an ADHD 'internal motor'. It had pushed me on and on and on, even when I was exhausted.

The medication also stopped my compulsive binge eating and I went down four dress sizes in a year.

This was a complete and utter revelation. At first I was totally self-absorbed and just thinking about myself and how this impacted me. But before long my mind went back to those boys at Aylesbury Prison. Three of the six had told me they were diagnosed ADHD as children. Keiran, Thomas and Aidan. But what about the other three? Was it possible they were ADHD as well, and was this potentially the reason I had bonded with each and every one of them pretty much instantly? Did we all have the same brain?

My mind went into overdrive, but for now I had to focus on these new Portland clients and they were flooding through the door after I had put the first twenty-seven in order of urgency.

More referrals were coming in weekly and, of course, I would help all of them but I could not forget those six boys at Aylesbury. Three who thought they had outgrown their ADHD, because they had been told it was a childhood condition you grew out of in your late teens: but look where all three had ended up – in Prison. And three who were now ringing big bells in my head, because some of the traits I was reading about me applied to them as well.

Beginnings and finding my way round

Finding my way round HMP Portland was going to be so much easier than Aylesbury for two main reasons. Firstly, all the Wings (bar one) were spread around the square Association area. So as you went in through the entrance gate, past the Admin block on your left and Health Care and Security on your right, on your far left stuck in the corner was the CSU, the 'Care and Separation Unit', known to everybody and his dog as 'the Block' or 'the Seg'.

Then, actually facing onto the Association area, were Nelson and Grenville Wings on your right, which housed primarily Young Offenders. On the far left-hand side were Raleigh, Drake and Benbow Wings, which held primarily adult men.

Just further on from Raleigh and Drake was a separate building and the Collingwood Wing, housing the induction unit. That's where everybody spent the first two weeks of their stay at Portland, whether they were new to the Prison system or had been moved from another Prison.

About half a mile past Collingwood, which took FOREVER to walk to, was the enhanced Wing, Beaufort. It really was one hell of a walk. Not so bad in the summer, still a good twenty minutes, but in the winter – absolutely bitter. No walls or trees to guard you from the elements. I did that walk to Beaufort Wing and back so many times in the freezing cold, with biting wind like I've never experienced anywhere else.

The only thing that broke up the torturous walk to Beaufort was there would nearly always be Prisoners from the gardening class planting flowers in the borders and beds, so talking to them did break it up a bit. But, my goodness, that was a very long walk. Occasionally, I would see an Officer walking the other way with a pained 'Jesus Christ, this is freezing' look on their face to match mine. You would share a very quick nod and a 'Hi' as you battled the elements to get to the other end.

My counselling room was on the ground floor in the Young Offender Unit in-between Nelson and Grenville Wings. Much cosier, though never warm enough to take your coat off in the winter. It didn't have any heating!

So everything was logically laid out and, not only that, I loved the fact that they had named the Wings after seafarers. Bearing in mind we were on an island and pretty much every boy had a sea view from his cell.

I think all Prisons should do this. I think it's lazy calling Wings A B C D etc. It doesn't take much innovation to come up with some names connected to your area and give the Wings actual names. It gives the boys and men a little bit of identity and community, which they desperately need.

The journey from my flat in Poole to HMP Portland was forty miles, so I was doing eighty miles there and back twice weekly. So 160 miles a week, but it really was the most beautiful journey through a lot of Dorset's most stunning countryside, passing by Dorchester, the county town, and then through Weymouth, around the colourful and bustling harbour, along the Chesil Beach Causeway and finally onto the island of Portland. The

Prison was built with Portland stone, so was a unique, white-washed grey colour.

I was almost ready to meet my first client. Something that had been decided in advance was that I would not be able to see anybody who was already under the Mental Health Team. I could understand the logic of this. If somebody was part way through an assessment, or having some sort of serious mental health crisis, me poking my nose in was not likely to help.

However, everybody else was up for grabs and from the middle of November 2014 I lived, ate and breathed HMP Portland. It was my whole life and I adored every second of it.

New clients
and stroppy mothers

So of course, my first client had to be on this one Wing that was half a mile from the main Prison didn't they? But were they worth the trek? Oh yes!

It was a bit of a strange one because there had been no referral form. I had been asked to see this boy to placate his mother, who was apparently on the phone complaining to the Deputy Governor on a daily basis.

I was copied into an email (that certainly never happened at Aylesbury!) explaining that Portland would be offering counselling to her nineteen-year-old son and doing everything they could to make his short Prison sentence bearable. This was after the mother had been threatening to get her MP involved. So off I trotted to meet Ashley.

Ashley was tall, probably just over 6 feet, had dark curly hair and quite a pale complexion. He had long trousers on for the first few sessions, but when I saw him in shorts for the first time I was staggered to see that both his legs were covered in tattoos. Brightly coloured ones at that. Nothing on his arms at all but legs covered from top to bottom in tattoos. You don't see that very often.

He was very eager to tell me why he was in Prison and very pissed off that he was there at all. Apparently, his family had their own successful business that he worked for and he drove a company car, a BMW. Not bad for nineteen, I thought.

Anyway, apparently one day he and his best friend were out in his car and the friend was driving. They stopped at a rental property, where the friend went inside to collect overdue rent due to his mother. There was some sort of kerfuffle in the house, definitely threats and a fight, but Ashley had sat in the car the whole time listening to music. He wasn't involved at all.

When his friend came out, jumped in the car and they drove off, Ashley had absolutely no idea what had happened in that house until the Police came knocking later that evening. He was arrested, charged, and sentenced to Prison for six months. Joint Enterprise. For those of you who haven't heard that term before, it was brought in originally to enable the Police to arrest gang members who covered for each other, but has subsequently been used in situations like this where somebody was just along for the ride and gets caught up through no intention, actions or behaviour of their own. In my opinion, there have been some serious miscarriages of justice due to Joint Enterprise. This one fitted the bill.

The whole thing was a horrendous shock to him and his mother as neither of them had had anything to do with the criminal justice system beforehand.

Ashley, not being a hardened criminal or Prison-savvy in the least, had been bullied mercilessly when he was first in Portland and had been moved onto the enhanced Beaufort Wing to keep his mother happy and to escape the bullying. He was exactly the sort who would get bullied in Prison because he spoke well and, although he wasn't quite an Eton type, he definitely wasn't your average street-wise young offender.

There were other concessions staff had given to keep his mother happy. One of them was to allow Ashley his guitar to be brought in from home, which was very unusual in any Prison. And Officers were also allowing him to continue with his A-level psychology studies, rather than do any of the other activities in the Prison.

I found Ashley instantly likeable, warm and friendly. He wanted to tell me all about his mental health issues, which had started when he was seven years old. His mum first had him in counselling when he was just seven. He discovered drugs at the age of sixteen, taking, in his words, 'anything and everything he could get his hands on'. His mother frogmarched him to the doctors on a regular basis, worried about the amount of drugs he was taking, and Ashley had been forced to try a variety of pills including antipsychotics, antidepressants and anti-anxiety medication. None of them had done a thing, and by the time he was nineteen, just before he came into Prison, he was having psychotherapy twice a week.

In our session 1 he told me how his biological dad had left when he was a baby and his mum's next boyfriend had sexually abused him for six weeks when he was aged ten.

Thankfully, his mum got rid of that man and was now married to a much nicer one, who Ashley actually liked. He was obviously a bright boy, because not only was he doing A-level psychology he wanted to do A-level chemistry too. I realised straight away from session 1 he was absolutely not the sort of boy who should've been in Prison. And I could completely understand the mother badgering the Prison, desperately trying to keep her son safe.

By session 2 Ashley was telling me he had been bullied at secondary school so his mum had had to move him to another school, and by session 3 he told me he thought that he might have ADHD. I was nowhere near ADHD savvy enough at this point to be able to pick it up in people, but I could bring in an ADHD screener, which I did the next week.

In session 3, Ashley talked a lot about what he thought were his ADHD traits and, with my very newly found knowledge of it, it sounded like he might have it to me. We did the screener and he scored off the scale. Really high. He begged me to ring his mum and tell her, because she had spent years with him in counselling and psychotherapy trying to find out 'what was wrong with him' and he had been right with his suspicions. He now believed he had had undiagnosed ADHD all along.

In sessions 4 and 5 he was telling me how he was struggling to concentrate to do this psychology A-level, much as he wanted to do it, and we both agreed that this was potentially because of his undiagnosed ADHD – being unable to concentrate and focus being one of the biggest problems. He told me he was 'more than curious' to find out if he had ADHD so he could get medication, which would hopefully help him concentrate enough to pass his A-levels.

Bearing in mind I had been copied into emails with the mother, I felt able to email her that night and tell her that we thought her son may have ADHD. I then went through all his traits with her over the phone after she asked if she could call me. She sounded hugely relieved to have a possible answer to her son's twelve years of mental health concerns, and straightaway said that she wouldn't worry about the Prison getting him diagnosed, but she would book an ADHD assessment privately for him the week after he was released. I think she had been so frightened for her son's mental health for over a decade that to finally have a completely previously unthought of answer was a huge relief.

Ashley and I carried on having sessions, chatting primarily about how his, as yet undiagnosed, ADHD had been missed despite all this counselling and psychotherapy, and being put on all the wrong medication throughout his teens. He felt stronger now he knew that there was potentially definitely something 'different' going on in his head.

Ashley told me he had terrible social anxiety, and I knew enough about ADHD by then to know that social anxiety was something that did affect many people with it, especially boys. So between us, we cobbled together information about ADHD before he left. We made lists of his traits.

He was only in Prison for three months and, as promised, exactly a week to the day he left the Prison he had a private assessment and was diagnosed with Inattentive ADHD.

I was so pleased for Ashley, more than pleased for his mum, and also pleased that I now had even more knowledge of ADHD than I did before I started seeing him. Many years later, Ashley would be one of the reasons I campaigned against Inattentive ADHD being called 'Girl's ADHD'. No 19-year-old boy sitting in a Prison wants to be told he has 'Girl's ADHD'.

Controlling Brummies, pregabalin and traffic wardens

My next client was thirty-one and had written all over the application form that it was REALLY URGENT he saw me and he couldn't wait and could I please fit him in as soon as possible? Please? So I did.

Michael was on Drake Wing, so that was nice and easy to find, just off the Association area.

This was the first client we threw the 'You can't see them if they're under Mental Health' out the window for. That didn't last long! Michael wasn't having much luck with Mental Health services so had made a big point of asking if he could instead see the counsellor. So once it had been approved by Mental Health, I of course obliged.

Michael had a huge personality when he came bounding into my counselling room. A Brummy from Birmingham who looked much older than thirty-one. Then I found out he had seven children, which is perhaps why he looked older than thirty-one! He had five daughters and two sons. He was fed up with his partner, because she lied all the time.

Michael told me very quickly that he had needed to see me so urgently because he was due for release in seven weeks and the Prison wouldn't put him on his ADHD medication. He told me he had been diagnosed ADHD as a child, and when he had come into Prison he was on his ADHD medication but they had taken him off it.

This was all new to me so I had no idea whether this was normal practice or not. He was a very strong and amusing character and told me that he was going to refuse to leave

Prison unless they put him on at least his anti-anxiety medication, if they wouldn't put him on his ADHD meds. He was certainly very wound up and hyper and said there was no way he was leaving Prison in this condition, so they had to put him on something.

He told me he was in Prison for stealing cars and anything else he could to feed and clothe his family. Getting a job, working and doing it that way didn't appear to have entered his head. He had been caught driving when he was disqualified, which had brought him back to Prison. It wasn't his first visit.

He told me he thought he was controlling in his relationship and sometimes 'out of line' and very possessive. He also told me Social Services were involved and, at the moment, he wasn't allowed to see five of the seven children. When I suggested a mentor might be useful for him on the outside Michael was all for it.

Very sensibly, I thought, he also asked me if I could get the details for Relate as he felt he needed couple's counselling if this relationship was ever going to work.

By session 2, Michael was telling me that he had been suicidal that Saturday. This was a huge change to how he had been in session 1. Then I found out he had taken himself off his antidepressants at the beginning of the week and by the time he was watching *The Voice* on TV on Saturday night he couldn't stop crying. I explained to him that when you come off antidepressants you're supposed to do it under the care of a GP, and gradually rather than just stopping. And this would probably explain his crash in mood.

He was only getting one or two hours' sleep a night but had good news from Health Care, which was that they were prepared to put him back on pregabalin for anxiety and also zopiclone for his sleep.

By session 3, he was much happier. He was back on his antidepressants, on the pregabalin, getting more sleep thanks to the zopiclone and had contacted Relate and made himself an appointment for just after his release date.

Michael was also very proud of the fact that he had booked a dinner for him and his girlfriend at a Chinese buffet on the night he was due out. He said he was feeling very organised, efficient and pleased with himself. Michael was thrilled that his girlfriend had agreed to go to Relate with him and was feeling much calmer and focused about being released.

By session 4, he was admitting he used to take a lot of drugs and he also used to sell them. But he had been clear of all unprescribed drugs for at least a year by then, and that's how he wanted it to stay.

He was still feeling organised by session 5, and was even in touch with Social Services about seeing his children. He asked if I would write a letter for him, confirming that he had been having counselling in the Prison, and I told him I would bring one in next week, which was to be our last session. There had only been one ruction this week when he kicked off because the Prison hadn't put credit on his phone PIN, meaning he couldn't call his girlfriend. He had apparently threatened to demolish the office unless they put the credit on his phone. It swiftly went on!

By our final session, Michael was assuring me that everything was all good. It had been approved that he would go and live with his dad and his father had, for the first time, told him that he loved him. This had made

Michael cry. Love was what I could see so many inside Prison were lacking. And craving.

I was slightly shocked when Michael told me his first Prison stay had been for shooting a traffic warden, and surprised it had come out in the last session – but perhaps that was on purpose. He talked a lot about having uncontrollable excess energy, due to his obviously quite severe ADHD being unmedicated, and knowing that he needed to channel it in some positive way. Not shooting traffic wardens would be a good way to start we agreed.

I hadn't had long with this client, but it had been a fun ride. He was certainly not boring! I wished him all the very best after giving him his letter confirming he had engaged in counselling, and just hoped that he and his girlfriend could get themselves sorted out with the help of Relate and Social Services.

I often wonder what happened to Michael and I do hope he managed to stay out of Prison. And that he is still swerving traffic wardens.

Bereavement, knives and life-changing decisions

I shouldn't (and didn't) laugh, but I put my next client near the top of my new client referral list because it said he had just lost his mother. So a forty-three-year-old gentleman called Dave, who was on Raleigh Wing, became my next client under somewhat false pretences.

I found out in the first session his mother was still alive. Bless his heart, I think he had learning difficulties because he had filled the form in himself saying he 'had bereavement issues having lost his mother a year ago', but when he turned up he said, 'No, she was still very much alive!'

I could hardly throw him out, so we carried on. His non-existent bereavement issues instead became 'carrying a knife' issues. He told me his pad-mate was actually a younger brother and his mother did have cancer and only months to live. 'Pad-mate' being the person you share a cell with.

The brothers both came from Weston-super-Mare. This was quite an adjustment for me because I was used to people in Prison sounding like they came from London or Essex, but in Portland many of them had a West Country accent. I found this odd at first. Because West Country accents make me think of farmers, not offenders. However, I had to get used to this. Dave had a very strong West Country accent and told me that he was as concerned about his brother as much as he was himself and would I see him too? So I gave him a referral form to take back to the Wing for his brother.

In the first session, once we'd overcome the confusion, Dave told me he was in Prison for knife crime. His actual words were that he was 'a horrible shit on the outside' and that he 'carries knives, has always carried knives and always intends to carry knives'.

I wasn't going to tackle this in the first session, especially after the confusion about his poor mother. I knew he was going to be a tough nut to crack. But if there is one thing I love it's a challenge.

In session 2, I found out Dave had two children, daughters, with his current girlfriend and she had four others, who were all in care. He told me he was not well educated but the one thing he could do was talk. He seemed to enjoy the session, although there was an awful lot of mentions of knives, when and how he had used them, and I decided to leave it until the next week to tackle that. He was still very upset about the fact his mum was dying of cancer at the age of seventy-one and that he was in Prison, so was his brother, and neither of them could be with her.

He talked a lot about his crime in session 3, and told me how he didn't want to go back to Prison but there was no way he was not carrying a knife. I listened intently and found myself disagreeing with absolutely everything he said, apart from the not going back to Prison bit, so I was going to have to tread very carefully. The rapport was being built nicely, but only if he could carry knives and stash approximately twenty at his home. If I disagreed with that, I could see this going downhill rapidly.

By session 4, I found out Dave had been in care for the majority of his childhood and he didn't agree with his brother carrying weapons. But it was perfectly okay for him! In fact, it was a necessity. Skewed thinking was something I was getting used to.

Dave was very sad in session 5, because his brother had been released and their mum had now been moved into a hospital. He agreed that we could do some CBT, especially around anger. He told me he wanted to stop being angry all the time, and for the first time he said he did know he needed to stop carrying knives. This was a major breakthrough.

By session 6 Dave had obviously been doing some thinking, because the first thing he said when he came into the room was that he had decided that it might be a good idea to stop carrying knives but he wasn't too sure how, because he would always have to protect himself.

I noticed in session 7 that Dave swore a lot. Not my sort of random, colourful, swearing but almost in a Tourette's style. I knew next to nothing about Tourette's but I did wonder if he had it. It would be many years hence that I would know Tourette's is often a coexisting condition of ADHD, as are learning difficulties. As was talking incessantly, not drawing a breath, and Dave certainly did that! But none of this entered my head at the time.

In session 8 we were going through the advantages and the disadvantages of changing or not changing. This was very eye-opening for Dave – he couldn't come up with any positives of NOT changing. I really felt we were making progress. He told me that day, just in passing, that he was abused in the children's home. This was not the first time I'd come across abuse in a children's home and it wouldn't be the last, but it was always cripplingly sad when I heard it. My heart broke for these kids who had already experienced the trauma of being removed from their own home and then faced abuse in the supposed safe place.

We were really rocking by session 9. Dave told me that he considered me to be very down-to-earth and easy to talk to, and I didn't look my age. That was very kind of him. If there's one thing I'm good at it's building rapport, but we weren't doing so well at getting rid of the twenty-plus knives.

In the next session, he started to open up about his time in the care system. All eight of his mum's children were in care. He told me he loved his mum a lot. He assured me he was a softy at heart, although he put on a hard shell. But he did tell me he became very emotional at times, which seemed to perplex him. Had I been more ADHD aware I would've known that this was another ADHD red flag – dysregulated emotions.

The following week he spoke about how his brother, on the outside, had taken all his own knives into the Police station and handed them over. Dave was a bit miffed. He said his brother now said he would fight with his hands and not knives as he didn't want to go back to Prison.

I was rather hoping this might rub off on Dave, but Dave was not at all convinced it was a good idea. He was more exasperated than anything with his brother.

Next session, he seemed more determined than ever not to offend or come back to Prison. He seemed genuinely focused on that, determined, and I just hoped it would last.

The following week he talked about the abuse and said he thought about it every single day. For a man in his 40s, how sad is that? He loved his mum, although she never sent him a birthday card. This had obviously stayed with him for life. His brother was now back in the Prison on a drugs charge. He'd only been out a fortnight.

And on the very last session, which was session 16, as soon as Dave walked in the room he said, 'I've decided – I'm going to hand all my knives into the Police station and I'm never going to carry a knife again.'

I was utterly shocked but tried not to show it. I said, 'Well, this is extremely good news. Can I ask what brought you to that decision?'

Dave said he couldn't be specific, but everything we had been talking about over the past three or four months had suddenly clicked in his brain and he realised that if he did not want to come back to Prison, which he definitely didn't, then he had to change the way he did things on the outside. And the first thing he would do would be to hand all his knives over to the Police and stop carrying one.

I was euphoric, especially as this was our last session and he was due to be released within days.

I tried to be as positive and congratulatory as I could, told him he had made the right decision, that if he stuck with it and managed his anger, which we had been working on, it was highly unlikely he would ever be in a Prison again.

And that was the last I saw of Dave. I hope, to this day, he's living happily and knife-free in Weston-super-Mare.

'Putting the ADHD to one side' and other nonsense

Running alongside my counselling at HMP Portland, my Level 5 in CBT was going well. There were a couple of nasty women on the course who were vile to the Tutor, which the rest of us thought was bang out of order. He was a lovely man, very knowledgeable and passionate about CBT and I learnt a huge amount from him. Stuart Rose was the CBT God in my eyes and I loved him.

Much as I had been seeing my supervisor Robin for approximately eighteen months in Buckinghamshire, now that I was studying CBT I was told I absolutely had to have a CBT qualified supervisor.

And now I had relocated I needed one in Dorset rather than Buckinghamshire.

The small college I was at had a recommended list of suitably qualified CBT supervisors, and I picked one called Ben, who initially I gelled well with. Ben was a font of knowledge when it came to CBT and everything was going nicely, until the day I told him that pretty much all my clients at the Prison were ADHD.

He said that he understood that, 'But when we are talking about your clients, we need to put the ADHD to one side.'

Hey? I didn't say anything at the time, but I thought, 'What on earth is he talking about? How can you put the ADHD to one side when you only have one brain and it's either an ADHD one or it isn't?'

I was still relatively new to this ADHD malarkey so I went straight home and rang the counsellor who had told me I was ADHD. Luckily she worked at the same college as Ben and knew him. She also rated him very highly but then I told her he had said I'd have to put the ADHD to one side, and I genuinely didn't know if this was right. It didn't seem right to me. ADHD seemed to be a massive part of who these clients were and I knew in my own head that everything I thought came from my ADHD so I just didn't see how you could put it to one side. But was I wrong?

'How utterly bloody ridiculous,' she said, 'Of course you can't put the ADHD to one side.'

I felt a huge wave of relief. I hadn't been wrong then. It was important that you accepted an ADHD brain for what it was, and you worked with it.

Lynda had been my counsellor at this point for about nine months, trying to get on top of this wretched cat phobia, and she was doing a pretty good job of it. We had reached the point where I didn't burst into tears the moment she talked about cats, and had made great strides in me not being so absolutely terrified of them.

I wasn't sure of the ethics of it all so I just asked her outright. 'Is it possible that you can be my supervisor instead?'

She answered, 'This has come up recently with another client.' Yes, she could be my supervisor, but if she was then she could never be my counsellor again. So I bit her hand off! And from that moment on, and for the next five years, she was my most amazing counselling supervisor. Lynda taught me vast amounts about ADHD and how to work with all these ADHD boys and men in

Prison. It's not an exaggeration to say that I wouldn't be the person I am today if it wasn't for this amazing woman and I owe her so much.

Travellers, speed dating and bouncing bunnies

My next client was from Nelson, one of the Young Offender Wings. He was twenty and his name was Caine.

He had referred himself, and his spelling of the word 'paranoia' on the referral form was enough for me to love him from the beginning. Shouldn't it just be spelt this way – PARONOIER? I could completely see his spelling logic. Caine came bounding into the room with a huge smile on his face, although his reasons for wanting therapy were to stop this 'paronoier', overthinking, and a serious desire to get his head straight.

It was no surprise to find out he had been diagnosed with ADHD after reading that lot. I was going to hear more and more sad stories as my time at Portland went on, but this one had to rate as a real heartbreaker from the word go.

Caine was originally from Southampton, but now lived on a Traveller site just outside Poole, so not far from me. He had been born into a Traveller family and it was the only life he knew.

When he was just four years old, his mother decided to leave his father. She turned up with a flatbed lorry, upon which she put all the possessions she was going to take with her. She picked up Caine and plonked him on the back, and then picked up his younger sister and sat his sister next to him. Then she picked up Caine again, stood him on the grass and shouted at the father, 'You can have him. I only want my daughter.'

What a thing to hear when you are four years old. And of course he's never forgotten it. It was the first thing he told me.

His father had begrudgingly taken him and then gone on to have two more sons with his next girlfriend. Caine, when he was four years old, before the split, had only just been diagnosed with ADHD, but because his mother left he never went for the follow-up appointment to talk about medication. So from the age of sixteen he had been in and out of Prison on very short sentences for petty offences like fighting and stealing.

I knew instantly, when I first met this boy, he just wanted to be loved. He had been rejected by his mother and then overlooked by his father in a new relationship with two new sons. My heart bled for him.

This was my first severely ADHD client. He spoke so quickly, just like he had a motor inside him. Apart from my own, this was the first time I had seen a very obvious internal motor in a client. It's a trait a lot of people with Combined or Hyperactive/Impulsive ADHD have and it was plain for all to see in this boy. He spoke at such lightning speed I literally couldn't hear half of what he was saying.

He told me that his sleep was dreadful and he used to smoke a lot of cannabis but had now stopped, and he thought his paranoia was a result of the amount of drugs he had taken.

Caine forgot to come to the second session – I had to go and fish him out of the library. He was mortified that he had forgotten his appointment but we still had a good session. He was telling me about his girlfriend, Paige. He had a lot of paranoia around whether she was faithful or not. This was where the overthinking was giving him trouble.

In session 3, I couldn't believe my ears when I heard that he was now going to dump Paige and he had sent two letters to two ex-girlfriends telling them that he loved them and wanted to get back with them. He said he was hoping at least one of them would say yes! He was very excited to have been accepted by the Prison Rugby Academy, but was worried that would mean he couldn't see me. I assured him I was in the Prison twice a week and we would make it work somehow.

In the next session he was back with Paige! Because she had gone to visit him and, apparently, 'looked better than last time'. What was this boy like?

Caine told me about some of his crimes, which included thieving a car and then driving while disqualified. He said he had been banned from driving three times.

The next session didn't go so well because he felt very poorly. He was sick, had a cough and felt very blocked up. He really wasn't himself and I felt so sorry for him. So many of these boys just seemed to need somebody to love them and care about them.

One of the ex-girlfriends had written back and said she would get back with him, but by the next session she had found out that he had sent the exact same letter to another girl, so she had changed her mind!

He was due out quite soon, this boy, and I desperately thought he needed a mentor so I offered to put him in touch with an ex-offender mentoring organisation and he readily agreed.

By the next week he was telling me how he had heard from the mentoring organisation and somebody was coming to see him about it, which he was very positive about. By the following week he was telling me that he was in love with the woman who was going to find him a mentor. He meant it too!

The next week Caine came into the room filthy because he had a new job on recycling. He told me he loved it there because he could use up all his excess energy, and by the following week he was in love with somebody else who had been to see him on a visit, and told me that 'she was definitely the one'. I couldn't keep up with this boy.

Caine's twenty-first birthday was coming up and he had yet another woman who had been to visit him, who had two children, and he told me she was 'definitely the one' and 'he was going to move in with her when he got out of Prison'. Those poor women, was all I could think. This boy could change his mind every ten minutes.

We had to miss the next session because the Prison was on lockdown, but Caine caught me walking across the Association area the next day and begged me to see him. I squeezed him in for an hour. He was hugely pissed off because they'd moved him onto Raleigh Wing, which was for adults, and he was quite happy with the Young Offenders.

The next time I saw Caine he was in a glassed-off area near the Education block. As I was walking along the corridor to collect a client, I could hear somebody shouting, 'Sarah! Sarah! Sarah!' When I finally located where the noise was coming from, I saw Caine jumping up and down like a bunny in this grassy glassed area, all alone.

Through the glass I asked him what on earth he was doing there and between bounces he told me, 'They've put me in here because I can't sit still in maths.' The poor boy had literally been locked in an area about 20 feet by 40 feet, behind glass, because he couldn't sit still.

We had one more session to go and all I could do was wish him the very best of luck. I asked him to give the mentoring a good go, because I thought it would help him a lot, and also go and see his GP about getting some ADHD medication. Only that was going to stop the overthinking, paranoia and this relentless latching onto women, and it only lasting five minutes.

I often wonder about Caine. I wonder if he found 'the one' and if he ever managed to settle. I do hope somebody is loving him and looking after him, because he had so much love to give. He just needed the right person to give it back.

Sausages, KitKats
and D Cats

My next client was quite high up on my list because he had only arrived at the Prison six weeks before and had received a seven-year sentence. He had to serve three and a half years of that inside and the rest on licence, but I felt he could still probably do with somebody to talk to sooner rather than later. And I was right.

Corey was thirty-one and although he had been in Prison when he was aged seventeen, for three and a half years, he had since spent all his 20s on the outside.

In the first session he told me that he honestly just wanted to see me to have 'a grown-up, normal chat', but if there was anybody who really needed counselling he would give up his space for them. Which I thought was very kind and he was the only person ever to offer to do that in all my years counselling.

Corey was actually from East London, but as he had been caught by the Police in the Bath area he had found himself in Prison in Dorset. At last I had a Prisoner who sounded like a Prisoner and not a farmer!

He, of course, swore his innocence, but when he brought the court papers into session 2 I did find myself questioning that innocence. It all looked pretty clear cut to me. Being found with £150,000 worth of cash in your snazzy BMW, when you were unemployed, was likely to raise suspicions with the Police. He had been charged with 'conspiracy to supply', along with seven other alleged drug dealers – the Police having watched them for many months.

In that session, Corey also told me that his neighbour in the next cell had tried to kill himself and desperately needed counselling. I could tell that Corey was genuinely concerned about this boy. Again, he offered to give his space up for this person who had been suicidal. And made me promise that if his neighbour asked for counselling, I would let him know so he could let him have his space. His kindness and concern were so lovely to see.

Corey started to tell me a lot about his life in London. He had had one girlfriend for nine years but now had a new one who was a paramedic. This was interesting because I knew that paramedic was the top job for people with ADHD, and also that ADHD people are attracted to each other. I hadn't had any other hint that Corey might have ADHD but those two things did make me think.

By session 4 all the talk was of 'ROTL'. This was the very first time I had heard the phrase, but it stands for RELEASED ON TEMPORARY LICENCE, which means you can go out of the Prison to work – temporarily. You have to go back to the Prison early evening. It didn't make sense to me because Corey had only been there six weeks, but apparently he was eligible for this relatively soon.

He also was talking about 'getting his D Cat'. This is something you hear of constantly in Prison. A 'D Cat', or Category D Prison, is an open Prison. There's a lot more freedom, and again the opportunity to go out to work, so right from the beginning Corey was looking for either ROTL or to be moved to a D Cat Prison.

He had been offered to move Wings to the miles-away-from-anywhere enhanced Beaufort Wing at Portland, but had turned it down because it would've meant sharing a cell – and he refused to share. He told me he was quite a snob and never ate frozen food! He had now admitted to me that, when he was younger, he did used to sell drugs. I think that explains his first sentence. But he still wasn't letting on anything about the most recent one.

In the next session, there had been a huge upheaval because a very well-known Prisoner, who 'ran the Wing', had been moved. It had caused uproar on the Wing and when Corey finally reached me all he wanted to talk about was places he wanted to go when he was out. Corey had dreams of going to New York, America, South America, and all sorts of other places. He also confided that he thought he was far too old to be in Prison now. He thought that by the time he was in his 30s he should've stopped all this nonsense and be settled.

The following week I couldn't see him because the Prison was on lockdown, but the next week he told me how his girlfriend said to say 'hello' and that he was always happier when he'd seen me. She said he had to carry on having sessions and stop thinking about giving them up for somebody else.

We talked about his heritage. He said he felt 50% Jamaican, although both his parents were born here in the UK.

Corey's girlfriend had visited him the day before and he told me he always felt very depressed after she left. The week after this he had an argument with the same girlfriend over her not telling him she was going to music festivals. She had told him to talk to me about his feelings because he didn't share them with her. Corey said he wished he could have her sitting on the couch next to him, because it was much more easy to be open when I was around.

He also told me that he'd asked his girlfriend to take a lie detector test when he was released, to make sure she'd been celibate. That was the first time I'd ever heard that. I can imagine it's torture being locked away for years while your stunning girlfriend is prey to every free man on the planet. But a lie detector test was pushing a bit too far in my opinion!

In the next session, when Corey walked in, he had both hands in his trouser pockets. When he pulled them out at the same time, he had a KitKat in one hand and a Snickers in the other one. Bless his heart. He had bought them from the canteen and saved them to have in our session.

I was terrified of doing anything that would upset anybody after my Aylesbury experience and said, 'Is it okay to eat in here?' He replied 'Of course it is.' He told me that the Officers often brought in sandwiches, sausage rolls, pork pies, quiche, cake and anything leftover from a wedding, funeral or christening. And if there were events in the Prison, and there was food left over, the Officers would always give them the food, so there was no issue with having a KitKat. So I did.

The following week, when he brought up the lie detector test again, I asked him if he felt that was not slightly controlling. He looked at me as if to say, 'Yes, I know it is but I'm not going to admit it.'

For session 10, I thought it was only polite to return the compliment, so I had taken in a Wispa and a Twix. Corey opted for the Wispa and told me he had a terrible craving for a Topic, which he couldn't get in the Prison. I promised I would bring him one the next week. Praying that wasn't breaking any rules.

This session was mostly spent talking about his wedding. He wouldn't be able to travel anywhere until 2020 and had brought in pictures of the ex-girlfriend, the current girlfriend, his mum and his sister. All very attractive and all very professional looking.

The next week it was his birthday, so I brought him in a birthday card and a Topic. He had been moved onto Collingwood, the Induction Wing. I never thought to ask him why he had been put on the Induction Wing. Looking back, I can only assume it was to prepare him for ROTL. When I arrived on the Wing, asking if he was there, one of the Officers said, 'Oh thank God, are you the counsellor? He's been stressing about seeing you. He didn't think you would find him.' Takes more than moving Wing for me to lose track of my boys!

Corey had even had a visit from his sister, mum and girlfriend all the way from East London and that is one hell of a trip from London to Portland, but they had come because it was his birthday.

We had a lovely session, apart from he was a little cheesed off that the Governor, James, had directly asked him that if they give him ROTL, would he bring drugs back into the Prison? Corey was deeply offended at this. As if! But the Governor probably did have a point.

The good news, however, was ROTL was getting closer. It had been decided he would be going to work at The Jailhouse Café, which was part of the Prison/Immigration Removal Centre a few miles down the road at HMP The Verne. Still on the island of Portland. He was very excited about this and couldn't wait to start. His only concern was he wouldn't be able to see me anymore, but as he would get back from work by about 4:30 pm we agreed we would swap our 2 p.m. session and I'd see him in the early evening. There were many nights when I didn't finish until 6:30 p.m. or 7 p.m. by the time I had fitted everybody in, so I was quite happy to wait to see him.

By session 13, Corey was really enjoying his job at The Jailhouse Café. If you ever get a chance to go there, please do. It has the most breathtaking views over Portland bay and the food is not bad either. Corey had been told he had to work there for ninety days, which at first he was happy about, but very soon was getting stroppy about it. He thought the manager was giving him far too much responsibility and Corey was doing a large amount of the cooking. The benefit for me was when I popped in for lunch he would never let me pay!

This led to us talking about what he was going to do when he was released and he said he quite fancied opening a Caribbean takeaway.

By the time of the next session Corey had had a huge row with his girlfriend on the phone, but I urged him to call her back because in two days' time it was her brother's wedding and I didn't want her to be upset by having had an argument with him and it ruining her day. So he did call her. That was sorted, but now he was fed up again because the Governor said he might have to do six months at the café. He was starting to feel taken advantage of!

Corey told me at the next session, 'I've now been put in charge of the café.' He was in a right strop about that. Thought the manager was taking the piss.

We missed the next session because of a Prison lockdown, but the next time he'd had a legal visit and was told it should be only two months before he would be moved to a D Cat. Corey was absolutely thrilled about this and in the session after that it was all he could talk about. Apparently he could choose which D Cat, and he had the choice of four. He was still running the café and still hating it, but thrilled to be moving soon.

In session 18 Corey surprised me by bringing a file to our session called 'Setting up in Business', which was apparently a course he had signed up for. Lord alone knows why he was doing that when the week before he had told me he was going to train to be an electrician, never mind the Caribbean takeaway. That's a sign of potential ADHD I missed – changing his mind every five minutes.

He was very angry in session 19 because the café wouldn't let him eat a sausage. When he was practically running the place, he thought it was very petty of them to refuse him a sausage. Small things can become very important in Prison. He was still pushing for his D Cat, but there was no news on that at that moment

What happened next set up a pattern for future clients. In session 20 Corey told me he was 'fixed' and he no longer needed to see me. But he would still like me to pop in for a chat when I was passing.

So next time I was in the Prison I popped by and we had a fifteen-minute chat, when he told me he had changed his mind and did need to see me again. I can't begin to tell you how many times this happened and sometimes several times with each client.

So the next session was for an hour and a half. Corey was buzzing because he had been awarded his D Cat! And couldn't stop talking about it.

He was going to HMP Springhill near Aylesbury in Buckinghamshire. Can you believe! Unfortunately, there was no transport to take him, which was frustrating him. Apparently the Prison said that his girlfriend could take him, so I offered too. As I was up and down to Buckinghamshire constantly I asked if I was allowed to take him. Surely I was as reliable as the girlfriend? So it was only polite to offer.

The next time, Corey was still at the café and there was still no transport to take him to Aylesbury. Despite his girlfriend and me both offering.

Both of the next two sessions turned into well over an hour with him still being frustrated and annoyed that he hadn't been moved to HMP Springhill. In the end he got so fed up waiting he put in a formal complaint.

And it must've worked, because the next week I went to see him he had gone! He finally reached his D Cat and got shot of the café! A win-win for him.

Corey was somebody I knew I would miss because I had so enjoyed our sessions, and I do hope that was the last time he ever went to Prison. He was such a nice man, so kind and thoughtful and I would hate to think that he has wasted any more years behind bars.

Silly GP's, nasty shocks and good dads

The next client I had was on Raleigh Wing. The very first thing Alex told me was that he had been diagnosed ADHD at the age of ten and been put on Ritalin, back in the days when they thought ADHD was a childhood behavioural disorder that you outgrow in your late teens. Typically, he had come off his ADHD meds aged eighteen. Now, here he was in Prison aged only twenty-one. He had realised that everything had gone wrong when he had come off the medication and was now trying to get back on it. But that was very difficult in Prison.

He wasn't due to be in for very long – a few too many fights involving alcohol had seen him put behind bars, and when released he was going to live with his dad, who had moved all the way from Northamptonshire to Portland to be near his son. I thought this was very positive as I had begun to realise how parents played a critical role in whether their adolescent ended up in Prison or not.

Alex told me that he was not very fond of his mum. She smoked a lot of weed, and had osteoporosis and sciatica. He said he hadn't talked to her for several years and was really not bothered.

Much more important to him was working on his social anxiety, which he hadn't realised was connected to ADHD until I explained the link. He told me he could only manage being in a class of six, or a maximum of eight, people and could not cope with thirty. When he was a child, he had had a Teaching Assistant and could only be taught in small classes. I thought he was a very endearing boy. Very grateful for me spending time with him, and neither of us had any idea of the shock that was to come.

In session 2, I brought in some very specific CBT social anxiety modules for him to have a look at and for us to work through together. He was so happy about that, because he wanted to conquer his social anxiety before he was released from Prison.

The shocking news came in session 3. His mum had died – very unexpectedly. She could only have been in her late 30s or early 40s. Alex told me he had been in shock for two or three days when it happened, but he was okay now. Not that okay though, because he also told me he was on hunger strike and was convinced someone had poisoned his peanut butter baguette with Spice. Spice being a relatively new but hugely popular drug that was running rife in the Prison system at that time.

I couldn't have him on hunger strike because of paranoia. Paranoia often comes with unmedicated ADHD, I had now found out, and also from smoking too much cannabis. Both of which applied in this case. I made him eat some chocolate chip cookie biscuits I'd brought in my bag to keep me going. He ate them because he trusted that I wouldn't have poisoned them.

In our fourth session, Alex was getting ready for his mum's funeral, which would be taking place the next day. This poor boy, aged only twenty-one, no doubt largely in Prison because his GP has taken him off his ADHD medication, was having to prepare for his mother's funeral. I gave him some more CBT paperwork to do after the funeral and before we met again.

In session 5, Alex told me that the funeral had actually gone very well. He had reconnected with a lot of his mum's family. He said he had been getting a lot of pain when eating so I gave him some food diaries to keep and I had the strong impression he liked the fact that I was 'looking after' him.

The following week I tried to see him, but an Officer told me he had gone to work so I popped a note under his door just to let him know that I'd tried to see him.

And before we knew it, we were at session 6, which was to be Alex's last one as he was due to get out of Prison on the next Monday. He said he now thought he was very well prepared and had asked me to find him a mentor from The Footprints Project, which I promised him I would do.

I thought with his dad on hand, and Alex being determined to go back on his ADHD medication, he should be okay and I really hope he has managed to swerve Prison ever since.

Self-harm, colouring
books and felt-tip pens

Ethan was twenty and on one of the Young Offender
Wings, Nelson. He had referred himself for
counselling, saying he had had a lot of family pass
away recently and was finding it hard to cope. When
I met him, the first thing he said was that he would
not be able to open up – and then talked solidly for
an hour!

I learnt a lot in that first hour because I just sat and
listened. He was a very interesting character to look
at. Half his teeth were missing. But underneath that
and a straggly goatee beard he was extraordinarily
good-looking. Ethan had very dark wavy hair and
was tall and slim, and I could see he had beautiful
features that had been ravaged, even by the time he
was twenty.

He had the most striking almond-shaped green eyes
and olive skin, and in another world could easily
have been a model. Or should I say probably, if his
own family background and upbringing had very
been different. He told me he was the oldest of four
children, the next down closest in age to him was a
sister and then he had two much younger brothers.
He was from one of the small coastal towns in
Hampshire.

Tragically, his mum had died four years before, of a
heart attack brought on by severe alcohol use. Ethan
told me she would usually drink four bottles of

sherry a day. He had been extremely fond of his mother and was heartbroken when she died. Typically for a lot of these boys in Prison, as soon as he had lost his mother, that's when he went off the rails.

On the other hand, he didn't have a good word to say about his father. And some of the things he told me blew my mind. Probably the worst was how his father had lied to his family, telling them he was 'imminently dying of cancer' so his father's parents and other family members gave Ethan's dad a lot of money to take all the children to Florida and on other holidays. He bought a flash car and frittered tens of thousands of pounds.

The father was later found to be lying and didn't even have cancer, let alone be dying from it. He was also extremely violent and had locked Ethan in cupboards for hours at a time when he was young because he was so out of control.

Ethan told me that he was diagnosed with four things, but he could never remember what all of them were. He knew one was ADHD and one was bipolar, but he couldn't remember the other two. He asked me if I would go and see the Psychologist and find out exactly what he was diagnosed with, so I did. The Psychologist told me, 'Oh him, he's just a complete pain in the arse,' as she rifled through his notes. She then told me he was diagnosed with ADHD, PTSD, EUPD and bipolar.

If those initials are unfamiliar to you, they stand for

- Attention Deficit Hyperactivity Disorder

- Post Traumatic Stress Disorder

- Emotionally Unstable Personality Disorder

- And the last one, obviously, Bipolar Disorder

EUPD had only recently been renamed and had previously been known as Borderline Personality Disorder.

EUPD is the one that is most commonly misdiagnosed when people actually have ADHD. Ethan was the only case, in all my years of counselling hundreds of Young Offenders, who I genuinely believe did have EUPD. It was the bipolar diagnosis I questioned. All the other three I firmly believe he had by the time I had worked with him for several months.

Ethan told me that he had a son and had lost another baby boy to cot death. He told me he was very violent but wanted to change. He focused heavily on all the family that he had lost in recent years, including an uncle, one of his grandads, two friends and his mum, all in the last four years. He told me that he had been sexually abused 'but did not want to go there', so we didn't.

I noticed he had very obvious self-harm scars on both his arms. I asked him if he minded if I checked them, to make sure they were clean, and he said, 'No', rolling his sweatshirt sleeves right up so I could see all of them. They literally went up from his wrists to his shoulders. They were the worst self-harm scars I had ever seen. Some of them had left permanent deep grooves in his arms. Some were obviously old, but a lot of them were new and weeping.

Ethan told me that he cut himself when everything boiled up inside him and he just couldn't cope any more, and gained a huge amount of relief by slicing into himself. He told me that he had tried to hang himself three times recently and had also drunk bleach, and had put bleach in his eyes in previous attempts.

I needed to go into a lot more detail with all of this, but he literally didn't stop talking for one solid hour. I would have to find out more next week.

In session 2 he had actually calmed down a bit and I managed to get a word in edgeways. He told me that he was already feeling better having somebody to talk to and, now he was seeing me, he didn't feel he would try to hang himself or self-harm this week. He said he had tried to hang himself the week before we started, but an Officer caught him tying bedsheets together. This shocked me, but was to become all too familiar the more clients I saw.

Ethan told me his family were very rich and his granny, in particular, was extremely rich. He was worried about his twelve-year-old brother, who was so much like him and already smoking and being very naughty. He talked a lot about his grandparents, who he obviously adored, and said they brought him up because his dad was so useless, lied incessantly, was always in and out of work, was always broke, and his mum was always drunk.

As he had said he didn't think he would be self-harming anymore I thought I would encourage him by telling him I would bring in some Bio-Oil, which we could put on his scars to help them heal, but we wouldn't be able to use it if he had actually been cutting. I was well aware that counsellors aren't to tell people to stop self-harming and I absolutely didn't. I just said that if he felt he could do something else instead (and I'd run him off alternatives from the internet), and the scars started to heal, we would be able to use the Bio-Oil but it was completely up to him. This worked. He didn't like the scars on his arms and because he knew Bio-Oil was quite pricey, but I had promised to bring it in, it pretty much stopped him from self-harming. From that week onwards we would spend sessions checking his wounds and putting Bio-Oil on the ones that were healed.

When I asked him what else he thought might distract him he said he absolutely loved colouring in but there were no felt-tip pens or colouring books in the Prison. That saw me stopping off at Sainsbury's on the way home and buying every mindfulness colouring book I could and a couple of big packs of felt-tip pens. If that's what it took, then that's what it took. And of course I checked with his Wing Officer if it was ok. He seemed surprised but pleased that I was happy to do this.

In session 3, Ethan told me he had heard from his sister and she was taking their father to court for both sexual and physical abuse. Now his sister was doing this Ethan felt he wanted to do the same. He still hadn't talked about the sexual abuse, but talked round it.

In the next session, he had drawn me a picture using only pencil but it was extremely good. It was an angel praying and he said he wanted me to have it. I'd been stopped on the way to the session by an Officer who told me to be wary because Ethan's other grandad had died the day before. I'm sure this was what the angel praying was connected to.

He had had a blip by the next session, and had self-harmed his left arm quite badly. Ethan told me it was because he had seen, on the television, a lady wired up on life support in hospital and it reminded him of how his mum had looked before she died. He showed me the scars and they were bad. I reported this to the Suicide and Self-Harm Officer – a wonderful man called Rick, who genuinely cared about all the boys and men in the Prison – knowing that he would alert Health Care about Ethan's wounds.

Ethan told me that his sleep was all over the place and he often slept in the day, and it was in the early hours of the morning when he was awake and alone that he tended to self-harm. This, again, I would find to be extremely common. With so many of these boys in Prison having ADHD, insomnia is very much part of the condition. And many of them told me that when they were awake in the early hours was when they felt most desperate and alone. Every time I was in the Prison I tried to pop in and see him, just to make sure he was okay and to drop in new colouring books and felt-tip pens.

There was another incident of self-harming evident in the next session, because it was his grandad's funeral that day. I was very glad I was seeing him and we talked a lot about his relationship with his grandfather.

By session 10 Ethan was feeling better, hadn't self-harmed and was talking about going to college to train to be a barber. I thought this was a very sensible idea. And I encouraged him.

He was now very concerned about being released from Prison. He did not want to live with his father, but his sister was in supported housing, and his two younger brothers lived with his father. He had a family friend in his 40s who had offered to put him up and he thought he would go there.

When we met for the next session, Ethan had been beaten up by three boys. He insisted he had no memory of it. That would be because telling the Prison who did it guaranteed you another beating for being a grass.

He felt he was being bullied on the Wing and another client of mine from Nelson Wing had actually told me, 'Ethan is a liability on the Wing because of his constant threats to hurt himself.' Very typical for people with EUPD.

Ethan desperately wanted to move Wing but I didn't think things would be different on any other Wing, and it was probably safest he stayed where he was known.

He asked me if next time I bought him colouring books would I mind getting him a word search, because that would really help him kill the time. So that went on the list for Sainsbury's.

When he had a fortnight to go before release he was excited but anxious, and most worried that he wouldn't have a television or a stereo, which he had in Prison. He agreed to me introducing him to the ex-offender mentoring charity, because I felt he desperately needed support on the outside.

Our last session was the day before he was due for release. He asked me if I had any sharp objects on me, which I found very strange. I, of course, said no and then he apologised and said he was really sorry because he did trust me but he didn't trust other people not to be carrying sharp objects.

I could see his anxiety building before he was due for release and it was worrying, but I had introduced him to the mentoring charity and given them a detailed history of his past. I just had to hope that Ethan would allow them to help him and then he would be in safe hands. Such a vulnerable client. But I kept a loose eye on him on social media over the years and he doesn't seem to have gone back to Prison, which I am thrilled about.

Football, noses and chicken sandwiches

My next client was also from Nelson Wing and was twenty-four. Eddie had asked for counselling because he was struggling to accept that he wasn't responsible for a car accident when a friend of his was killed. He wasn't even driving at the time, but for some bizarre reason was initially charged with manslaughter. Although these charges were dropped he had spent seven years blaming himself for the loss of his friend, and when he first came to me was absolutely wracked with guilt

Eddie was 6 feet tall, well built, had light-brown neatly cut hair and a very warm and smiley face. I instantly liked him. He was from Wiltshire and told me he had a much older girlfriend, who unfortunately was still married to somebody else, but he had plans on getting her away from her even older husband!

He told me he had been in Prison once before, aged eighteen, having been caught twice in a fortnight carrying drugs, but he'd varied it a bit this time and was in Prison for biting part of someone's nose off. He maintained he was being attacked and it was only in self-defence, but had been given twenty-four months inside for it and was not amused in the slightest that he had another twenty to go.

In session 2, he told me how he had been a very successful footballer in his teens and had actually played for the Junior England team. He was very competitive and apparently showed huge amounts of potential but, aged fourteen, discovered cannabis and kept turning up for weekend football training out of his head on weed. He was given a straight choice by the England coach – you either carry on your football career giving up the drugs, or you leave. Eddie had argued that he was just as good a player having been on the cannabis as he was off it, but the trainer was firm; there was no way his reactions and timing would be as good if his brain was addled by drugs.

Eddie decided to stay on the drugs and that was the end of his football career. He was not only on them, but selling them and making vast amounts of money. He already owned one property at the age of twenty-four and was about to buy his second.

Sadly, this was a very wrong decision in my view and I started, about now, to wish I could get hold of these boys when they were younger and help them make the right decisions.

Eddie went on to explain he had also become sick of travelling all over the country every weekend and wanted some time to himself to see his mates. I suppose I could understand that, but giving up a potential football career playing for England? And now here he was sitting in HMP Portland.

Eddie was very driven in the Prison and wanted to be a 'Red Band'. Red Band Prisoners are considered more responsible than other Prisoners and have access to usually banned places. They are trusted with senior jobs around the Prison and have a lot more freedom to move around than other Prisoners. So his first goal was to be a Red Band and then to get his Cat D as soon as possible.

We talked a lot about the car accident and he eventually, begrudgingly, agreed that if it was another sixteen-year-old in that situation he would be able to forgive them, but he just couldn't forgive himself.

In the next session Eddie started to open up about his drug use and how it had escalated after the car accident. He brought up the subject of the possibility of him having ADHD and asked me if I could bring some sort of test into the Prison for him to do. I said I would and we talked quite a lot about the traits. He said he was almost positive he had it. He told me he couldn't concentrate at school, still couldn't read books, and actually hadn't read one book in his entire life. He said he couldn't read magazines or anything else at all because he couldn't concentrate. So I offered to bring an ADHD screener in for him.

Eddie arrived for our next session saying he was ill and wouldn't last long, but ended up staying for the whole hour. I gave him the ADHD test and asked him to maybe do it in his cell when he felt better and bring it back to me next week. And I hoped he would be feeling better.

During session 5 I marked the ADHD screener he had filled in. He had come out very high on both the subscales of hyperactivity/impulsivity and inattention. This seemed to please him a lot although I made it very clear this was in no way a diagnosis, but it was an indicator that there were big red ADHD flags that could and should be investigated – for example, him having been to Prison twice before the age of twenty-four and throwing a football career with England down the toilet in favour of drugs. If it was indeed ADHD then he needed to stop ballsing up his life – being too focused on making money fast but breaking the law in the process. I didn't mention anything after red flags, but I definitely thought it.

Eddie said it would explain a lot of his past. He told me he'd been reading about ADHD during the week 'and it was literally' all him.

Deep joy. When I arrived for session 6 he had been moved to the Wing miles away from anywhere – Beaufort. I trucked over there. In the driving rain and wind that whipped your face so hard it hurt.

The weather at Portland honestly has to be experienced to be believed. I've never known anything like it. When it was windy the howling noises would be quite spooky, especially as it became dark. The wind would literally be screeching at you. And the force of the wind – if you stood still – could knock you off balance. There were numerous times I had to drag myself one bar of the ever-present railings at a time, to get to my counselling room. The wind was that strong. I guess that's what being up high, on an island that juts out into the sea does for you.

I had a really good session with Eddie. He'd tried going to Mental Health to get an ADHD assessment, but when he went to see them, because he wasn't shaking his leg, they said he couldn't have ADHD! It was roundabout then I started to lose faith in Prison mental health services.

Eddie and I had done a lot of work around the car accident and he was finally beginning to see that because he wasn't driving it could not possibly have been his fault. He had carried so much guilt and shame for so many years for somebody so young. I really wish he had had some therapy at the time rather than waiting nearly eight years for it.

I think it had taken a stranger like me, who wasn't involved at all and didn't know him at the time, to help him realise that it just made no sense whatsoever for him to take responsibility purely because he was in the car and it was his friend who died. He had absolutely no control over it. I was finally allowing him to accept that there was nothing for him to take responsibility for.

Session 7 didn't happen, because Eddie had just woken up and was feeling dreadful, so we agreed to meet the next week. By session 8 he was very angry, saying that somebody had grassed him up as a drug dealer in the Prison. He was all over the place. He didn't want to see me at first and then decided he did. He'd been told he would have to move Prison. He explained he might have even gone by the next week, but if not, it was his birthday and he definitely wanted to see me.

To cheer him up, I asked him if I could bring in something nice for his birthday. Something that was allowed. He told me he had a terrible craving for a chicken and bacon sandwich. I took food into the Prison anyway for myself, because often I was in there for six or seven hours, so I could easily slip in another sandwich, which I did.

He was still livid that somebody in the Prison had said he was a drug dealer, but the next day he was going to have a visit from his dad and his girlfriend, which he was really looking forward to. He still thought he was going to be moved out but said if he hadn't been moved he did still want to see me.

The next week Eddie was still there but was very concerned as his girlfriend was now being threatened with deportation. He was really fed up and worried about his girlfriend and told me that he'd been sleeping a lot. A sign of depression, which didn't go unnoticed by me.

The following week, his session 11, was our final hour. He had been granted his wish to move to a Prison nearer home, but thanked me for helping him understand that the death of his friend was not his fault.

I was very glad that I had at least allowed him to do that but still felt the England football team had missed out, because ADHD people always want to win and are very driven. I suspect Eddie could've been a bloody good footballer had drugs not got in the way.

IPP Prisoners, Crohn's disease and a government minister's worst decision

Alfie was going to be unique in my Prison career. He was the only person I ever counselled who was on an IPP sentence. For those of you unfamiliar with the term it stands for 'Imprisonment for Public Protection' and was brought in in 2005 in the UK and abolished as inhumane in 2012. The reason it's considered inhumane is because there is no end date to the sentence.

Originally it was brought in for people who were potentially going to be dangerous if let out, even after serving a 'life' sentence. In practice what it meant was nearly 9,000 people being given this utterly ridiculous sentence, and as I write this, in autumn 2024, there are still nearly 2,800 people behind bars serving an IPP sentence in the UK, despite it having been abolished as 'inhumane'.

Alfie was the first and only Prisoner I worked with who was on one of these sentences. When I met him he was thirty-one. From London. Tall, slim, fair hair with a very kind face, but he looked totally defeated. He had been in Prison since he was twenty-one on a GBH charge. He told me he had seen people coming in for attempted murder, stabbings, kidnapping, arson and all sorts of other crimes, and get out before him.

I actually saw Alfie for twelve sessions and I found them incredibly hard. One trait people with ADHD have is a heightened sense of justice and this inflamed mine.

Alfie was the first to admit that he had been naughty when he was younger. And of his three brothers and one sister he was always known as 'the naughty one'. Nobody had ever explored ADHD with him and neither did I, because we had had two much bigger issues to deal with, but being 'the naughty one' and in Prison at twenty-one, it wouldn't have surprised me in the least if he'd had it.

Looking back, I am annoyed with myself that I didn't discuss ADHD with Alfie because now I have a strong suspicion it was what was prolonging his sentence. One kick-off, meltdown, telling a Prison Officer to 'Fuck Off' or any kind of adjudication meant your release date was delayed even further, so if Alfie did have undiagnosed ADHD and was having these blips every now and again it would've done nothing but give him more time to serve behind bars.

Alfie told me that he had 'stropped out' of his last Parole hearing because he was so frustrated. He asked me if I would speak to his Offender Manager, a lady called Karen. I did and she told me that Alfie was his own worst enemy and just needed to get in touch with her and re-engage.

Alfie told me he couldn't even get to a D Cat Prison, because he had been at one once and had been found with two bags of, as he called it, 'naughty stuff', which amounted to several mobile phones and some cash. And he had also set fire to his cell bin! Back to enclosed Prison he went.

I tried to get Alfie to focus on the future, knowing that at one point he would have one, although Lord alone knows when. He told me he wanted to work in some sort of youth work role to try and keep young people away from the horrendous life he had had as a late teenager and in his 20s, and which was now following him into his 30s.

I reported back that his Offender Manager was very happy to have a meeting with him if he would like to get in touch and be polite! He agreed to do this and by our next session he had spoken with her, had a good chat and things were back on track there.

He had also taken me up on my suggestion of going to the library to try to find some information on any Open University Youth Work courses he could do in Prison, and he had done.

Halfway through our sessions Alfie was diagnosed with Crohn's disease. He told me he had lost two stone in the last three and a half months. He was relieved to have the answer to the pain he had been in, and the weight loss, but said he was getting absolutely no help from the Prison whatsoever on what he could eat.

So that night I went home and ran off as much information as I could about Crohn's so he could understand the condition, and also numerous lists of food that he could eat and what he couldn't. I also ordered a book from Amazon for people recently diagnosed with Crohn's. When I took all of that in the next week he was very relieved and grateful.

Alfie was a very good writer and I suggested to him that it might be a good idea to write to *Inside Time*, the Prison newspaper, and offer to write 'The Diary of an IPP'. He thought this was a great idea so together we composed the letter and I sent it off for him.

He managed to get an appointment with the Prison Doctor to go through the food lists I had taken in to make sure that he was eating Crohn's-friendly food.

Alfie found out he'd been given funding for the OU course on Youth Work. I was absolutely thrilled for him. Also, a lady had been to see him from the kitchens regarding his Crohn's diet. And he said he had learnt a lot from the book I had bought him on the subject as well.

Alfie and I only had twelve sessions face-to-face because he was moved to another Prison, but that was certainly not the last help I was going to give that man. He had given me contact details for his mother and sister on the outside and I spent the next eighteen months helping them get Alfie out of Prison.

His mother had been a Headteacher before retiring and was a very sensible woman, and his sister was feisty. The mum told me that, the more she had learnt about ADHD 'she was pretty sure Alfie had had it as a child'. I explained to her that ADHD is a lifelong condition and it was my concern that it was the odd ADHD kick-off/meltdown/blip inside that was keeping him in there.

Between the three of us, we worked extremely hard over the next eighteen months and I wrote reports on how Alfie had engaged with counselling, was trying to improve his life by studying to be a Youth Worker, had re-engaged with his Offender Manager, and how many positive steps he had taken purely in the twelve weeks I had been seeing him.

I also explained about his potential undiagnosed ADHD and how this may explain why he was constantly having the odd blip and it wasn't likely to change until he was assessed, diagnosed and medicated, but it needed to be taken into account now.

At the next Parole hearing Alfie had all our evidence presented and I am thrilled to say he was released. I can't take credit for doing most of the donkey work – that was down to his mother and sister – but I do think it helped that I had encouraged him to take up the Open University course, and to re-engage with his Offender Manager. I'm just so glad I could do that for him.

And all the other IPP Prisoners still serving their sentences? I think it's an utter disgrace and they should all be released. Even David Blunkett has admitted it was the biggest mistake he ever made in his position as Home Secretary.

How can something be outlawed over twelve years ago as being inhumane and yet we still leave people in Prison serving that sentence? I'm ashamed to live in a society that does that to people. Let's hope I have to update this book when they've all been released.

Six-month review time

My six-month review wasn't actually instigated by the Prison. It was my idea that I would put together a six-month review of the counselling service I had been providing at HMP Portland. Everything was very disjointed in Prison, so I thought a report of what I had done and who I was helping, and how, would be quite useful for staff in different departments.

I still have the report and it tells me that after six months I had seen fifteen clients, totalling 101 counselling hours. The longest-running clients were one who had been seeing me for fifteen weeks, and one for twenty-one weeks.

The report details who was referring the clients, and they were coming from a variety of sources. Approximately 50% had self-referred, either from the initial cell drop or by asking Wing Officers or their Wing 'chat room' for a referral form. I was also getting quite a few referrals from Rick who was in charge of Safer Custody, and as he was also the Suicide and Self-Harm Officer he had his finger on the pulse of those most at risk. Some referrals were coming from the Substance Misuse Team and some from Chaplaincy. A fair few were also now coming from Mental Health.

I then listed all the reasons people were seeking therapy and this list gives you a good idea of just what some Young Offenders and adult males are dealing with in Prison. The issues included:

- bereavement, including death of own child, father, mother, grandparent, primary carer/aunt, best friend, friends, cot death of son

- suicide of parent
- having to turn off parent's life support machine
- anger and violence, both outside and inside Prison
- suicidal feelings, with many having made previous suicide attempts
- depression and anxiety
- paranoia and social anxiety
- self-harm
- eating issues, i.e. not being able to eat at all, or being sick after meals
- pre-release anxieties, especially around relationships, children, work, housing and health
- ADHD issues, especially overactive brains, overthinking, paranoia, inability to sleep and relax
- childhood sexual abuse by father (two clients), uncle, staff in children's home
- low self-esteem
- relationship issues.

The document went into a lot of detail about the Through the Gate Support I was offering people upon release. This included: referring them to ex-offender mentoring projects in Dorset, Somerset, Hampshire and London; sourcing employment agencies in different geographical areas who specifically help ex-Prisoners; supplying details of The Prince's Trust Enterprise

Programme for clients wanting to set up in small business, and sourcing any other services clients wanted support from on the outside, like Relate, the NHS and local housing authorities.

I was blissfully happy doing what I was doing and felt I was making some small difference to people's lives. I wasn't being paid a penny, no travel expenses or any of my other expenses, but I didn't care. I was doing this out of pure love because I cared about these boys and men and I genuinely thought I could help them improve their lives. Just believing in them was more than enough in most cases as many felt they had been given up on.

Basketball posts, Cadbury's Creme Eggs and gung-ho Probations

My next client had to rate as the most unusual introduction and first session ever. I was walking across the Association area one day when an Officer caught up with me and told me there was somebody on the Seg who was refusing to communicate with anybody.

For the whole of that morning, this boy had spent five hours sitting on the top of the basketball post, with hard concrete underneath him, surrounded by Officers terrified he would fall.

After five hours, he had come down of his own accord but was now refusing to communicate with absolutely anybody. Mental Health had tried. Officers had tried. Psychology had tried. But nobody could get a word out of him. The Officer said, 'You can have a bash if you like, but don't go in with any expectations.'

So I made my way down to the Segregation Unit, fascinated to know who had thought sitting on the top of a basketball post for five hours was a good idea. Must've been blooming uncomfortable if nothing else.

Once I'd passed Security and gone through all the extra gates, I opened the door into the room where this boy was sitting in a bright orange boiler suit.

I looked at him. He looked at me. We both burst out laughing and I said, 'What in God's name have you been doing, love?' I was pretty good at rapport but this was instant.

We only had half an hour, because I was due to see another client, but he chatted easily and told me he had just been 'bored stupid', so sat on top of the basketball post for something to do.

I found out he was twenty-six years old, from Somerset, and called Nathan. He was tall with white-blond hair, was very thin and told me that he was completely pissed off with everything, hence the refusing to communicate, but would definitely see me if I could fit him in. I promised I would and we arranged to meet the next week.

That following week he was back on Nelson Wing, which seemed to be my spiritual home. Young Offender Wings were my Holy Grail. Nathan told me that he had terrible racing thoughts and changed his mind like the wind. He actually said he couldn't keep up with his own thoughts. He hated everybody in Psychology and Mental Health because he didn't think they understood him. And because he had walked out of a Psychology session, they had struck him off their list. He didn't care, because he didn't feel seeing them was helping at all.

Nathan told me he had two brothers and a sister. Also a mum, and he did have a dad, but his dad had now passed away. He had started taking drugs and drinking very young and had always mixed with older kids, and he was incredibly worried about being released – which was only six weeks away. He told me he suffered with chronic paranoia and would be very interested in doing some CBT around his racing thoughts and his head that just wouldn't 'stop'.

I promised him I would be back the next week with some CBT exercises we could do and we would tackle this paranoia and anxiety together. Another big problem was that he was finding it very difficult to eat and, when he did eat, he was always sick. Eating disorders were something I was not experienced in at all, so I took this to supervision.

In the next session Nathan said he'd really been looking forward to seeing me all week. And after our first short session he 'felt so much better' and like he was eighteen again. Heaven knows why, but we did seem to have exceptionally good rapport. He talked about his need for adrenaline and how he loved nicking things.

He was very upbeat and chatty in the next session. I had taken an ADHD screener in, along with the CBT paperwork, because there were so many ADHD red flags with this boy and – surprise, surprise – Nathan scored highly off the scale. Especially on the hyperactive elements, which would explain him sitting at the top of a basketball pole. I'd brought a couple of Cadbury's Creme Eggs in my pocket and, when he told me he hadn't been eating, I asked him if he fancied one. He said he fancied both of them and ate them, which I thought wouldn't hurt, bearing in mind he was looking even thinner than before. They were what I'd brought in for my lunch that day, but how could I deny him.

Nathan had told me at the end of the last session that he had had chest pain and a dead arm, which I had reported to Health Care, but this week he said nobody had been to see him about it, which I was alarmed about. He was incredibly thin and I was really worried about him not eating. Cadbury's Creme Eggs weren't the best for nutrition but they were all I had on me.

By session 4 he was in a much better place and told me that he was now eating fine and sleeping much better. The next day at 10:30 a.m. he was due to find out from Probation where he was going on release. Nathan definitely wanted a mentor as he said he knew he was going to screw up the minute he set foot outside the Prison.

In session 5 we talked a lot about ADHD, because he said he had been talking to others in the Prison who had it and, finally, he thought he knew what was going on in his head. Everything about ADHD resonated with him. He was congratulating me, saying that I had worked him out in five sessions and he now felt happy and chilled.

This was all good, but I was still concerned about him being released from Prison, because he seemed like he was at the severe end of ADHD to me, but obviously undiagnosed and unmedicated.

In session 6, he was still chilled and happy. Nathan was talking about what he was going to enjoy most when he got out. It was primarily McDonald's, a KFC Zinger burger and a cappuccino! He told me he spoke to his mum every other day on the phone, although he still considered he had a very bad relationship with her. He also had a bad relationship with his older brother, but liked his younger brother and sister.

He told me he had decided that he wouldn't drink alcohol at all when he was released, because he knew it was bad for him. Said he used to be a very heavy drinker. The better news was he was still eating loads, but I still thought he was painfully thin.

Session 7 was supposedly the last time I was going to see him. He had been told he was going to a bail hostel in Gloucester. Nathan was looking the healthiest he ever had, and gave me two big hugs to say goodbye. He thanked me for sorting out his head, and I thought that would be the last I would see or hear of Nathan.

However, I was wrong because within a few months I was contacted by his Probation Officer. Nathan had asked her to ring me so I could explain why I thought he had ADHD. I literally had to start from scratch because this enthusiastic Probation Officer desperately wanted to help him, but didn't have the first clue about ADHD. By the end of the conversation she was profusely grateful. She said, 'I've been a Probation Officer for twenty years and you're the only person who's ever told me anything faintly useful about a client.'

What happened next was very unusual, I've only heard of it happening once, and it's definitely not recommended, but Probation had obviously confiscated some ADHD medication from somebody and gave it to Nathan!

Probation put him on ADHD medication for two weeks, which they shouldn't have done – because you have to have all sorts of tests, including heart tests and obviously an actual ADHD assessment, before you start somebody on ADHD medication – but this Probation had been a bit gung-ho and put him straight on the ADHD meds.

The heart-warming thing was that Nathan rang me during these two weeks and said, 'Sarah! Honest to God, I feel if I had been on this medication all my life – I don't think I would've committed any of my crimes, because I feel completely different.'

Now this boy had been a prolific offender. Silly things. Stealing and offences connected to alcohol, where he had been self-medicating what I was absolutely convinced was his severe ADHD. And he had been in and out of Prison many times before the age of twenty-six. But here he was, telling me that had he been on this medication all his life he truly didn't think he would've committed any of those crimes, because he felt so completely different.

Sadly, before being put on the meds, Nathan had committed another minor crime and was sent to Bristol Prison. However, his Probation Officer and I were determined to help this boy and between us, with me giving her the ADHD assessment pathway information and her having the power to make it happen, we managed to arrange for the Bristol Adult ADHD Centre to go into the Prison and assess him – where they diagnosed Nathan with severe Combined ADHD. This is the one and only time I have ever managed this, and it was purely because he had an excellent Probation Officer.

The Psychiatrist would only put Nathan on a non-stimulant ADHD medication, because stimulant medication had quite a high sale value in Prison. I said to the Probation Officer, and to Nathan himself, 'I'm afraid this isn't going to touch the sides with severe ADHD.' And it didn't, to the point that he came off the medication a few months later because it wasn't doing anything for him.

Infuriatingly, and this was the first time I became really angry with Prison mental health services, a Psychiatrist in that Prison took his ADHD diagnosis OFF him, told him he didn't have ADHD and instead said he had three personality disorders. Nathan actually rang me up and said, 'Sarah, I'm not ADHD. I've got three personality disorders, but I can't remember what they are.'

I said, 'Good! Don't even try and remember, because you don't have any personality disorders. You have severe ADHD, you have just never been on the right medication for it.'

I was so angry that I put in a formal complaint and involved the Bristol Adult ADHD Centre, whose diagnosis had been rubbished.

I'm now rather famous for my formal complaints and I have honed them to perfection over the years. I will not have 'professionals' mess with peoples' mental health. It's life-threatening and dangerous, and this was a classic case of screwing with a young offender's head.

The last I heard from Nathan, he was still in Bristol Prison and had the hump with me when I wouldn't give him money to pay off a drug debt. That's something I will never do. So, as I write, he's currently not speaking to me, but I hope he does again one day, and more than that I hope he manages to get the correct diagnosis reinstated.

When you have been bored to the point that sitting on the top of a basketball post for five hours is preferable to sitting in your cell, the wrong diagnosis and incorrect medication is not going to help you.

Short-term clients, corned beef and psychopaths

Some clients didn't stick around for long – I hoped not due to my crap counselling! Usually it was because they had been moved to another Prison, which happens more than you would ever think.

Moves happen for a variety of reasons, often because somebody has been moved from a C Cat to a B Cat, or any other category Prison. Sometimes it's because a Prisoner has had a birthday and needs to be moved from a Young Offender Institute to an adult male Prison. Very often it's to stop gangs forming or to break gangs up. Sometimes it's because there's been a hostage-taking or a riot situation and those involved have to be split up.

Sometimes a move happens because a course the Prisoner has been instructed to do as part of their sentence plan isn't available at the Prison they are currently in, so they have to move to one where it is.

Often it's because they fall out with people, have beef with people, and think things will be better in the next Prison. This is nearly always not the case. Boredom is another reason – it has certainly been a big reason for a lot of my clients moving. So many told me they were bored stupid in the Prison they were in and needed to see some new faces.

So my next four clients were all incredibly short-term. The first was a thirty-two-year-old South African man who was on ruddy Beaufort Wing, meaning that twenty-minute walk in the driving rain with gusts of wind either pushing or pulling you.

His referral form was interesting. The person who wrote it said that Harrison was 'struggling to manage his emotions, anger, frustration and upset.' I wondered if anybody there had any clue about adult ADHD and emotional dysregulation and all his other issues that were ADHD classic traits. Probably not at the time, because adults had only been diagnosed with ADHD since 2009 in the UK and this was only six years later.

But I'd been told that South Africa was far more advanced when it came to ADHD and, indeed, I found out this polite man had been diagnosed as a child but was not taking ADHD medication, which was his choice. The wrong choice I assumed, because here he was in Prison. Something had obviously gone wrong and it would no doubt be due to that anger and frustration. Medication would've almost definitely sorted that.

We only had two sessions, but what was interesting and unique to Harrison was he didn't sit down for one minute of either of them! He was either walking around the room, hanging on to the back of a chair and rocking it, leaning against the window frame or walking/shuffling his feet on the spot. He just could not even sit for one minute to talk to me.

I found out that although he was born in South Africa he now lived in Dorset. Harrison was the second oldest boy of four children and had two sons of his own, aged thirteen and three. He firmly believed his problem with violence was brought on by alcohol. He was in Prison for putting somebody in the boot of his car after she had tried to inject him with crack and heroin. He had obviously lost the plot and thrown her in the boot.

In the second session, we went through his history of violence. Harrison said he was 'just born to be a fighter' and as he was a very tall, big, imposing man I could see why he had been given that label. He told me he knew his violence was 80% alcohol-related, and if I had known more at the time it would've clicked in my brain that this was him self-medicating his ADHD and talked to him strongly about going on ADHD medication. Sadly, I didn't know enough at this stage and I literally only saw him twice – for two very exhausting sessions because he just couldn't sit down.

The next referral was from somebody I had a huge amount of respect for. Her name was Cathy and she was the Head of Resettlement. Cathy was somebody who cared. Just like the Governor. And me. Cathy and I had many a chat about our joint clients. I remember her vividly saying to me, 'I can always find something to love in each of them, can't you, Sarah?' and me massively agreeing. She was a kindred spirit.

She had a twenty-six-year-old client who was due for release within five weeks and thought it would help him to see me. On the referral form Cathy had put that he was dyslexic with ADHD, but sadly I never actually met this boy because every time I went to see him he was at work. But I did notice he was yet another who was already diagnosed with ADHD.

Next I was referred a twenty-two-year-old boy on Drake Wing. Near the Association yard thank goodness. Lewis self-referred and, when I met him, he was such a timid and gentle person. Only twenty-two but he looked much older. He had different skin shades on his face, which I later found out was because he had had hot corned beef and hot fat thrown in his face. I never found out who by, but I assumed before Prison. The scars looked old.

I was to have eight sessions with Lewis so I was able to get to know him a bit better. He was well spoken and very polite. He told me this was his first sentence and he had to serve four years. He only had eight months to go. He could also be let out on tag even sooner.

Lewis said his main issue was with the staff. That he hated the rude ones! He said it was approximately a 50–50 split, with 50% being nice and 50% being rude. He referred himself to counselling after having referred himself to Mental Health when he was twenty, to see if he had bipolar. He told me he had strong highs and lows and went from dark to manic.

His dad was addicted to heroin and crack, and his mum was very anxious and paranoid. He absolutely loved his mum to bits and he liked his stepdad and brother and sister, but he had mostly come to me to see if I could work out whether he had bipolar or ADHD.

I told him that I couldn't officially assess him for any condition, but I could bring in some screeners and I would do that the next week. And I would also run him off some information from the NHS website about both conditions so he could read up for himself. He was very happy about this.

Lewis said he didn't really think he needed counselling as such, he just wanted to know what was going on in his head and why he had these extremes of euphoria and then almost suicidal thoughts.

We agreed that I would pop in every week and see him and if he wanted to chat we could, and if he didn't that was equally fine. When I saw him the next time he was in a cooking class, but as I opened the door he threw down his spatula, rushed towards me, and said he definitely needed to see me. We walked over to my counselling room and Lewis told me that he had completed the screeners for ADHD and bipolar, which he showed me, and he had scored extremely highly on both. He had put in another request to see Mental Health, but he hadn't been seen by anybody yet.

The following week he had seen Mental Health. He told me, 'They were useless.' He said that they had just told him he had 'low mood'. I felt his frustration because we both knew there was more going on than that.

Lewis talked about his mum a lot. She had told him she 'thought he was better than this,' i.e. using drugs. He was gently opening up, but his main issue was finding out what mental health condition he had, if any, and getting the right medication for it.

The next time I went to see him he had moved Prison, so I can only hope that he pushed to find out whether he had ADHD and/or bipolar, which can coexist. And I hope he accessed the right help because he was such a mature and polite man who was trying his best to work himself out and find out what on earth was going on in his own head

My final short-term client was the shortest of all. And the most perturbing. I was sitting with Rick one afternoon going through the latest referrals as a lot of new ones had come in. Rick knew all these boys and men well and he wanted to go through some of them with me.

He removed the top referral from the pile and said, 'You can't see him. He's in hospital.' This was a first so I asked why. Rick picked up the second referral, showed it to me and said, 'Because this one, his pad-mate, attacked him and nearly killed him. He's on life support and we don't know yet if he will live.'

Bloody hell. I was horrified and sad at the same time. And it turned out they were best friends on the outside! Rick asked me if I wanted to see him as he was on the Seg and in disgrace. I think Rick was rather keen for me to move onto the third referral, but I was too fascinated and had to meet this boy.

So, later that afternoon, I trundled off to the Seg and was shown into a very small room where a boy, who can't have been more than twenty, was sitting wearing a bright orange boiler suit and looking about as disinterested as it's possible to be.

This is the only time I have sat in front of a client and not felt ANY rapport. I started with my normal friendly introduction, but I could tell this lad was not faintly interested in anything I had to say.

I asked him about the incident and how he was. He brushed off my concern, said he was perfectly okay and that the friend had deserved the battering because he had told him he had slept with his mother.

There was obviously logic to this in his brain. I asked him how he felt about his friend being in hospital, potentially not going to make it, and he said he couldn't care less. I could tell he really didn't.

As this was only a pop-in introduction meeting, after about fifteen to twenty minutes of banging my head against a brick wall and the coldest meeting I have ever had with anybody, it crossed my mind that this boy might be a psychopath. I didn't know anywhere near enough to be sure, but it did enter my mind. He seemed to have absolutely no feelings about his best friend being in hospital on life support. With him having put him there.

I decided to make my excuses and leave, which I did very politely saying that if he wanted to have counselling he was very welcome and just to let Rick know. As I stood up to leave, his final words to me were 'By the way, my mum's best friend is a mental health nurse. She thinks I'm a psychopath.'

I said, 'Okay, interesting. That might be something you want to pursue.'

I left and I never went back. There was definitely something very strange about that boy. God alone knows he could've come from a very traumatic background, which most of them had, and maybe his was more traumatic than anybody else's, but he definitely made me feel extremely uncomfortable. Not scared, because there were always Officers on the other side of the door. But sitting close to somebody with absolutely no emotion or compassion was unsettling to say the least.

He didn't ask for counselling and I suspect was moved out of the Prison quite rapidly. So he became my shortest-ever client of approximately eighteen minutes.

I never found out what happened to the friend either, but I do hope he made it.

Tattoos, CARATS and ADHD assessments in Prison

My next client had come via Chaplaincy. Chaplaincy in Prisons caters for all different faiths and is a lifeline for many. If there is a bereavement in your family, it will be the Chaplain who breaks the news to you. And many people turn to Chaplaincy when they are feeling desperate and need somebody to talk to.

My next client had been seeing the Chaplain who had recommended he had some counselling. The introduction session alone blew my mind.

I was told this client was on Drake Wing and I was waiting at the bottom of the metal stairs for him to come down from his cell on the third floor. I've never seen anybody come down a set of stairs like this man did. To say he was like Tigger from Winnie the Pooh would be an understatement. This man bounced, literally bounced all the way down the stairs.

From where I was standing, I could see the top of his bald head and it was covered in tattoos. I'm used to tattoos in some pretty strange places, but I had never seen the whole of the top of somebody's head smothered in tattoos before.

Once he had bounced down three flights of stairs, he bounded over to me with the biggest smile on his face and introduced himself as Mikey.

Drake Wing had its own 'chat room' and we often used this for counselling sessions rather than drag people across the Association area into my counselling room. Especially as the weather at Portland was nearly always like a monsoon and a typhoon combined.

This man was not only coated in tattoos, but also had nose studs and earrings. He was very heavily adorned! He also had on bright green trousers and a multicolour jumper. He exuded energy.

In the first session he told me that his mother had died in May, but he felt no emotion about that and didn't understand why. He had one son of his own and one stepson, who he considered his own. That all made sense but the next bit didn't. He told me he had come back to Prison on purpose to stop drinking and taking drugs, and also to find out 'what was going on' in his head. He then proceeded to tell me how he managed to get himself put back in Prison.

Mikey was forty-six and lived in a small town on a main road. Opposite his flat was a petrol station. He had decided that he would rob the petrol station but he didn't want to upset anybody. In particular, he didn't want to shock or frighten the two elderly ladies who usually worked behind the counter. But he knew there was one night a week when only the male manager was working. Mikey was determined not to scare either of the ladies, so he waited until the manager was there alone, put on his balaclava, grabbed his fake gun, nipped over the road and robbed the place.

Mikey was absolutely adamant that nobody should get hurt, and he only had a fake weapon, but he also knew he had to make this look serious enough to necessitate a Prison sentence as his goal was to get a decent amount of time inside. I had never heard anything like this before in all my years working in Prisons!

He ideally wanted to get a sentence that would see him inside for two years as he thought it would take that long for him to sort out his excessive drinking, moderate drug taking, and to find out why he felt his head was a chaotic mess. He was very disappointed to be put in Prison for only nine months, but told me that he was fully prepared to punch an Officer the week he was due out to make sure he stayed inside longer!

So I started off with, 'Well let's hope nobody needs to get punched. I would much rather we managed to work out what is going on for you and you leave here when you are due to be released – having sorted out the drinking, drugs and whatever other issues we need to. Can we make that the goal instead?'

He agreed to that, but said it wasn't very likely to happen in the time he had.

Mikey also told me in session 1 that he already liked me and had told me stuff he would never tell anyone else, so we were off to a good start.

Session 2 was only a quick half an hour because the Prison was on lockdown and Mikey was on 'Railways'. Railways was a very popular and oversubscribed training course in the Prison and he had managed to get on it. It pretty much guaranteed you a job on the railways when you got out.

He told me he was depressed and after he had been so bubbly in our first session I was concerned and told him I would definitely see him the next week for a full hour.

In week three, he told me he thought he was bisexual. He said this was huge for him because he had been married twice and had children. He also wondered if he had ADHD. I had more than wondered. I had pretty much made up my mind by the time he had bounced to the bottom of the stairs for our first session. I've never seen anybody with so much hyperactivity, including in our sessions when he couldn't sit still. He came across as such a genuine, considerate man with a warm personality, and I wondered if it was his sexuality or the potential ADHD that was actually at the root of his problems.

By session 4 he was opening up more and we spoke about ADHD and its traits. He had decided to put an 'app' (or application) into Health Care every day asking for an ADHD assessment. He thought if he did it daily he might actually get one.

Mikey told me that he had had one gay relationship and honestly didn't know who he was or what he wanted in life. I had brought in an ADHD screener and left it with him to complete in his cell.

In the next session, session 5, he told me that he had taken his ADHD screener results in to the Prison Doctor, who had scanned them into his notes and said that he would put him forward for an ADHD assessment. Unlike Eddie, Mikey must have been shaking his leg!

During session 6 he told me he was having a lot of therapy. He was seeing the team who offered 'Emotional Wellbeing' sessions, CARATS, which I had never heard of before, and having counselling with me. I asked did he not think that was all a bit too much, but he said no, he wanted to carry on. He also told me he nearly climbed onto the Prison roof earlier that week, but he managed to hold himself off!

When I arrived home I had to Google CARATS, and found they helped people with substance misuse issues in Prisons and CARATS stood for CARE ASSESSMENT REFERRAL ADVICE and THROUGHCARE. That was a new one on me and I was surprised I hadn't heard of them before. Initials are banded around constantly in Prison, everything is reduced to initials for speed, but that was one that had passed me by.

We could only have half an hour for session 7, due to issues on Mikey's Wing. He was extremely hyperactive and kept telling me that he was not diagnosed yet. Despite still putting an app into Health Care every day.

By session 8 he was much more relaxed and told me he had still not had the ADHD assessment. I assured him I was emailing the relevant people and trying to push this through for him, but I had never managed to get anybody an ADHD assessment in Prison before and I had no idea whether it was possible. Mikey told me he was depressed and started telling me about old crimes and repeating how he'd been desperate to get into Prison to get off the drugs and the alcohol and sort his head out.

Session 9. He was looking well and was much calmer. He still hadn't had the ADHD assessment but had been told it was imminent now.

During session 10 I realised it was Mikey's birthday the next day and I was very annoyed with myself because I had forgotten to bring him in a card. Something so small can mean so much to people in Prison. However, he had finished his Railway course and it had gone well. He thought he would pass. He said he was still waiting for the ADHD assessment, but he could see that getting out was going to be a positive thing and he had dropped his plans to punch an Officer. Hallelujah! Heaven be praised. And I'm an atheist.

I told him in session 11 that I had missed seeing him the day before as there was a lockdown for a football match between the Officers, but I had managed to catch him that day instead. He was very happy and smiley, and told me he had avoided the 'Spice' that was circulating round the Prison, thank goodness. He had also finished the 'Emotional Wellbeing' with Tracy and was looking happy and healthy. His face had filled out, he'd put on a little bit of weight, and looked much better for it.

Session 12 – Mikey was starting to panic about getting out again. I'd already introduced him to Jo from The Footprints Project, who was going to find him a mentor, but he had started to be very hard on himself. I realised that underneath all this bravado there was low self-esteem.

Sessions 13 and 14 both went well. He was still concerned about getting out but he had met Jo from the ex-offender mentoring charity and liked her very much. He said he had opened up more to me than anyone, which he was grateful for, but he had also had two panic attacks in his cell that week. Health Care have given him amitriptyline, which he said was helping.

In session 15 Mikey told me he had had a telephone call with his Probation Officer, also called Sarah. He said he LIKED her, but he LOVED me! Bless him. He was very happy because the doctor had said he must have the ADHD assessment before he left Prison. That was interesting. I wonder why they said that? We'd been asking for absolutely weeks. He was back to being terrified of getting out but said he was ready now, and he didn't think he would be.

He also told me he had heard from Elaine, who was his new mentor. There had been no ADHD assessment as yet but he had been accepted into a 'dry hostel', i.e. one where no alcohol was allowed, which he wanted. But he had no idea where it was. He was quite high and happy, but still with some anxiety around getting out.

Session 16 wasn't so good. Mikey was so hyperactive it was difficult to get a word out of him. He told me he had thought about hanging himself on Saturday, but thankfully he hadn't. He had met Elaine, his new mentor. She was in her 70s, God love the woman, but he liked her. He had been told the dry hostel was in Wells in Somerset. He'd also be getting a full neurological psychiatric assessment. Both he and I were very relieved about that. It would take place in Dorchester Hospital.

That day it crossed my that mind Mikey might be bipolar, as well as ADHD. I just hoped he did get a thorough assessment.

For session 17 Mikey was very upbeat. He gave me some paper with notes on it from our last session. He had been worried when I had used the word 'mood', meaning low, and he had taken it as 'moody'. Mikey did concern me because he was so up and down. I still suspected ADHD and bipolar.

And, in our final session, he had some very big news for me. He had had his ADHD assessment and had been given an official diagnosis. Severe ADHD, Combined type.

I was absolutely thrilled to bits for him because this had all happened before his release date. He was getting on top of both his alcohol and drug addictions with the targeted support he was receiving in the Prison. He had found out what was going on in his head, he was going to be medicated for it and, even better, no Officer had to get punched to keep him in Prison longer!

The icing on the cake? Mikey was the only client ever to tell me this – he said he was so thankful and grateful for the counselling I had given him, it had inspired him to train to be a counsellor. I told him I thought he would be wonderful at it, because I genuinely did think he was so warm and caring, had been through so much himself, and his life experience would make him an excellent therapist.

Wicked stepmothers, anxiety and chronic low self-esteem

My next client couldn't have been more different to the last. Justin was thirty-nine years old and had asked for counselling as he had had a lot of recent deaths, including losing a grandmother and a grandfather.

When I met him for the first session he seemed extremely nervous, on edge and very anxious. He also seemed excessively keen to please. He had brought in lots of photographs to show me. It was almost like he was trying to impress me in case I rejected him. I would subsequently find that I hadn't been wrong about this. He was terrified of rejection.

Justin told me his father lived in Tenerife. Justin had been with his partner, Lucy, for twelve years. Together they had a daughter called Tilly, who was eight.

His mother had died in 2006 and, unusually for a first session, he told me why he was in Prison. It was for taking drugs into another Prison for a friend of his on a visit. This was the first time I'd ever met anyone serving a sentence for taking drugs into a Prison, although I knew it was a punishable offence.

I had always thought it was the most reckless thing anybody could possibly do, but I wouldn't have dreamt of saying that to this very timid man. I had a feeling he could beat himself up perfectly well without anybody else helping.

In session 2 I found out Justin had adored his mother, who had died eight years before, but his father had since married somebody he called 'his wicked stepmother' and proceeded to give me numerous reasons for not liking her. I have to say she did sound like a piece of work.

Justin told me he desperately wanted to work on his self-confidence and anxiety in session 3, which pleased me because I had never met such an anxious, timid and seemingly scared-of-everything person in a Prison before. He was one of the last people you would expect to see locked up.

By session 4 he had moved, but I found him on sodding Beaufort Wing. I was getting used to the twenty-minute trek there and the twenty-minute trek back by now. I must've lost a stone just doing this walk. Justin looked very glassy eyed, which I mentioned. He told me he was on medication for hepatitis C. He didn't look himself at all. I had brought him in some mindfulness colouring books and felt-tip pens, which he'd tentatively asked for. He was falling over himself with gratitude. As I left, he touched my forearm and thanked me for my time. I thought then, what an absolute sweetheart AND what a plank for trying to take drugs into a Prison.

In session 5, he cried for pretty much the whole hour. This was the first time I found out that Tilly had been taken away from Justin and Lucy and was actually being brought up by Lucy's cousin, who lived on the island of Jersey. He told me he'd been crying in his cell that morning too. He had come off the hepatitis C medication as it was making him ill.

Justin told me in session 6 that he had absolutely no idea who he was without drugs and had no self-esteem. He seemed such a nice, kind person, but I didn't think he had a clue, so in session 7 I thought we'd go through his life history.

Justin told me that he had been taking drugs from the age of fifteen and was expelled from school at sixteen. He first went to Prison at the age of seventeen and had been in and out ever since then. He told me his mum was a Gypsy who gave birth to him when she was very young, aged sixteen. His dad was older, in his 30s at the time. He seemed to be a bit less anxious that day. Maybe he was getting used to me.

In session 8 Justin had decided he would like to send a card and a letter to his daughter, which I said we absolutely could do. I told him I'd pop into town before coming in the next week and would bring in what he needed. I asked him what he wanted the card to say on the front and promised I would go and find one as close to that as I could.

During the next session, I found out Justin's girlfriend, Lucy, had once been put in Prison for a year for bringing drugs in to him in Prison. For goodness' sake! Tilly, who at the time was aged one, had been taken off them for that reason. Why did these people risk taking drugs into a Prison? I thought it was absolute madness. I'd wet myself even bringing in Cadbury's Creme Eggs!

In session 10 he told me he had a rash on his testicles and he was a bit worried. I was more worried that he was going to show me! He reached to undo his trousers, but I was quicker off the mark and said, 'Absolutely don't do that. There are cameras in here.' I don't think there were cameras, but it was the first thing that came to mind. He said he had been into Health Care about it and was waiting to see somebody.

Justin had also brought in his criminal record. Dear God. I've seen some long lists but this one beat the lot: loads of criminal damage, burglary, theft and car crime. He'd been banned from driving, but had never passed his test. This, to date, was probably the longest criminal record I've ever seen. It went on forever – and then he told me we'd only got halfway through!

By session 12 Justin was in a right pickle.

He had seen his dad and brother for a visit. But they left early because he was so anxious. He asked me if I would call his aunt and pass on a message for him, which I did that evening.

Session 13, Justin was looking better and more chilled. We agreed to write the letter to his daughter the next week, which we did in session 14. Justin wrote extremely slowly and couldn't spell even the most basic of words. I had to help him with everything from spelling to sentence construction to punctuation. I strongly suspected he had dyslexia or dysgraphia, but we eventually had that letter written.

In session 16 we did some life coaching exercises to try and find out what Justin's values were. 'Being clean' came out top, followed by family, relationship and stability. I had bought him a brand-new blue file to keep all his CBT paperwork in, and you would've thought I had just given him a million pounds. He was over the moon with it.

He told me he wasn't happy on Beaufort Wing because it was full of Young Offenders. That pleased me, because I hoped he would move to one of the Wings nearer the Association area.

It wasn't until we did a proper CBT formulation exercise that I found out Justin had ADHD. He was diagnosed as a child but had never told me. That would explain the potential dyslexia or dysgraphia, which are coexisting conditions of ADHD. He definitely didn't seem to have the hyperactivity element. Possibly Inattentive ADHD.

A lot came out in the formulation. His early experiences were: the bad treatment from his stepmother, not being with his own mother, and his father being away a lot with work, so he felt very unwanted.

His beliefs were that he was lonely, alone, loving, caring, insecure in himself, and he protected himself by keeping things inside. That certainly rang true from everything I'd seen.

Justin told me his biggest fear was that he would become institutionalised, but he thought he might already have become so. Having spent twenty years in and out of Prison I suspected he might be right. He felt strongly that his life would never be 'right' without his mum. And he felt second best, particularly to his stepbrother who was treated like a prince, while he was 'the naughty boy' in and out of Prison all the time

He thought the 'critical times' in his life were when he was aged two, having to go and live with his stepmother and father when his parents split up. Also, when he first took drugs and was sent to Prison for the first time. Then losing his mum when she died. He had left home when he was sixteen, met his partner when he was twenty-seven, and had his daughter when he was thirty.

He told me that his anxiety made him feel a tightening in his chest, he got sweaty and shaky hands, his whole body became hot, his heart beat faster, and he had butterflies and a dry mouth. He felt he was constantly anxious, uptight and wary. He said his overriding thoughts were that he would always have an anxious brain, he would always have ADHD and much as he wanted to overcome it he just couldn't. He also thought he had OCD and it was only the drugs that managed to turn off his brain.

He desperately wanted to be more confident in himself, to have more self-worth and to be able to remember to take his medication.

The drugs he had taken from sixteen onwards included solvents and cannabis. He was expelled from school for the cannabis. He had only ever felt 'right' when he was with his mum. Because she was a Gypsy, she lived in a caravan and there was a time when his father let him live in a caravan next door to his mum. That was the only time he had ever felt happy and loved. My heart broke for him.

Justin was first arrested when he was seventeen for stealing a moped and by the time he was eighteen he had his own flat which was, by his own admission, a disaster because he spent the whole time partying, hosting raves, taking and dealing drugs, sleeping with random women and never working. Then at eighteen he first went to Prison.

There wasn't one mention of ADHD medication, seeing an ADHD Psychiatrist or any sort of support for his ADHD. I realised he was yet another one who thought ADHD was something that related to his childhood and not his adulthood. Yet there he was, having been in Prison on and off for twenty years. Had he been on

ADHD medication I doubt that would've been his life path.

When he was twenty-three he had received his first court order for drug treatment. If only somebody had realised at that time his drug taking was self-medicating his ADHD, the next seventeen years of his life could have been so different.

Justin had had such a tragic, sad life and was the most anxious person I ever worked with in any Prison.

After that session he was moved from Portland, which we had known was coming. I truly hope he found our sessions helpful and, more than that, that he has gained some self-confidence and self-belief. I so badly wanted that for him.

Insomnia, paranoia and clocking-up 1,000 cars

My next client was referred to me by Rick, the Suicide and Self-Harm Officer. This client was on an ACCT, which in Prison stands for ASSESSMENT, CARE in CUSTODY and TEAMWORK. People who are thought to be at risk of self-harm or suicide are always on an ACCT. It amounts to an orange cardboard file with several sheets of white lined paper inside – when you have any interaction with that particular client, you record what happened and anything that might be relevant regarding their mental health and state of mind. Anything out of the ordinary, any concerns you have, and any action needing to be taken.

I had many clients on ACCTs over the years and my next one, Billy, had been on and off them for quite a while. It's quite common for people to be on them, off them, on them, off them as their mental health either improves or deteriorates.

Billy was twenty-three years old, very tall, lanky and had red hair. He came from Plymouth. In our first session he told me he had never had counselling before and talked incessantly for an hour. That was an indication of ADHD if ever I heard it! But there was no mention of him being diagnosed, so I said nothing.

When I had first seen my counsellor, the one who worked out I had ADHD, apparently I had talked incessantly for the first three hour-long sessions.

I didn't know if Billy was ADHD yet, but I couldn't get a word in edgeways in session 1. Time would tell.

Billy told me his mum and dad had split when he was younger. He had an older sister and a younger brother, who was by very far the favourite. There were also twins, who were half-siblings to him as his mum had twins with another man. One of the twins was autistic.

He told me only his sister understood him, because she saw 'all that happened in his childhood'.

And what had happened in his childhood was absolutely tragic. Billy told me his own father had physically and sexually abused him. He gave me no further information on the sexual abuse, but told me he had been physically locked in his bedroom for weeks at a time and his father had punched him and beaten him on a regular basis. He also told me his mum 'had an inkling' about the sexual abuse, but did nothing about it and he could never forgive her for that. As an adult he had assaulted his father seriously three times for the abuse. He never talked about what the abuse was, specifically, and I didn't ask. I knew he would tell me if, and when, he wanted to.

Billy had a cousin, Simon, who was very important in his life. Very important – but also led him into trouble a lot. Simon was also currently in Prison, but not HMP Portland. Billy wanted to talk about how to have a life without risk and how to behave when he got out, because he had absolutely no idea how to lead a crime-free life. I knew I was going to enjoy working with this boy and I just hoped he would open up the longer we saw each other.

In session 2, he paused for breath and we managed to have good interaction. Billy was still chatty but a little bit more subdued. He told me how his mum was 'good', as in, she fed them, they always had clean school uniforms and the practical stuff was done. But when it came to emotional support, he felt he had had absolutely none. She didn't believe him when he told her about his dad and the abuse, and instead phoned up all their family members, in front of him, to ask if they knew anything about it and whether it was true. He had found this horrendously embarrassing. And cripplingly painful that his mum didn't believe him.

Billy talked about his cousin Simon again. He said they had met when they were both sixteen and had been best friends since the age of eighteen. Simon seemed to be the 'good person' in his life and he readily admitted his pet hate was his mother.

Billy told me he was supposed to be coming off the ACCT the next day, but he was not keen to. He said they wanted to give him medication, but he didn't specifically say what. And he didn't want it anyway. He then told me that he was not sleeping. Just the odd hour here or there. He'd been moved to the Vulnerable Cell next to the Wing office so he could be kept an eye on.

Again, he didn't say specifically what his father had done, but he did use the words 'sexual abuse'.

I had been asked by Rick the Suicide and Self-Harm Officer if I would complete a review in session 3. I did this in conjunction with Billy.

During the review, he told me that he knew he needed to 'get it all out' about his dad and he wouldn't feel better until he did. But didn't go further than that.

He also told me he used to drink up to thirty cans of lager a day with his cousin. It was a miracle he was alive.

There was literally nothing of him. I've no idea where those thirty cans went. He was adamant that he was not using any drugs or alcohol in Prison. Rick told me that Mental Health wouldn't get involved or give him any medication while he was having counselling. This struck me as odd. Why ever not?

During the review I learnt a lot more about Billy:

- Sleep – he averaged three hours of sleep per night. Would go whole nights with no sleep. Sometimes he would have just half an hour's sleep at night.

- Lack of appetite – some days he ate absolutely nothing. On a good day, he would just have a baguette in the evening.

- Childhood – abused between the ages of eight and eleven.

- Lack of contact with family – this was an issue. He believed his mother was guilt-ridden.

- Anxiety – paranoia could be extreme. When he heard people talking, he believed they were plotting and planning, and he felt vulnerable. He hadn't been to the gym for ages as he had not left the Wing for five weeks. He would get himself ready to leave his cell, but when the Officers opened his cell door, he turned to stone and could not physically propel himself out of the door.

- Billy felt his main issues were lack of sleep, paranoia, anxiety and he said that he had not felt himself for the last five weeks.

He felt like somebody else:

- He heard voices when he was aged nineteen, was drinking a lot and taking amphetamines.

- He felt he had no enthusiasm; no get up and go.

- Substance misuse – he had not used alcohol or drugs in Prison. Between the ages of fourteen and twenty-two he used cannabis a lot.

- Dreams – he had vivid dreams three to four times a week. Would wake up drenched in sweat when dreaming specifically about his childhood.

- Personal hygiene – Billy would only shower once a week as he was too anxious in a small space with lots of people and no Officers for protection.

It was agreed he needed a mental health assessment, but when he saw a junior person it was decided he needed to see someone more highly trained and would be referred to the Prison Psychologist. He had not heard anything since.

By our session 4, Billy was feeling better in all respects. Said he was now sleeping three to four hours a night and eating better. He had been moved onto Drake Wing and said he had already made four or five friends, which had made him happy. He was in a single cell and looked so much better. He said he was still not brave enough to go to the gym or library, but he did have an appointment with the Psychologist the next day

In our next session, number 5, things were even better. He was eating properly. He smiled a lot. Still not sleeping well, but he was actually asleep when I went to get him, so I went back later on in the evening. The last thing I was going to do was disturb his sleep when he was actually getting some.

His main issue now was his cousin. Although Simon had written to him, and said he wanted to go straight, Billy looked disappointed. He told me that when he was at college, between the ages of sixteen and eighteen, he was actually very well-behaved, but when he met his cousin Simon, at eighteen, it all went very wrong. It would appear Billy was incredibly easily led. I needed to get him focused on his future. I wasn't actually sure he didn't have some kind of special needs. He had a very slow delivery, with a smile on his face at all times. I was becoming fond and very protective of him.

In our session 6, Billy was back to not sleeping. He was very chatty and seemed happier. Said he was eating okay. He told me he was an adrenaline junkie and, although he didn't like driving cars, he used to steal cars a lot. He would get his cousin to drive! We had a fascinating conversation about this.

When Billy told me he was in Prison for stealing his 1,000th car I asked him if he ever thought of the consequence before he stole each one? He looked at me for a good thirty seconds, thinking about it. And then he answered, 'Honestly, no.'

He said, 'This last one – I was walking past the car, I tried the door, like you always do–'

And I thought, 'Well, no, I don't always! In fact ever! But okay.'

'–and then the keys were in the ignition.' He looked at me wide-eyed and said, 'What else was I to do?'

He genuinely didn't know, so I thought I'd better go slow with this. I asked him if he ever thought of the consequence of any of his actions, including this. And he said no. And it was at that point I first suspected he had ADHD.

There were too many red flags and they were all adding up: prolific petty offending, as in stealing cars and driving them away; chronic sleep problems; in and out of Prison from a young age; and never thinking of the consequences. Oh, and being an adrenaline junkie.

By session 7 he was regaling me with his additional health issues. We spent the whole session talking about them. He asked me if I would email Health Care about it, and I did. He told me that he was now averaging one and a half hours sleep at night. He felt he had a pain in his kidneys, and he was getting pains in his chest and his left arm. This was obviously dangerous when it came to the heart. He was very underweight. He was 6 feet 2 inches, and only 9 ½ stone. It was even more difficult to get him taken seriously because he looked so well but said he felt 'utterly crap'. Anyway, I'd told Health Care all of this and I hoped they would take it seriously.

In session 8, Billy said he was feeling much better. Was eating okay again. He said he was not sure if he was sleeping or not, but he was lying there and trying. I got that, because that can be my problem as well. I suggested that he try turning off the TV earlier, i.e. at midnight, and getting up at 8 a.m. and forcing his body into some sort of routine. I could talk – it had never worked for me, but it did work for some people. He thought this was a good idea. He also wanted to do some CBT the next week on what he saw as his problem of not wanting to go back to Prison but knowing he would. I went off to find some CBT to help him with that.

We had a proper CBT session in session 9. We filled in an initial assessment form. Billy had decided he wanted to fill in the ADHD screener alongside the CBT. He was okay that week. Very shaky. Said he was eating, but sleep was still odd. He also brought up his father by saying that he needed to 'resolve what happened' with his dad. This was the first time he'd mentioned it in several weeks.

The last session I had with Billy, we went through the ADHD screener and he couldn't believe that he ticked every single box. He had ticked 'sometimes' or 'often' to every single trait. When I explained that insomnia, anxiety, paranoia, eating disorders and petty, but prolific, crime could all be red flags for ADHD he was amazed that all his issues could possibly come under one banner.

As this was going to be our last session, I explained to him how important it was to bring this up with the Psychologist. The reason he knew he would be coming back to Prison was because his impulsive and compulsive ADHD brain just couldn't stop doing what it had always been doing. And doing that, repeatedly, had always led him back to Prison.

But if he were to get diagnosed and medicated for ADHD then all of that would stop. He would no longer be an adrenaline junkie because his brain would be getting all the dopamine it needed. And he would be able to control himself when he walked past a car door that was unlocked!

He was incredulous that this could be possible, but I promised him it absolutely could. And he promised me that he would insist on getting an ADHD assessment when he saw the senior person in Mental Health.

I truly hope Billy found the right diagnosis, the right medication to help him, and that the people of Plymouth are now safe if they forget to lock their cars.

Red Bands, OCD and tags

My next referral was an absolute joy. I really can only describe him as a joy to work with, but he was struggling with some issues of his own, which had brought him to counselling. He was a thirty-two-year-old who I would find on Raleigh Wing, which was just off the Association area. So that was good for starters.

This was also the first time I had met anybody who was a Red Band. I had had plenty of clients who aspired to be one, but this was the first client I worked with who was already a bona fide Red Band.

Honestly, you would think someone could have come up with a bit more of an exciting title than 'Red Band', and just slap an elasticated red armband on these men, wouldn't you? Job titles are important to people! They raise self-esteem and give people a sense of pride and responsibility. Which is much-needed when you are in Prison. It's a golden opportunity to give somebody a nice job title to aspire to, and to keep hold of when they get it.

I'm sure I could come up with fifty different titles for somebody who had more autonomy, was considered to be more senior and responsible, and as such could have access to pretty much anywhere in the Prison. But no, 'Red Band' it was, and to my knowledge still is.

Ricky had again been referred by somebody in Mental Health, which was another step in the right direction after having been told initially that I couldn't see anybody who was. Now there was a steady flow. This pleased me for two reasons: one, it meant they trusted me, and two, so many of my clients just wanted someone to talk to.

As a Red Band, Ricky didn't only have access to walk freely around more places in the Prison, he was also eligible for slightly more challenging jobs than sweeping the Wing. I found him the first day in the industrial workshops, where he was working in the office. Anything clerical was considered to be a very responsible job. We settled into a nice little routine of me staring through the glass strip in the door and he, waiting for me, would spot me approaching the door and be up at lightning speed, out of his seat, dropping whatever paperwork he was working on and literally run to the door. We would then walk over to my counselling room.

Ricky was a real character and we bonded immediately. He told me he was in Prison for organising a 'Punch Up & Punch Party' which was a huge success, primarily because Ricky was supplying a wide variety of illegal substances for his guests. Until the police raided it. The irony was he didn't even drink or take drugs himself but pretty much everybody else in his circle did. And those circles were the music business because he was already an established drummer before he came to prison. He was charged with 'Intent to supply class A drugs' and sent back to Prison. He had been in before. Nothing major, just several short sentences for petty crime.

In the first session he told me he had two children – a girl aged seven and a boy aged eight. Very unusually, he told me that he had 'selected' the work colleague of his who he thought would be the best mother to have children with. She wasn't his girlfriend, but he just knew she would be a good mother. You don't hear that very often.

He was from Herefordshire and told me he was diagnosed with OCD and anxiety, and immediately I suspected undiagnosed ADHD, but didn't mention it that first session.

In session 2, he told me that he was eleven when he found out his dad wasn't his real father. He wondered if this was where his anger came from. I suspected so. He seemed quite bright, and told me he passed seven GCSEs, and was very ashamed of the fact that he was violent with an ex-girlfriend. He wanted to work on that.

By session 3, he was telling me that he was extremely violent in the past. He genuinely didn't know why he got so angry. He was seriously thinking about doing a 'Thinking Skills' course because he strongly believed there was something wrong with his brain. He told me more about the mother of his children – how he absolutely didn't love her when he suggested having children with her, but he 'does now'. I became more sure he was ADHD in this session but still didn't say anything. He had already made some disparaging comments about 'the hundreds of ADHD kiddie boys on the yard' – getting on his bloody nerves!

Our session 4 didn't happen because the Prison was on lockdown. And, unbelievably, session 5 didn't happen because the Prison was on lockdown! The amount of petrol I wasted driving over to that Prison when it was on lockdown I can't begin to tell you. However, because it was on lockdown for the second time I did manage to pass some CBT paperwork underneath his cell door, and we had quite à good chat through the observation panel.

I loathed it when the Prison was on lockdown. I hated letting people down. While I understand, for security, it had to be the case, when it got in the way of me seeing my clients and them being let down, it was so frustrating. I know it affected literally everybody else and not just me, but I found it exasperating when I was there ready to see somebody, and they were there waiting to see me, and yet we couldn't do anything about it.

Thankfully on session 6, we did get to meet up. I gave Ricky some CBT exercises specifically about anger and thought processes. He talked a lot about his OCD. Heaven only knows how he managed this but, in a Prison where it was difficult to get one shower a day, he told me he had four showers a day and also changed his clothes four times every day. Fair play to him for managing that. However, he was convinced he was covered in whitehead spots. He thought the people in the laundry were using too much washing powder and was going to ask them to cut down! I couldn't even see the spots despite him shoving his face and hands at me and insisting they were there.

In session 7 he told me he hadn't brought his CBT paperwork back as he didn't feel Prison was the best place to work on his OCD or anger, because of how dirty it was. I had to agree. Instead, he decided he would like to work on courses and anything positive to impress his Offender Manager and his potential Probation. He said he felt his head had been going in a bad direction and Probation wanted him to fail. I mentioned this was overthinking at its best.

In session 8, he was happier because he had seen the doctor, who told him that the spots were due to the water in Prison. He had been given some cream. He was much more upbeat and we filled in the skills application form. He showed me pictures of his girlfriend and their two children – absolutely beautiful children – and he started to talk about being very keen to get his tag.

In session 9 he had had a visit earlier that day from his girlfriend and their two children, which had made him very happy. He told me he had been an apprentice footballer at a northern professional football club between the ages of fourteen and seventeen, but was sacked because of his cannabis use. We've heard that story before haven't we? How many of these boys were exceptional at sports but blew it when they discovered cannabis? I was becoming even more convinced he was ADHD. Using cannabis to calm an ADHD brain often starts in the teenage years and I was seeing it time after time in my clients.

In that session he told me he was sexually frustrated. I could understand that but, as he was going to be out soon, we agreed it was a problem that wouldn't (hopefully) be troubling him for too much longer. When an Officer took me aside afterwards and told me that Ricky was considered a serious risk to women, and they'd always watched me when I was with him, I was very surprised. I had never felt this at all, but took it on board. There were no cameras in my counselling room and I had never felt anything different with him than I had with anybody else.

Ricky had given me his band's name, so I could listen to him drumming, and I promised I would listen to some of his music online. I wasn't a fan of heavy metal but was interested to see if this was Prison bravado or true.

In session 10 he was thrilled when I told him that his drumming was excellent and I had been very impressed. He blossomed in front of me. He was jubilant, confident, desperate for release now, and asked me if I would go to his tag hearing with him on Monday. This would be a first for me, but I said, 'Of course.' Anything to help these boys.

I thought now was about the time to suggest he might have ADHD. It could potentially help him get released if he had been undiagnosed all his life and, very importantly, undiagnosed and unmedicated at the times he committed his offences.

He still didn't think he was the same as 'the dozens of hyperactive, noisy, fighting, little ADHD twats on the yard,' but listened when I assured him I was not a little twat, if we were to believe Thomas, and I had just been diagnosed with ADHD at the age of fifty-one

I had to tread very carefully here because of his opinion of ADHD twats, but when I explained that anxiety, overthinking, OCD, ruminating, not understanding what's going on in your brain and violence were all red flags for ADHD I could see him seriously considering it for the first time. Now I'd finally got his attention on this, I took the opportunity to mention numerous short sentences for petty crime, just like his own colourful criminal career, were also a red flag. To my relief, he said he would definitely consider it and would fill in a screener. I felt sure this was the answer to him not coming back to Prison again and he was such a nice guy,

I wanted to get the message over that this could be behind his petty offending.

The tag meeting went well. There were about five of us in the room and the Parole Officer was speaking to all of us via a very strange looking contraption in the middle of the table. Ricky presented himself well. I was honest about how he was trying to understand his previous violence and had engaged in counselling, and also how I suspected he had an undiagnosed neurodiverse condition, which could have contributed to his previous violence. We both left the room feeling hopeful.

By session 11 everything was okay, apart from the fact that Probation now had a problem with him living at his cousin's house. He was really pissed off about this as he had banked on it. He insisted he was 'Hanging on waiting for release,' and nothing else mattered. He just wanted to get out. Worryingly, he also told me he hadn't a clue how to earn money, because when he was dealing drugs he was making good consistent money, but he didn't want to go back to Prison so I was faced with the familiar dilemma – a talented footballer, who had made too much money selling drugs, and was now looking for a new direction. It's very difficult to entice these boys into a career where they are only going to earn a tenth of what they made dealing drugs, yet none of them want to go back to Prison. Luckily, he had his music career, which could potentially earn him very good money.

He had filled in the ADHD screener and I said I would take it away with me, mark it, and bring it back with me the following week.

In the next session everything was good, but now he was feeling tense because he knew his tag had been approved but he hadn't actually been given a date when he would receive it. He was getting very stressed about it. He told me he had been an escort before, only part-time, and had only actually had sex with two clients. One time because somebody asked and one time because he decided to give it for free!

In the next session he was still very tense over this tag. He said he knew the application was on the Governor's desk, but he also knew there were hundreds of others sitting there as well.

Then he told me that he had a meeting the next day, as a Red Band, in the Governor's office. I said, 'Well, there's your golden opportunity!' He didn't have a clue what I meant. So I explained, 'Look, YOU – not all the other people who are waiting to hear about their tag – YOU are going to be in the Governor's office. YOUR application is on his desk. Speak to him!'

It was his brother's eighteenth birthday party coming up and he was desperate to be out for it. So I explained, 'Give the Governor a reason for you needing your tag before other people. He's a decent bloke. If you explain you are desperate to be at your brother's eighteenth, he will listen.'

In our last session he was ecstatic, because it had worked. He had managed to speak to the Governor one-to-one and explained about his brother's eighteenth and the Governor, being the compassionate man he was, had agreed to put Ricky's tag application at the top of the pile.

I gave him the results of his ADHD screener. He had scored high enough to warrant further investigation and I could almost guarantee a diagnosis. He was still saying he didn't want to be 'a little twat with ADHD'.

I said, 'No, you don't have to be. But you could think about the fact that it's potentially what has brought you back into Prison this time. As you are so determined not to come back, have a serious think about getting an assessment and potential diagnosis on the outside. And a serious think about medication if you are diagnosed – because that alone could stop you coming back to this place.'

This absolutely stopped him in his tracks. He hadn't realised that an ADHD diagnosis and medication could actually help stop him going back to Prison, and that was his goal.

As it was his last session I impressed upon him how important getting assessed was. He didn't need to be in Prison. He was a talented drummer and had also taken up weight-lifting competitively, which he was proving to be good at as well. Not to mention he had two gorgeous children who needed their dad.

He had options for what he could do, and that did not need to include drug dealing, so my parting words, for the first time to a client – and because it seemed appropriate – were, 'Please don't fuck up and please don't come back to this place.'

And I'm very happy to report, because he writes occasionally, that he hasn't fucked up and he hasn't gone back to Prison. I still don't know whether he ever had an assessment for ADHD though! I doubt it. He was so determined not to be a 'little ADHD twat' like the other hyperactive Young Offenders. But I'd bet my life he is as ADHD as me.

An insistent client, damaged heels and the travelling trainers

My next client wins the award for trying hardest to see me. Every time I was on his Wing, Drake, picking somebody else up or dropping them off, he would beg to see me. I kept giving him the referral forms to fill in, which he said he had done, and chatting with him for as long as I could as he was obviously desperate to talk, but he still wasn't getting an appointment. However, eventually it worked. I was given a referral form for him and booked him in as soon as I possibly could, because the poor man had tried harder than anybody else.

Tony was thirty-five but looked older. Like a lot of them do in Prison. A life of crime and constantly evading the Police takes its toll, not only mentally but physically, and Tony could easily have been forty-five. Having said that, he was still a good-looking man with the most piercing big blue eyes and blond curly hair.

He told me straight away he had been on heroin and cocaine since his late teens. He was currently being medicated with methadone and pregabalin, which is a strong anti-anxiety medication, in the Prison. Methadone being what they give you to reduce and then hopefully stop your addiction to heroin.

That bit didn't surprise me, drugs play such a big part in how and why so many people end up in Prison, but what he said next did. He told me his mother had also been on heroin and cocaine as far back as he could remember, and all through his childhood she insisted he inject her. How horrific! He said he never wanted to inject her, but she would be screaming at him and writhing in agony, begging him to inject her with heroin, so he had to, especially in his teenage years. Heartbreaking. So when I was at home watching *Blue Peter*, having my hard-boiled egg and tomato sauce sandwiches and doing my homework, there were people injecting their mothers with heroin. Two such different worlds.

In our first session Tony told me he had two daughters aged fourteen and eighteen, and the eighteen-year-old had just had a baby, making him a grandfather. He was also dealing with bereavement. He had recently lost his grandad, stepdad and two very good friends. His main complaint in session 1 was that they were reducing his methadone too quickly in the Prison, and I noticed he talked a LOT. An ADHD red flag there along with the addiction, but the only two red flags I noticed in the first session.

By session 2 he was much more subdued and told me that he felt quite depressed. Then came the story of his wrecked foot. Unfortunately, for him at least, his last house burglary had gone badly wrong and he'd been caught by the Police after jumping out of a third-floor window. This had had a catastrophic effect on his left foot and he was in agony. He couldn't put his foot down on the ground. I had never heard of anybody with a broken heel before, but apparently it can happen.

Tony was so horrified about the state of my crumbling counselling room that he had already asked his Wing staff if he could decorate it for me! He was waiting on a decision.

In session 3, he told me he took Spice, the horrible synthetic cannabinoid drug that was still rife in the Prison system. I asked if he was seeing the drugs team and he told me he was, so I didn't meddle as I knew they would be taking that seriously, especially as he was on methadone and pregabalin. I asked him if he was being honest with the drugs team about what he was taking and he said he was. We talked about how he must be completely honest about what he was putting into his body for them to be able to do their best to help him. He said he got that and that was why he was being completely honest, because he genuinely did want to be clear of all drugs. I admired him for this. When you have been brought up by an addicted mother it's a complete lifestyle change, which is difficult for anybody before you add addiction into the mix.

Tony told me he felt very sad about the lack of contact with his daughters, although he was not restricted from seeing them. I suggested that he start by writing to them, which he thought was a good idea but one that hadn't seemed to enter his head before. He told me he was not enjoying being in HMP Portland and, 'Their Mental Health services are shocking.'

He was still very concerned about the state of my room!

In session 4, Tony was now worried about his Offender Manager, Probation Officer and Parole hearing. He asked me if I would speak to his Offender Manager, Sam, which I promised him I would do. I could now see why he was desperate to see me. I was positive he thought engaging in counselling would gain him brownie points.

For our fifth session, I actually saw Tony for ninety minutes as the two previous clients were no-shows. He was very stressed as he didn't believe the Prison Doctor was taking his needs seriously. Apart from that, it was a good session until he found out that I was not paid. He was stunned into silence (almost!) about this. He had seen me coming and going for a year and had assumed I was paid staff. He was now not only outraged about the state of my room but also the fact that I was not being paid. I did explain that the Governor was trying his best to get funding for me, and it was apparently quite imminent, but Tony just couldn't believe I'd done everything I'd done for a year and not been paid a penny. I didn't dare tell him I didn't get any expenses either or I think he would've imploded.

Session 6 and everything was okay, he was just having a general moan about Health Care.

By session 7 I realised Tony was a professional moaner! Gosh he was good at it. That day he hadn't been given his methadone until twelve noon, instead of 8 a.m., so he was very angry with Health Care. That warranted a good moaning session and I empathised and sympathised appropriately.

In session 8, he told me he wanted to be an escort on the outside. Most Prisoners do become sex-starved in Prison, so I can understand why some have thoughts of doing this sort of work when they are released.

Tony told me he had his Parole hearing coming up and for a change was very happy that Health Care had apologised for taking him off his methadone too quickly – but now he had changed his mind and said he was glad they did!

In session 9 he had a good old moan about Probation having put the hearing date back, but said I was 'helping him a lot' and he really liked seeing me. I think I just gave him an outlet for his moaning. However, counselling can be all about that if it's what the client needs at that time. And Tony definitely did.

I was realising Tony had a very heightened sense of justice about everything – from the state of my room, the fact I wasn't being paid, Health Care being late with his methadone and Probation putting his Parole hearing off – so as having a heightened sense of justice is an ADHD trait I tentatively introduced the possibility of ADHD.

He was a bit surprised because he thought ADHD only related to kids, but when I told him I'd been diagnosed at fifty-one, and addiction was hugely linked to ADHD, he started to wonder whether he had it and not only him, but also his mother. When I explained that it was usually hereditary he became even more keen on doing a screener.

I have that screener in my hands right now and to every ADHD trait question he had ticked 'sometimes' or 'often'. In fact, he had only ticked 'sometimes' four times and 'often' fifteen times. Not once had he ticked 'never' or 'rarely'. There was zero chance this one wasn't ADHD in my opinion and we put in a request for an ADHD assessment there and then. I didn't think he would get it before he was released but I thought it might help with his Parole hearing.

Tony was one of the people who I did stay in touch with when he left Prison shortly afterwards. It tended to be the boys and men without parents who kept in touch – or parents whose parenting skills included forcing their teenagers to inject them with heroin. I think they saw me as a constant support and stability in their life, which so many of them hadn't had. Who was I to take that away from them? I never would. And having been an ex-offender mentor for the best part of twenty years I knew I was more than qualified, experienced and trained to help them on the outside. I'd loved mentoring and having reached the point where I was training new mentors, I knew mentoring inside out.

About a year later, when he was in another Prison, Tony wrote to me and asked me if I wouldn't mind sending him a second-hand pair of trainers. Apparently his heel was still giving him agony and he didn't have any shoes with any sort of soft padding. He didn't want me to spend much money and just asked if I could possibly go into Oxfam or another charity shop and pick him up the cheapest pair of squishy trainers, and he would reimburse me.

Well, I have a 'thing' about anything second-hand, and I thought no way am I buying him second-hand trainers. Instead I would get him a cheap but half-decent new pair from Amazon. I checked with my young trendy niece as to what was vaguely with-it and spent no more than £15 on a pair of trainers that had good, padded bottoms. When they arrived she assured me they were surprisingly okay for the price, so I packed them up and sent them as required to the Prison.

If you knew then what happened to those trainers! This hopefully will give you something to smile about. Firstly, it took about three months for them to get into the Prison. Lord alone knows where they went, but Tony and I kept trying to find out what had happened to this pair of trainers and apparently they were in various different departments in the Prison he was now in. Eventually, I put in a complaint to find out where the trainers were and, after many letters backwards and forwards, I was told they had been sent outside the Prison to be screened for drugs.

Dear God. I have never so much as smoked one cigarette, let alone taken any drugs, but I guess as Tony was a known drug user they were suspicious there were drugs coming in in the trainers. There really weren't.

However, what happened next is either laughable or tells you how much the Prison service wastes money. These trainers had to be sent off-site to a specialist service to be screened for any traces of drugs.

And then guess what they did. They blew them up! Yes, I had a letter to say that the trainers had been blown up because, potentially, there was drugs in them. Unless Amazon and I had decided to take up drug dealing, there were absolutely no drugs in those trainers, but it took the best part of six months for us to find out where they were, what had happened to them, and eventually that they had been blown up.

And by the way, HMPS, you still owe me fifteen quid for the trainers (never mind thousands of miles in petrol and hundreds of pounds in counselling hours). But it's those bloody trainers that irritate me the most, because all I was trying to do was help that man not be in pain and the Prison service had to blow them up in case there were drugs in them. FFS.

Twelve-month review time

To be honest, Tony did have a point about me not being paid a penny. I was getting a bit incredulous about the situation now. I had passed all my counselling qualifications by then so I was a qualified CBT Therapist, qualified coach with 25 years' experience working with clients as a mentor, Tutor, Trainee Counsellor and a qualified Level 5 Counsellor.

I was the only counsellor at HMP Portland. It was literally just me. I was supporting the Safer Custody department when they were concerned that people were going to attempt suicide or self-harm, often seriously. I saw their clients immediately.

I was taking referrals from Mental Health, which we had agreed at the beginning would be beyond me, but it wasn't and I honestly thought I was doing a pretty good job! – the Governor did too and I knew he appreciated everything I was doing and was fighting to get funding for me. I thought I would do a twelve-month review to back him up and show that I was needed in Portland.

This report started off a bit differently to the six-month review. I now had quite a lot of feedback from clients to include. These were just some of them I had received:

'It's the only hour a week I don't feel I'm in a Prison.'

'I felt amazing after seeing you the first time – I remember asking if I could see you twice a week'

`'I'd definitely be down the block if I didn't see you once a week.'`

'It's so good to talk to a normal person and not to have to watch what you say, like I do to Officers and Prisoners.'

'It's helped me so much – I was really depressed when I first saw you. I only realise that now I feel so much better.'

'I've felt guilty about that car accident (where a friend was killed) every day for six years. Since seeing you I honestly hardly think about it anymore. I get it wasn't my fault.'

'It's so good to clear my mind once a week – it stops me kicking off in-between sessions.'

'It's just so good to be able to talk for an hour and not be judged.'

'You've made it so much easier for me to open up and talk.'

Then the report stated that I had single-handedly been providing the counselling service at HMP Portland for a full year by 19 November 2015. I had seen thirty clients in total and at that point provided 290 counselling hours (there were more hours to come) and was still coming in on a Wednesday and Thursday from Poole to Portland.

It stated that the longest-running clients had received thirty-eight, twenty-seven and twenty-five hours of counselling.

Referrals were still coming from Safer Custody, the Substance Misuse Team, Chaplaincy, Offender Supervisors, the Head of Resettlement, and clients could also self-refer.

The reasons people were seeing me had obviously diversified and still included bereavement, suicide of parents, having to turn off life support machines, and the very common depression, anxiety, paranoia and social anxiety. There were also numerous cases of self-harm, eating issues and pre-release anxieties.

Then pretty much every client had either diagnosed or undiagnosed ADHD issues. Cropping up most were overactive minds, overthinking, paranoia, hyperactivity, boredom, insomnia, having a heightened sense of justice about help they were either receiving or, more usually, not receiving in the Prison, and every other ADHD trait known to man.

On top of this I was dealing with childhood sexual abuse, suspicions people might have bipolar, anger with the judicial system and wrongful imprisonment, a partner having a stillborn baby, Wing bullying, fear of attacks, and flashbacks to crimes and the death of a best friend.

I was also seeing clients with severe depression, an IPP Prisoner with no release date, fear of returning to offending, not wanting to come back to Prison but not knowing how to live a crime-free life, knife crime, and anything and everything in-between.

I stated in this report that around 75% of my clients had been diagnosed ADHD as children, but I was recognising undiagnosed ADHD in pretty much everybody else. And every single one of those diagnosed as a child had either not been on medication or had been taken off their medication when they came to Prison.

I was also working outside the Prison with some of the most vulnerable clients alongside their Probations. So I was putting in hours outside the Prison liaising with Probation Officers, and one case that had to be reported to the Police as it included historical sexual abuse.

As if that wasn't enough to keep me busy, I had an empty property and was housing some of these ex-Portland clients, in conjunction with their Probation Officers, because the alternative was that Probation supply them with a tent. I couldn't have that when it was bitterly cold, especially on the coast with the severe weather coming from the sea, when I had three spare bedrooms. So several of them stayed in my property for many months.

I was giving my all to help these clients and I loved every second of it. But surely I was worth something? The wonderful Governor James thought so. He bounded into my counselling room one day saying, 'I think we've got you funding. I've tried everywhere but it looks like we can get money from the drugs team.' It wasn't definite, but it was looking likely, and I was so grateful for him trying.

Cod and chips, crying and heartbreak

I only cried once at HMP Aylesbury and that was the day my supervisor and the paperclip numpty laid into each other, they stripped me of my Prison belt and keys and threw me out. And even then I wasn't only crying for me, I was crying for the boys I was leaving behind. But it was definitely only on that one occasion. Every time I left HMP YOI Aylesbury I drove half an hour home and still felt I was quite geographically close to my boys.

Leaving HMP Portland was a different matter altogether. For starters the Prison is on an island. As you leave the Prison car park you have to wind your way down the hill, past the signs for HMP The Verne, down through Portland Village itself and onto the Causeway. The Causeway takes you over Chesil Beach and into Weymouth.

Except, more often than not, I didn't make it to that Causeway before I had to stop the car. I would have to stop because I was crying and couldn't see through my tears to drive.

And I would just sit and sob. Unfortunately, the only safe place to stop was near a fish and chip shop, so I did get some very strange looks from people going in for their chippy teas.

I would sob at leaving those boys behind. So many of their stories broke my heart. So many of them, I felt, didn't deserve to be there. I knew so many of them, if they had been born into my family, with my mother, they wouldn't have gone near any Prison. She wouldn't have let them. Not that she was perfect, but she would not have let a child of hers get into trouble with the Police. One of my brothers came close in his early teens, for stealing from a shop, but she was down on him like a ton of bricks and he never got into trouble again from that day onwards.

So many of these boys didn't have mothers. So many of them had lost their mums when they were at that critical age, between sixteen and eighteen. All of their mothers had died from either alcohol or drug addiction. And as pretty much all these boys were ADHD, it was safe to assume that either one or both their parents were too, and had been battling addiction due to undiagnosed ADHD. This is what broke my heart.

If there had been more education and knowledge around adult ADHD their mums, and sometimes their dads, wouldn't have died when they were so young and from that minute the kids wouldn't have gone off the rails. I had seen it in so many of them. Everything was going perfectly fine until at sixteen, seventeen or eighteen their mum had died and after that they had thought, 'What's the point?' They just didn't care anymore. They had nobody else that they looked up to as much as they did their mum and she was gone so what did anything matter?

Then there were the boys who went into the care system. I had seen how that had destroyed them. The rejection they felt was absolutely horrendous. One trait of ADHD is Rejection Sensitive Dysphoria. It's something that only ADHD people have. It's an extreme reaction to either rejection or humiliation, and the reaction can be equally painful, whether there is actual rejection or humiliation or not. If an ADHD person perceives rejection, it hurts just the same. So I had seen how cripplingly hurt and rejected these boys had felt when they had been put in care. Especially the ones whose brothers and sisters hadn't been put in care too. It had utterly destroyed their self-esteem right from the beginning. And, after that, nothing mattered anymore. So many of them just didn't care about what happened to them because their mum was gone or had 'rejected' them by putting them into care.

I've honestly never cried as much as I did when leaving Portland. It was a rare occasion when I arrived home with no tears at all. And the wrong song coming on the radio made it ten times worse. It took me an hour door to door and, if I was lucky, I'd have stopped crying by the time I reached Poole.

I loved the bones of so many of those boys and young men. And the more of them I met, and the wiser I became about ADHD, it was very obvious I had the same brain as pretty much all of them and that's why we bonded so instantly. I got them and they got me.

I'd never been a typical twinset and pearls, scarf round the neck counsellor. I'd always been a ripped jeans and T-shirt counsellor who swore far too much. But that worked extremely well in a Prison! Boys would much prefer you to say, 'Shit that sounds awful,' than, 'How does that make you feel?' in response to anything they said. I was them and they were me, and I adored all of them.

So leaving Portland twice a week and driving home was one of the hardest things I'd ever done in my life. I sometimes wondered whether I was emotionally strong enough to do the work but nothing, absolutely nothing, would've let me walk away from those boys.

When I say I loved every second of working with them and being in that Prison, I mean every single second. It was the most satisfying thing I have ever done. And I wouldn't change it for the world.

Punching, Probation
and weddings

One of my clients was extremely long-term and I had been seeing him since almost the very beginning. He looked like a child. He was short, approximately 5 feet 6 inches and looked very underdeveloped for his age.

His name was Darren and he was from North Dorset. He was based on Grenville Wing, which along with Nelson was one of the Young Offender Wings. He had very short, jet-black hair, which was always gelled into spikes, and the brownest of eyes.

He was very striking to look at. But everything about him was underdeveloped. Almost like a pocket-sized version of an adult. I was to find out why I was right as time went on.

Being small hadn't stopped Darren having quite a reputation in the Prison for being extremely violent. And I had been warned about this in advance. When I saw him and how tiny he was, compared to the other men, I couldn't possibly imagine him being violent.

His referral form alone had broken my heart, which is why he was near the very top of my pile. Darren had lost both his parents in his early 20s and spent most of his life either in the care system or in Prison.

I had been assured that taking the odd bit of confectionery into the Prison, both for my own lunch and afternoon snacking, wasn't considered the crime of the century, so with this boy, and pretty much all the rest, I had begun stopping at Portland Post Office and Newsagent on my way in to the Prison and picking up their favourite sweets. Darren had a particular love of liquorice allsorts. So I would sometimes get them from the very limited post office pick 'n' mix or buy a whole bag for him.

When we started our sessions he told me his release date was nearly two years away. He was in Prison for attempted murder after beating somebody up with a metal pole. But he had the goal of getting out for his oldest brother's wedding, which was in only ten months. He came from a family of seven and all the rest were younger than him, some in care, some adopted and some fostered. Honestly, you couldn't make it up. But he had spent most of his adult life in Prison, and when I found out his background, I wasn't surprised.

He was typical in that both his parents had had severe alcohol problems and his father was not only a drug user but also a drug dealer.

By the time this boy was twenty both his mother and father were dead. Both through addiction. And the seven children had been scattered throughout the country, a couple of them fostered together but most of them split up.

Getting Darren to talk was easy. He was warm and friendly and very open.

He told me how, as children, they would come home from school to find their mother drunk on the sofa and their father either beating her up, sorting his drugs ready to be taken out later that evening, or 'out' and coming home heaven knows when. He was known for staying out for two or three days at a time. So, between them, the children had had to go out and steal whatever they were going to eat for their tea. The girls in the family had been the cooks and the boys had been the robbers.

Darren was very honest about his violence and his anger. He was yet another one who had been diagnosed ADHD early as a child, at the age of seven, but had never been on medication for it. From what he told me of his brothers and sisters, I suspected there was a lot more ADHD in the family than just him. Two parents with addiction issues almost guaranteed undiagnosed ADHD when a son was diagnosed with it. At that time, just he and one of his sisters had been diagnosed, but none of the others to his knowledge. At that point he wasn't in touch with most of them.

Darren wanted to work on his anger and his violence and he was a very willing student. I thought he was perfect for CBT because there really was only one main issue and that slotted beautifully into the CBT framework. So right from the beginning I was using CBT modules on anger and violence, and how to manage them. Obviously ADHD medication would've helped manage it even more, but that wasn't an option there so we worked with what we had.

Every week, Darren would fill in his CBT homework and bring it back to me.

He understood that a lot of his anger and frustration as a teenager was due to not being medicated for his ADHD, but he also believed it came from living in a very angry and violent household, where punching somebody was the norm and slapping somebody was considered weak.

I was determined to help this boy. One of his problems, and something he had quite a reputation for, was punching Prison Officers. He explained to me that he had a reputation to keep in the Prison and was known for never walking away and never avoiding a fight. I am absolutely sure him being undernourished as a child, and his very small frame, had meant he had had to develop this tough persona. He'd have been mercilessly bullied without it. Although he was small, he had worked hard in the gym and was very muscular and, I would imagine, strong. He had punched several Officers in his time in this Prison and many other Prisons, and this was what we worked on initially.

I talked to him about the power of walking away, of telling somebody that you wanted to punch them but you were choosing not to, and how powerful that could feel. He was very, very dubious about this at first but I said, 'The next time you feel the need to punch an Officer, why don't you just give it a go? Why don't we use it as an experiment just to see how you feel?'

Darren thought this was going to be hard, largely because he was known as a fighter and the boys in the Prison would always egg him on. He didn't want to be seen as a pussy for walking away. I said, 'That's why you have to make it very loud, clear and heard, that you COULD punch somebody, but you are choosing not to because they are not worth it and you are walking away.' I promised him it was powerful and he should see if he could do it just once for starters.

I didn't have much hope this would happen quickly, but to my surprise, about a fortnight later, he came in and told me that he had done just that. The boys had been baying for him to punch an Officer who had been rude to him, but he said in a very loud voice, 'I could pulverise you. I've done it before but you're not worth it, so just fuck off out of my face.'

Not quite the ideal language but better than punching. So I congratulated him on that element of it and said we would work on better put-downs later! I asked him how it had felt walking away and he said, 'Surprisingly good.'

And just as I had dared to dream, this became his standard behaviour from then on. Darren even reached the point where he wouldn't say anything. He would just stare at them, turn his back and walk away. He said the more he did it the more powerful he found it, and he actually enjoyed it and had no desire to punch anybody.

We talked about blips. I explained how it's very difficult to change ingrained behaviour and if you have the odd slip-up we must see it as just that and not a return to your original thinking and behaviour. He understood that and sure enough a blip happened about two months into our time together.

The best thing about it was his absolute, urgent desire to tell me of it. Darren had arrived at my counselling room before me that day and literally as I opened the door to come in he said loudly, 'I've had a blip, Miss.' I hadn't even sat down.

I thanked him for being so open and honest and asked him to explain the blip from start to finish, with absolutely no judging from me. Well, the blip was he'd become embroiled in an argument in the food queue at lunchtime, thrown his plate of food across the room and had some sort of ADHD meltdown. Nobody had been hit, punched or even hurt, as his plate didn't hit anybody. It was just messy.

So we spent the next hour analysing exactly what had happened, and what had irritated him – which turned out to be him being given a smaller portion than the boy in front of him – why he had lost his temper so quickly, and how he could've handled it differently.

By the end of the session he was feeling so much better about it and knew if it happened again he would handle things differently and how.

I impressed upon him that we just used each blip like this as a learning experience. There were going to be blips, that was just a fact that we had to accept, but the blips were good in as much as we could use each of them as a learning experience. He seemed to like that. That there was a use to these blips. They weren't just a step backwards – he was actually gaining knowledge and awareness of how to do things differently in future.

This really worked with Darren and there were only one or two more blips – once, when he ripped a basin off a wall, and the other time when he punched another Prisoner. But he learnt from them, very quickly, how he would do things differently in future and never again were they repeated.

His behaviour was improving so much, to my detriment, they moved him onto bloody Beaufort Wing, the enhanced Wing that was twenty minutes' walk away! I couldn't complain could I? He was doing everything I had asked him to do. He was becoming less and less violent, to the point that he had been moved onto a Wing where he had his own cell, a shower to himself and a phone in that cell, and it was new and in much better condition than the rest of the Prison. I don't know who was more surprised, Darren, the other boys in the

Prison or the Officers. Numerous Officers then came up to me and said, 'Jesus Christ, what have you been doing with him? There was no chance of him being on that Wing, ever.'

Nobody could believe that Darren was on Beaufort Wing. It had been sanctioned by the Governor, apparently. It was only six months earlier that he had the reputation of being the most violent person in the Prison. Now, suddenly, he was enhanced, because you had to be enhanced to be on that Wing.

It was around this time that I happened to bump into the Governor on one of the corridors. He was rushing somewhere, and so was I, but I had to take this opportunity. I said, 'Have you got literally one minute for me to ask you one question?' and he said, 'Yes.'

'Darren,' I said, knowing full well the Governor knew who I was talking about. 'It's his brother's wedding in October. What are the chances of him getting out for it?'

'Absolutely none, I'm afraid,' came the quick answer. I was crushed. All the work we had been doing was to try and improve his behaviour to give him some chance of being out in time for his brother's wedding. I had to think on my feet, and fast.

'Ok,' I said. 'Would it be possible for nobody to tell him that, because I'm working with him to get him out in time and I know he will lose momentum if he thinks it's not going to happen.'

The Governor thought about this for about ten seconds, and then said, 'Absolutely. I'll have a word with all the people who work with him and tell them that, as far as Darren is concerned, it is a possibility if his behaviour keeps improving.' I thanked him profusely. I could've hugged him, but he was soon on his way and so was I.

Darren's behaviour continued to improve, the blips became fewer and fewer, and I could tell he was much happier in himself. It just goes to show that if you move somebody onto a good Wing with humane conditions, treat them with respect and show them you believe in them, their behaviour improves dramatically. So, between me and the Governor, we were doing a good job of keeping Darren's fists away from Officers' faces.

It was one day when I was over on Beaufort Wing looking for Darren that I saw something odd as I passed a corridor. It seemed to be a beige pile of some sort on the floor and there was a lot of hullabaloo going on, so much so that I stepped backwards to have a look. I then saw there was a boy flat on his back on the ground and the beige pile was actually the Governor's jacket, which he had flung off, and he was on the floor giving CPR to this boy. I was told by several concerned Prisoners and Officers standing near me that the boy had had a serious Spice attack, was unconscious, and the Governor was doing his best to bring him back to life.

I moved away swiftly as I didn't want to be in the way, but my estimation and admiration for the Governor went up that day, even higher than it already had been. I had never seen a Governor before who would throw off their coat and get down on the floor to give CPR to one of their Prisoners.

Work with Darren carried on and he was the most calm, relaxed and easy-going anybody had ever seen him.

Initially some of the Officers had thought he would screw up and get thrown off Beaufort Wing, but that never happened.

What happened instead blew my mind and Darren's, all at the same time. He was given an early release date! Three months before his brother's wedding. I can't remember if I cried but I probably did. I was so happy for him. And also so happy for his brother. This disjointed, dysfunctional family, who had had everything life could throw, thrown at them – something had finally gone their way.

Darren was told he would have to go to approved premises, and would still be on licence for the rest of his sentence, but he had no problem with that. He was just thrilled to be out for his brother's wedding.

When he left Prison, I helped him get to the approved premises in Bournemouth and kept an eye on him there from a distance. The last thing I wanted was him going back to Prison before his brother's wedding.

As the wedding drew closer he told me he had no way of getting there. He had spoken to Probation and they had said they would pay his train fare, but his brother was getting married in Doncaster. Bournemouth to Doncaster is one hell of a journey.

Darren tried to work out how to do it but it involved numerous trains and changes, and with his ADHD he just wasn't convinced he would ever be able to get there. So I offered to drive him there and back. I asked Probation if instead of the train fare would they pay for the petrol for me to drive him there, and they readily agreed.

As the day drew nearer I was dreading it. I, of course, wanted him to be at his brother's wedding but it was nearly 250 miles away. I couldn't possibly do that and back in one day and as Probation weren't coughing up for a hotel, I booked two rooms in a B&B: one for Darren and one for me.

On the day, I woke at the crack of doom, drove to pick up Darren from the approved premises, and started the journey from Dorset to Yorkshire. It was absolutely exhausting and by the time we arrived I was fit to drop, but Probation had insisted I keep an eye on Darren at the wedding and to make absolutely sure he didn't get drunk. Plus, I was to ring them before midnight to confirm that he had left and was back in the B&B.

Shattered as I was, we hurriedly put on our wedding outfits in the B&B and just made it to the wedding in time. His brother's face made it worthwhile. There were many tears as they were reunited at his wedding. Not only was he reunited with his brother, but all the fostered and adopted siblings were at the wedding as well. There wasn't a dry eye in the house.

Although their parents were sadly both dead, their grandparents, aunts, uncles and cousins were blown away that the family had managed to reunite for this wedding. I was knackered but euphoric at the same time.

I felt like a spare part all day, but had to keep my eyes on him in case he disappeared or got rolling drunk. Thankfully he did neither and Probation received their phone call at midnight to say that he was back in the B&B and would be back in Bournemouth the next day.

Then, the next day, I had to drive from Doncaster to Bournemouth. And guess what. Not only did I pay for the B&B but Probation never paid a penny towards that petrol! Absolutely hundreds it cost me to get that boy to his brother's wedding, and it porked me off that Probation went back on their agreement, but I didn't have time to argue. I was just glad I had managed to get him out of Prison in time and then managed to get him to his brother's wedding.

Darren was very appreciative and I was happy that was a job well done. Somebody who had no hope of getting out when they wanted, given time, attention, no judgment at all, and new tools to manage their behaviour, coupled with unwavering encouragement – that miraculous change could, and did, happen.

And thankfully it happened in time for him to attend that wedding where 150 guests were extremely surprised but thrilled to see him. Especially his brother.

I like a challenge but this one genuinely felt like beating the odds. Just like it did when Dante and I had taken on the Foreign Office all that time ago at Aylesbury.

Pretty nails, happy dads and miscarriages of Justice

Much as James the Governor at Portland had been right when he said, 'We can keep you busy,' I still didn't write off HMP Guys Marsh near Shaftesbury in North Dorset. They had welcomed me exceptionally kindly when I went there, battered and bruised from the Aylesbury experience. The Officers were so nice, but I didn't have any more time left for counselling in the week. I was still studying, having counselling supervision, seeing my own counsellor, tackling my very annoying cat phobia, and doing ridiculously huge amounts of counselling homework. So, although I was only in HMP Portland for two days a week, there were a lot more hours that went into it than that. But I was still keen to do anything I could to help at Guys Marsh at weekends.

Barnardo's asked me if I would like to get involved in their Family Days. I had never been to one of these, ever, but I offered my services for the next one and was accepted. I was soon to find out that Family Days are one of the best things to ever happen in a Prison. It's the day when mums, partners, brothers, sisters, aunts, uncles, grannies, grandads and very importantly, children, can come and see their family member in a much less formal environment than the Visit Hall. And for several more hours.

You can imagine how every dad in the Prison was desperate to see his family on one of these days, and places were very hard fought for. Some people were always disappointed because there were never enough spaces for all the dads who wanted to spend time with their children.

The Family Days at HMP Guys Marsh were held in the gymnasium, which was a huge rectangular room, and on the first Saturday I turned up it had been transformed. There were thick, squidgy gym mats on the floor, and lots of designated areas assigned to different fun, active and creative activities suitable for young children right through to teenagers. It was a room full of hundreds of colourful toys and play equipment, with volunteers having little tables around the edge offering different family friendly services.

Rather than when sitting in a formal Visit Hall, the dads didn't have their Prison bibs on and instead were in jeans and sweatshirts and allowed to sit on the floor and play with their kids.

When I had been volunteering for Crisis, the homeless charity, just one of the very many hats I wore over the years had been Head of Hairdressing Services. There was always a huge queue of anything from 50 to 100 people waiting to get their hair cut. And a lot of volunteers kicking around doing nothing, because there were only so many basins and so many hairdressers available. I had the idea to set up single tables with a chair either side and start offering hand massages to guests in the queue. This started off small but quickly went on to become a full-blown Nail Service. I have always loved painting nails and I'm very proud that I set this service up at Crisis because it exists to this day and is a very popular part of what Crisis now offer people at Christmas. I missed painting nails, so I asked HMP Guys Marsh whether me painting nails would be of any use to them? They thought it would.

Barnardo's told me there were always a lot of little girls visiting, and also their mums, who they were sure would love to have their nails painted. They thought that giving Dad some time on his own with the children, while Mum had herself pampered, was a great idea.

I have always owned a full Nail Technician's box, with a vast array of nail varnishes, so I set up my little table and didn't quite know what would happen next. But I'm thrilled to say, just like at Crisis, it proved very popular and I had customers constantly all day.

I worked at several of these Family Days and I loved every minute of them. I even had some regular customers! They were all aged five and six and were tiny little girls who were thrilled to have their nails painted for free. When the doors opened they would run towards my table trying to get in first! I adored them all and I used to paint their nails, making them very pretty and sparkly – and then some of the girls would insist their dad came over and had his nails painted as well! The dads were all good sports and many of them left the gymnasium with sparkly nail varnish on as they made their way back to their cells at the end of the day.

It was very good to have a one-to-one chat with the mums and girlfriends, especially as I was a counsellor and some of these mums were quite distressed and upset seeing their kids with their dads, knowing it was only for a few hours. There were definitely tears shed at my nail table, but I tried to make the mums feel as special as I could. I wouldn't only do their nails; I would give them hand and arm massages.

At my very first Family Day I was running round helping as much as I could, especially when it came to giving out teas and coffees, cakes and then the lunch. It was all hands on deck at that time and the Prison had put on an amazing spread for the families. There was a young man who I was working with a lot and I really didn't know whether he was a very helpful dad or brother, or a volunteer like me. He looked like he could perhaps be somebody's older son, helping while the younger children played with their mum and dad.

He certainly didn't look like he belonged in Prison. He was tall, slim and dark haired. We ended up on the bin bags together at the end of that day clearing all the lunch tables, and it was then that I realised he was a Prisoner rather than a volunteer. I only realised when all the mums, relatives and children had left, and he was still there with me clearing tables.

When we had finished, and finally sat down, I had time to speak to him properly. It was obvious by now that he was a Prisoner, but I couldn't imagine what on earth he had done. He looked like an American college freshman: incredibly well presented, smart and the last person you would expect to see in a Prison.

It wasn't long before his story came tumbling out. This wasn't the first or last of what I considered to be a terrible miscarriage of justice I would hear, but this one was particularly unfair I thought.

Gavin was from Worcestershire and told me that he was in Prison on a nine-year sentence. He didn't look older than twenty-one.

It didn't take much for Gavin to start talking and we were left on our own for about half an hour before they came to release us volunteers. He'd been out in Worcester, admittedly drunk, on a Saturday night. I don't think there are many people who can say that hasn't been them at some point in their life. He was seventeen, out with his mates, and had had a few too many pints of lager.

Outside a bar, there was a bit of a verbal rumpus that involved two boys who eventually started punching each other. Gavin tried to step in, because one of the boys was his friend, but instantly he stepped in the other boy fell to the ground. He had been punched by Gavin's friend.

Gavin had absolutely no memory of what happened next because he admitted he was three sheets to the wind.

But apparently he kicked the boy on the floor before him and his friend walked away. He told me that there were numerous witnesses who said he had kicked the person on the floor and he was perfectly prepared to accept that he had done it, which he had been clear about in his statement to the Police.

Tragically, the person on the ground died and Gavin and his friend found themselves arrested. Because Gavin had not punched the boy and it was the punch that had killed him, not the kick, Gavin was advised to plead not guilty. His friend, who had actually punched the boy, which had been unequivocally proven to be the cause of death, pleaded guilty to manslaughter.

And this is where I think our justice system is skewed. Gavin's friend – who had admitted punching and ultimately killing the boy on the ground – because he had pleaded guilty to manslaughter was given three and a half years in Prison. Gavin was given nine years because he had pleaded not guilty. Because he wasn't. And on the advice of his solicitors. How can that be fair?

So this very smart, intelligent, kind and hard-working boy was going to lose most of his 20s inside Prison – for one kick, which had not caused any damage.

I felt dreadful leaving the Prison that day. That boy should not have been there and he should've been walking out with me. The only positive was that he was in a modern, clean, well-kept Prison, only built in 1960 rather than Victorian times. I've never forgotten him.

Gun dealers, spaghetti hoops and HMP Aylesbury

Rick, the Suicide and Self-Harm Officer, asked me if I could squeeze in somebody he was really concerned about. I never said no. Ever. However late it meant me staying in the Prison, I would always fit in clients who needed it. I sometimes didn't leave Portland till gone eight o'clock at night but I would've moved in if I'd had the chance. The more time I spent there the better.

Robbie was only twenty years old and the third child in a family of nine children living in Cornwall. The first seven kids were all born to the same mum and dad, but the last two girls had a different father. Robbie's dad had been very ill following a stroke and was now quite disabled and in a wheelchair. Robbie firmly believed it was this that led his mother to taking drugs. Then she took to selling drugs, and in Robbie's words, 'Became VERY well respected and the biggest drug dealer in the area.' I wasn't impressed but I think he thought I ought to have been. I wondered why on earth the woman had had nine children if she didn't have any plans on being a terribly good mother.

All nine children had been removed from the parents due to the drug taking – I'm not even sure the drug dealing was common knowledge, but the drug taking was – and given to various members of the family. Robbie was given to an aunt who had another three children of her own. Bringing up three children and one nephew, and working full-time, I'm sure she took her eye off the ball at some points and certainly off Robbie who, when he was only eighteen, had been involved in a robbery where a knife was used. Somebody was stabbed, but thankfully it wasn't life-threatening. Initially he was given a fifteen-year sentence, but that was reduced to eight years on appeal. He told me he would be out in three and a half years.

Rick had told me that Robbie had been a model Prisoner with absolutely no adjudications for two years. He was also a 'Listener' in the Prison, which meant he had been trained by the Samaritans and would go and sit with Prisoners who were feeling anything from sad to desperate, and especially those who were thinking about self-harming or even suicide. He told me he absolutely loved the work and he had the sort of manner that I thought would be very reassuring to other people. I liked him immediately. Not sure he liked me so much at the beginning.

Rick told me that the aunt had died of cancer just three months before and in those three months Robbie had changed completely. After having no adjudications whatsoever, from doing nothing wrong at all for two years, Rick told me it had all gone to pot in the last six weeks. Robbie had started to hit Officers and everyone was very concerned because it was so out of character for him.

In session 2, Robbie told me about his life when he was still living with his mother. I thought I was getting shockproof, but that proved to be optimistic.

Robbie recalled one evening when he had been about five years old. He was sitting at the kitchen table, eating spaghetti hoops on toast, when his mum went to answer the front door. Outside was his nan in a white van. Robbie watched as loads of neighbours descended on the van and his nan drew back the big sliding door, displaying an array of guns. Robbie's nan was a gun dealer.

Robbie came across as very grumpy in that moment and was asking me if I could please get him twenty-eight days in a Prison nearer his mum and disabled father. He hadn't seen them in two years. He also had a 3 ½-year-old son who he wanted to see as well, but he needed to be nearer Cornwall.

I promised him I would contact Rick about this, who I thought would probably be able to help him get an 'accumulated visits' move somewhere nearer his parents. Accumulated visits are given when a Prisoner is in a Prison far away from home. The Prison service can move them, for a temporary period, to a Prison nearer their family and friends, usually for twenty-eight days.

Because I had been filled in by Rick beforehand, I felt I knew a lot about Robbie before I met him and the first session seemed to go well as I promised to help him. Not so session 2 – he was extremely grumpy, primarily because I'd woken him up. I had tapped on his cell door not knowing he was asleep. He didn't like me very much that day at all.

Robbie told me he hated Portland and wanted to move. He did say that he had only not kicked off in the last couple of days because he knew he was going to be seeing me. But he was still grumpy about it! This was on a Wednesday and Robbie asked me if he could see me on Thursday as well. That was a challenge as I was chock-a-block with clients, but I said I would absolutely pop in if I could.

He assured me there was no real reason for his agitation, just that he was sick of Portland, the faces and the Officers. I did gently ask him if he wanted to talk about his aunt and he said no. Robbie told me he was closest to his sixteen-year-old brother and it definitely wasn't the easiest session we ever had.

I did pop in the next day as promised. Robbie looked tired and emotional. He told me he'd put in an application to see the doctor for sleep medication and antidepressants. He also told me he was starting to go to English classes from Monday, just so he 'gets paid'.

In session 4 Robbie was very unenthusiastic again. He told me he didn't go to English as his mum had sent him some money. He only wanted to go to English for the wages for phone credit.

Robbie told me he knew he would get an IEP (standing for 'Incentive and Earned Privileges') and that would mean he probably went onto 'Basic', which means no TV and reduced, or even no, what is known as Association in a Prison. And what you and I might call 'socialising' out of your cell but still on the Wing.

He had an appointment booked with the doctor the next day, but he had only requested it because I 'told him to'. Robbie didn't seem very keen to engage much and I found it quite a difficult session. I actually thought he was very depressed. He said he didn't feel that he wouldn't come back to Prison. I always find it worrying when they say this. I dumped the idea of CBT and decided to wait till I saw him the next time. I just let him get it all out.

The next session, Robbie told me he was too sick to see me.

The next session, he said he was too busy to come because he was moving cells.

The next session, Robbie said that he wanted to stop counselling because he was 'okay'. I was really not sure. I told him he could come back if he wanted to and would go straight to the top of the waiting list if needed. Somehow I knew this wasn't going to be the last time I saw this boy. I knew Robbie wasn't okay, but obviously he wasn't ready to talk about it.

It took two months for him to come back. And in those two months I had seen him occasionally on the Wing, and always smiled and said hello whenever I saw him. But eight weeks on Robbie told me that he definitely wanted to come back and have proper sessions. Hallelujah! I knew he needed them.

Robbie was really fed up because he admitted he'd been selling drugs in the Prison and had barricaded himself in a room, and now they wanted to move him to HMP Aylesbury. He was very sad and down.

In the next session, Robbie told me exactly what his crime had been. He had become involved in a row with a takeaway delivery driver. He said it was to 'protect his friend', and told me he always carried a knife. He hadn't gone to Aylesbury yet and I so hoped he wouldn't go. I knew I could help this boy if he would only let me.

He then started to come regularly for counselling. ADHD didn't enter my head at the time for this one, but looking back he was very erratic with his moods, his emotions were very dysregulated, he became angry quickly and had a very strong, heightened sense of justice, so who knows. He could've been, I just didn't explore it.

After three very productive sessions I turned up to my counselling room one day and Robbie was sitting at the nearly deceased desk with his head buried in his hands. Sobbing. Great big heaving sobs. Standing beside him was Rick.

Straight away, I went over to Robbie and said, 'Whatever is it? What's happened?'

In-between sobs he managed to tell me that it was definite – he was being moved to HMP Aylesbury. And he was terrified, because he had heard it was the roughest and toughest Young Offender Institute in the country.

I tried to assure him that it really wasn't, that it was hardly any different to Portland, apart from the fact that they were all Young Offenders in Aylesbury and there were now adult males in Portland. But nothing seemed to console him.

He just couldn't stop crying and I think all the pent-up emotion of the last few months was finally flooding out of him.

Quietly, to Rick, I said, 'You know I own a house in Buckinghamshire? It's literally only about twenty-five minutes from Aylesbury Prison. Am I allowed to go and see him?' After the Aylesbury debacle, I was always paranoid about asking permission for everything. They probably thought I was a right wimp at Portland, but when you've been through what I'd been through at Aylesbury, you become an anxious, nervous wreck.

Rick, being the kind and caring person he was said, 'Do YOU want to go and see him?'

I replied, 'Definitely. If that's allowed, then yes I'd love to go and see him.'

Rick said, 'Of course it's allowed. I'll be very grateful for you keeping an eye on him.'

Robbie was now listening in to this conversation and his mood immediately changed. Once he knew I would still be coming to see him in Aylesbury he stopped crying and gave me a hug. I could tell Rick was relieved, because he obviously had a lot of time for this boy, and now he could see I did as well.

It was only a matter of a few weeks before Robbie was moved up to HMP Aylesbury, and although I was based both in High Wycombe, Buckinghamshire, and Poole in Dorset I made sure every time I was in Buckinghamshire I went to see him.

And it was after one of those many happy visits, that Rick, Robbie and I all desperately wanted, my world crashed all over again.

Texts, tears and a new determination

As soon as he moved to HMP YOI Aylesbury, Robbie put me on his visit list and I made absolutely sure that each time I was in Buckinghamshire, which was usually weekly if not fortnightly, I booked a visit to go and see him.

He was a changed boy. Aylesbury hadn't been as bad as he was expecting and he had actually met some old friends in there. He was thrilled that I was visiting him and we had several chatty visits where I was just so relieved to see him happy. I think everything had got on top of him at Portland – he had been there two years and some new scenery and new faces was doing him good.

I always reported back to Rick when I had seen him and Robbie would often send his best wishes to Rick and his gratitude for all he had done for him. Everything was hunky-dory. Or so I thought.

On one particular visit, Robbie told me that he had been in a fight. He said it was over something and nothing and he regretted it already, but he had damaged his shoulder. He was obviously in quite a lot of pain during the visit. After I had filled him up with chocolate, drinks and crisps, and everything else I could buy him, I said goodbye and that evening drove back down to Dorset, because I had clients in Portland I was due to see the next day.

I was constantly on the motorway in-between High Wycombe and Poole at that time, 100 miles door to door, because nothing would allow me to leave Portland Prison. Even though I had bought a house in Buckinghamshire, that I was supposedly moving into, I had no real wish to move in because I was so happy at the Prison.

After I had seen Robbie that day he sent me a text. Now, obviously, boys in Prison shouldn't have phones, but I wouldn't like to guess the high percentage who do and a lot of them actually have two phones. The text I received from him said, 'Thank you so much for visiting. It was really good to see you.'

I immediately texted back, 'Brilliant to see you as well. Take care of yourself. Don't go getting into any more fights and look after that shoulder.'

He texted back, 'Lol I promise I won't – see you soon.'

And I replied, 'Yes you will and please just take care of yourself.'

And thought nothing more of it.

Until I next went into Portland. I tried to get my keys out of the security box and they wouldn't come. I just couldn't remove my keys from the socket and I couldn't work out why.

I went over to the Officers on the gate and explained that I couldn't get my keys out, innocently thinking there was a technical issue, but I was told that there was a message for me to go and see the Head of Security. I hadn't a clue what was going on, but was shown into his office.

This man could not have been nicer to me. I'd never met him before. He said, ' Sarah, I am so sorry and we don't want to do this, but we've got to let you go.'

I could feel tears prick the back of my eyes straight away as I asked him, 'Why?'

He said, 'Trust me, this hasn't come from us. We do not want you to leave, but we've been told that you have got to, by Aylesbury. They haven't given us any choice.'

He went on to explain that when Robbie had texted me his phone signal had hit the mast, and because Aylesbury had my mobile phone number they knew he was texting me and I was texting back.

And that was me – quite spectacularly – sacked twice by HMP Aylesbury, yet again for trying to help somebody. Had the paperclip numpty anything to do with this? I wouldn't be surprised.

This time it appeared it was even more serious than the last. I was told that I was on a ban from working in the entire Prison service for two years and from HMP Portland for ten years. Working? Bit of a joke. I'd not been paid a penny since I was a Tutor at HMP The Mount. It had cost me a fortune to do it, but I'd have gladly paid twice the price. I loved it so much.

The first place I went was to see my counsellor, Lynda, who was now my supervisor. I was beating myself up badly this time because it hadn't entered my head that texting somebody back could have such serious ramifications. I was telling my supervisor that I was 'livid with myself', 'it was all my fault', 'I totally deserved everything I got', and 'I was bloody stupid and I hated myself'. And obviously crying. A lot. After I'd gone on like this for about twenty minutes, she stopped me and said, 'Just wait a minute.'

'I appreciate that the Prison has rules, but I want you to think about this from the counselling point of view for a minute,' she said.

I said, 'Okay', but I really wasn't sure where she was going with this.

'Now, that boy, when he texted you, if you hadn't responded to that text, what could have been the worst-case scenario?'

I thought about it and replied through tears, 'Well, the absolute worst-case scenario would have been that he would feel rejected again, could have gone back to his cell and potentially self-harmed or even taken his own life.'

'Yes, exactly,' Lynda said, 'and that's why, in the counselling world, you have done nothing wrong.' She said, 'It would've been far worse if you had ignored that text and something like that had happened to him. For starters, you would never have forgiven yourself and the Prison service would've had another suicide on their hands.'

So she forced me to stop beating myself up – and God bless the most amazing, supportive supervisor ever, Lynda, for holding me together during that time, because I can't begin to tell you how much I hated myself.

I had absolutely adored everything about Portland Prison. From the Governor, to Rick, to the Head of Resettlement, Cathy, to the rotting ground floors that nobody could have lessons or classes in because it was so damp, wet and disgusting that the boys all had to be on the first floor and up. To that bloody Beaufort Wing, that was horrendously windy and cold to get to, but when you got there it was wonderful. I loved everything about it, but there I was, through my own stupidity, chucked out yet again.

Had I been a bit more ADHD savvy at this point, I would've known that an ADHD brain doesn't ever think of the consequences. I certainly hadn't thought of them when I texted Robbie back. It was only when I was put on ADHD medication afterwards that I ever started to think of the consequences of anything. And I was in my 50s.

I'm not blaming my ADHD for this. More my ignorance around what was allowed and what wasn't allowed. Nobody had ever specifically told me I couldn't text anybody in a Prison, so I didn't know it was against the rules. Yes, I knew it was against the rules to have a phone when you are in Prison, but when I was subsequently diagnosed with severe dyspraxia, with 1% processing and 1% motor skills, it made complete sense of why I hadn't thought beyond the fact that he had texted me and it was only polite to text back. My 1% processing didn't take the thought any further than that.

And something had to force me out of that Prison and into this new house I had bought in High Wycombe, that had been sitting empty for the best part of a year. My mum had severe Parkinson's by now and I wanted to be near her in Bucks. Plus, now I would finally have time to do what I had so wanted to do for such a long time, and that was go into private practice – getting hold of these boys when they first ran into trouble and stopping them from going into Prison in the first place.

I had realised, the more of the boys I had worked with, that I was getting to them when it was too late: they'd committed the crime, been sentenced, their self-esteem had plummeted, their mental health had deteriorated, they hated themselves and they thought they had blown every opportunity they had. I knew I had to get to them before they started on the slippery slope that ended in Prison.

I'm never kept down for long. I'm a very optimistic person. So I was straight back up to High Wycombe, setting up my therapy room and advertising myself as an ex-Prison Counsellor who was determined to keep boys and men, girls and women, out of the Prison System. Particularly those with ADHD who seemed to make up most of that population. I was not done yet.

And little did I know that over the next few years I would become more involved in the criminal justice system than I ever had been before. Just on the other side of the bars.

PS. Please don't think I ever let Robbie down. I went to visit him in every Prison he was moved to until he was released.

PPS. The saddest thing for me was that I had just been referred a new client who had been traumatised when arriving at Portland. 'Spooning' wasn't something I'd come across, but apparently it was quite common. Assuming, when someone arrived in Prison, they had brought drugs or phones in with them, hidden up their back passage, it was commonplace for them to be held face-down by several Prisoners and a spoon or similar utensil shoved up their bottom to dig out any hidden spoils. This had just happened to my last referral, who was hiding nothing. He had been physically ripped and torn, and was terrified and traumatised. And Portland begged me to see him. I was on my way to see this boy that day when Aylesbury intervened. They stopped me seeing and helping somebody who was absolutely desperate. I never met him, but I've never forgotten him. And I just hope he was able to get support from somebody else.

Pre-Prison Counselling and my first 'arrested but not yet sentenced' teenager

So here I was, with my brand-new house in High Wycombe and a therapy room that I'd never used because I'd been too busy at Portland. I set to work furnishing it beautifully, chose and registered my company name, which was 'Headstuff Therapy', and cracked on looking for these boys who were getting into trouble at a young age. I knew if I could get hold of them soon enough I could change their life trajectories. I just had to find them!

It's a bit difficult to market yourself as that sort of therapist. 'Heading for Prison? Head here first!' Hardly appealing.

So I just put on my brand-new website that I specialised in ADHD and waited.

Within just a few weeks I received a phone call from a mother in a panic. Her son, Archie, aged thirteen, had been arrested and Archie was convinced he was ADHD. She didn't think he was, but he was adamant, so could she bring him to see me?

It was a very entertaining hour with this thirteen-year-old and, at the end of the session, I invited his mother in and told her that as far as I was concerned Archie was screaming ADHD and the best thing we could do would be to get him diagnosed and medicated as soon as possible.

Archie hadn't done anything terrible, but had been arrested under this wretched 'Joint Enterprise' charge because he was present when a couple of incidents had happened. And even they weren't that serious .

His mum, thankfully, believed me and immediately booked him in with an ADHD specialist paediatrician, where he was diagnosed with ADHD and put on medication. However, there was still a court case involving him and a large number of other young teenagers to face.

The Judge seemed particularly determined to make these teenagers pay and, although they were only aged thirteen and fourteen, sentenced them all to three years in juvenile Prison. Not only that but he scattered them all around the country, which was horrendous for some of the mothers who I also happened to meet in other circumstances. Suddenly, their thirteen-year-old was 500 miles away.

However, Archie was lucky. Much as the Judge didn't like any of this group of boys and girls, he waved the ADHD diagnosis in Archie's face and said he would like to send him to Prison for as long as the others, but he couldn't, based on this medical evidence. So he would give him a community order. One part of this court-instructed community order was that he had to come and see me on a Friday evening at six o'clock for the next eighteen months, as well as seeing Youth Offending Services and doing two days a week community service at weekends.

That hour on a Friday night became the highlight of my week. Archie was very mature for thirteen and I learnt so much about 'teenage boy ADHD' from him. He was quite severely ADHD, and some of his antics had me in hysterics, but the undercurrent was me most definitely trying to talk him out of doing anything like that ever again, and to never again come into contact with the criminal justice system.

There were a few blips along the way and a couple of things that were a bit more than a blip. There was the time he bought drugs off the internet and hid them by burying them in his auntie's garden. I told him he couldn't leave them there because if his auntie had her house raided, and the Police found drugs in her garden, she would be sent to Prison.

I made it very clear that he couldn't sell them, as that would make him a drug dealer, and he couldn't give them to his mates as that would get him arrested for supplying. So they had to be disposed of very carefully with a lot of thought.

In the next session, he proudly told me that in the early hours he had retrieved the drugs and put them in a skip at the end of the road. And was adamant that nobody had seen him. Thankfully, this was many years before Ring doorbells were commonplace.

Then there was the time he bought a gun. I nearly died when he told me this, because I had the big therapy room windows wide open. It was the height of a hot, humid and sticky summer. I've never closed my windows so quickly in my life. When I asked him why in God's name he had bought a gun he told me not to worry, because when he went to pick it up it wasn't where it was supposed to be, so he was more concerned that he had been ripped off financially.

This boy was severely ADHD and risk-taking and thrill-seeking to the max.

But together, we worked through every aspect of his ADHD till he knew exactly why he had done certain things in the past. And by the end of our sessions he was as ADHD savvy as I was. He understood his own brain wiring, why he thought a certain way and was prone to risky and thrill-seeking activities. He was more self-aware than most adults I knew at that time with ADHD.

He realised how he must catch himself when he was going to be impulsive. That he had to force himself to think of the consequences, because his brain naturally wouldn't. That he was at high risk of addiction because of his ADHD. And that he wouldn't have a verbal filter, so he would be saying things to people that might upset them!

I don't think there was one aspect of the condition we didn't cover and Archie complied with everything, and was so mature about the whole situation that the Judge let him off after twelve months rather than eighteen.

This had been a massive learning curve for me as well, because I had no idea that not having an ADHD diagnosis and/or not being medicated for the condition meant you 'were not of your right mind' at the time of any offending behaviour. And this was most definitely 'mitigating evidence' and usually showed 'reduced culpability'.

This set me up in very good stead for what was going to happen over the next few years. And Archie was the first in a very long line of ADHD teenagers I saw at various stages of going off the rails. A lot had been arrested by the time the parents found me. Some were already on that slippery slope heading towards juvenile Prison. I'd found a new purpose. I was determined that NONE of my ADHD teens were going anywhere near the criminal justice system.

Cautions, paramedics and DBS's

It wasn't long before my next teen-in-trouble arrived. Or rather his mother did. The poor woman was desperate to get Alex, her eighteen-year-old, in to see me, but he didn't turn up for the first five session times she booked. I spent more time talking to his mother than I did to him.

Every time it was for an 'ADHD-related' reason, so I forgave him. Often he had overslept, because he'd been awake in the night and we now know insomnia often features with ADHD. Another two times he completely forgot to come – poor short-term memory also goes with ADHD. Another time he became hopelessly lost on the way and was so late he gave up, yet another ADHD trait. But he actually turned up for session 6! Late and flustered, but I managed to get him through the front door and into my therapy room.

His mother had begged and pleaded with me not to give up on him and I didn't and went on to see him for about eighteen months.

Initially, when I saw Alex, the main problem was he had been thrown out of his very good grammar school because they had failed to identify his ADHD, and he had been misdiagnosed by child and adolescent mental health services (CAMHS) as having Borderline Personality Disorder. He had made two quite serious suicide attempts and his parents were worried out of their minds, and, if we thought that was enough to deal with, worse was to come.

By the time he saw me, he had only recently received the right ADHD diagnosis for which his parents had had to go private, having despaired of CAMHS ever getting it right, but Alex hadn't yet started on the medication.

He was a phenomenally bright boy and I was soon to find out that he also had a wonderful personality. Yes, he had had troubled teenage years, but largely because nobody had spotted his ADHD nor medicated it. But he was coming out the other side with the correct diagnosis and was about to be put on the correct medication. He was kind, caring, compassionate, had a quick-witted sense of humour and was extraordinarily humble for somebody with such a brilliant brain.

The main issue was having been evicted from his grammar school – Alex needed to get A-levels and go to university to fulfil his lifelong dream of becoming a paramedic. His mother told me that ever since he'd been a little boy all he'd ever wanted for Christmas and birthdays were doctors' uniforms, ambulances, stethoscopes and first aid kits. He'd been utterly obsessed with being a paramedic for most of his life.

His ever-resourceful and incredibly supportive parents had found a college Alex could do A-levels at privately and it was at this point I met him. At first he was struggling with three A-levels and it was agreed that he would drop down to two. That wouldn't stop him from becoming a paramedic.

A lot of our sessions focused on Alex's social anxiety, because he found travelling on public transport very difficult. He travelled by train to the private college and sometimes even standing on the platform with so many people was too overwhelming for him. Sometimes the train was just too full of people for him, but he made it into college more times than he didn't, and because he was so incredibly bright he was still doing very well in his A-level studies, despite missing quite a few classes.

Towards the exams we spent our sessions going over and over and over revision. Alex used to bring in cards that he had written facts on and I would test him in the sessions. When it came to the exams, he achieved high grades in both A-levels and was interviewed and accepted by two universities to train to be a paramedic. Everything could have gone as smoothly as that.

However, there was a problem. And that problem was his DBS.

Just at the time he was being put on the ADHD medication and, as they call it, 'titrating', which means going up and down doses and sometimes switching over to different ADHD medications, he had done a couple of minor but naughty things. On one of these occasions he had forgotten to eat for a day and a half before having a very small amount of alcohol. One of the side effects of the medication is wiping out your appetite. With no food in him it went straight to his head and he did something very out of character – he had punched somebody. For the first and only time in his life.

Both of the 'incidents' were not serious enough for any sort of criminal charge, but he did accept two cautions from the Police, which, unbeknown to him or his parents at the time, would cause havoc later on.

So Alex found himself in the position of having been accepted by TWO universities to train to be a paramedic. No surprises there – he was so likeable and

I doubt they'd ever met anybody as keen as Alex to be a paramedic! However, because of the cautions on his DBS, ACRO – The Association of Chief Police Officers Criminal Records Office – barred him. You had to have a completely clean DBS for them to even entertain you training to be a paramedic in the UK – in fact to train for any position working in Health Care.

At the time we were all absolutely incredulous about this. His parents did everything and anything they could to overcome the situation, including numerous appeals to ACRO, letters to MPs, and even going to the Houses of Parliament and meeting MPs, asking for every intervention they could, but there was absolutely no leeway. Despite these two minor incidents having happened when Alex wasn't medicated properly for his condition, therefore 'was not of his right mind', nobody seemed to be interested in how critical that was. It counts in law and in a court, so why not with ACRO?

His mother and father put in so many hours trying to overcome the situation, but there just didn't seem to be any way round it. However, they couldn't stop this boy wanting to train in medicine, so they came up an innovative solution – he would train abroad.

When he should've been off to university that autumn, training to be a paramedic, Alex was actually on a flight to another European country where he was going to train to be a doctor! He couldn't do paramedic training abroad but he could train to be a doctor, and this boy was bright enough to do just that.

And I'm thrilled to say that, despite two Police cautions as a teenager, the same year as this book comes out, Alex will qualify as a doctor.

His parents haven't given up fighting and at some point, we hope in the not-too-distant future, misdemeanours by ADHD teenagers when they were either not diagnosed, not medicated, or not titrated on the right dose of the right medication, will not be held against them for life.

Alex will make the most wonderful doctor and his parents both deserve medals for fighting for their son to achieve his dream.

Arsey teenagers and the Houses of Parliament

My next client, who had been arrested by the time I met him, had the most unusual first session of any client ever, both in the Prisons and out!

I'd had many conversations with Jason's mother on the phone before he finally agreed to see me, but she told me Jason had said, 'If I don't like her, I will tell her to fuck off.'

I told his mother to tell him that, 'If I didn't like him, I would tell *him* to fuck off.'

Apparently, that impressed him enough to come and see me.

However, on the day, Jason could not have been in a worse mood. I was standing outside waiting for him, and his mother said, 'He's in a really foul temper and he doesn't want to come in.' So I insisted she didn't force him. But eventually, to both our surprise, he walked in the door. His mother quietly removed herself and waited in the car.

We sat down and I went through my normal introduction of who I was, how everything was confidential, especially as this boy was fifteen – they do like to know that you aren't going to tell their parents everything – and I thought things might go okay, although Jason was resolutely refusing to meet my eyes! But as soon as I asked him a question all I got back was a snarling – 'No comment.' I asked him another question, and still, 'No comment.' After about eight of these 'no comments' I explained that this was not a

Police interview and if he didn't want to be here, he didn't have to be.

At which point I didn't get a 'no comment', but I did get an, 'Oh, Fuck off.'

So, as I had promised, he got one straight back. And a hell of a lot more! I told him that I had a queue of people waiting to see me, how he was wasting my time, how he could fuck off out of my therapy room and take his attitude with him. He left.

His mother then came in and asked if she could have the rest of the session, which I gladly gave her. A lovely woman!

Over the next six months I didn't see a whiff of Jason but I spent a lot of time helping his mum and dad deal with his school. The school had the most appalling lack of understanding of ADHD, and I went to one memorable school meeting at the request of Jason's parents. There were approximately ten people in the room, including Jason's Head of Year, two staff from Youth Offending Services – who he had become involved with – a Social Worker, and some other teachers and welfare staff from the school, but the only people who seemed to understand ADHD were Jason's parents and me.

Between the three of us, we contradicted pretty much everything they were saying and told them that these techniques would just not work with an ADHD brain. The meeting was getting heated until Jason's father exploded and said, 'Well, quite frankly, everything you've been advising us to do and everything you've done hasn't worked, so shall we give Sarah's way of handling Jason a go?'

At that point, the Social Worker snapped her large notebook shut and said, 'Well, I'm obviously not needed here,' and walked out.

Things did improve marginally at the school and Jason's mum continually drip-fed that, despite him telling me to fuck off, I had worked very hard on his behalf and was constantly fighting his corner with his teachers. She was hoping that this might one day make Jason curious enough to see me.

This sounds like a terrible name-drop, but it's true. One day I was at the Houses of Parliament at an APPG – an All-Party Parliamentary Group – on ADHD. The main meeting had finished, I was checking my text messages and there was one from Jason's mother. It was a message saying that Jason would like to speak to me and was there a good time for him to call. I said absolutely, I would be free the next day in the afternoon and he could call me whenever he wished.

The phone rang the next day and, before I could say a word, Jason garbled all in a rush, 'Sarah, can I just apologise for my absolutely appalling behaviour. I am really, really sorry and I would like to come and see you.' He had obviously built himself up to say this!

I replied, 'Of course you can come and see me, and I apologise for my appalling behaviour as well. I'm not in the habit of telling clients to fuck off and I will gladly see you.'

The appointment was arranged, and Jason came back and stayed for about eighteen months. And I can hand-on-heart say I love the bones of that boy. We went on to have the most successful, transformative and life-changing sessions. We also realised that although his mother had spent thousands sending him to a private special education school for five years, they had missed numerous learning difficulties Jason had, so no wonder he was struggling. Both schools had not recognised the comorbidities, or coexisting conditions, of his ADHD.

Jason was frustrated because the Police still had his mobile phone and his computer. He had been arrested for, but not charged with, 'threats to kill' and 'sending threatening messages'. Sounds a lot worse than it was. He was purely threatening the new boyfriend of his ex-girlfriend not to treat her badly. But when seen by the Police those words can be interpreted in a very different and more serious way.

We spent a lot of our sessions trying to work out exactly what conditions Jason had and we realised that we actually had some of the same. Through working with so many clients I had come to realise I had dyspraxia and so did Jason. And the same with dyscalculia. With a lot of research and Googling – we were pretty sure we both had it.

All through this, Jason only had one ambition and that was to be a footballer. He knew he wasn't the best, but what he lacked in skill he more than made up for in enthusiasm. He played for a weekend football team and was utterly obsessed with football.

One day Jason's mum sent me a screenshot of a newspaper advert regarding forthcoming trials for youth apprenticeships with a local football team. The text said, 'I bet he won't go, but look at this.' I was seeing Jason later that day so I replied, 'Leave it with me.'

Jason had severe anxiety but he also had a dream of being a footballer. So for the whole session we talked about how there was the possibility of trialling for this team, and the worst that could happen was that he wouldn't get in. I explained to him how trying and failing would at least give him some idea of how good he was.

If he didn't try, he would never know whether he was good enough and he would be left questioning for the rest of his life – if he had tried would he have been good enough?

'How about we just see it as an experiment? Go, do your best, and let them tell you whether you are good enough. You don't actually have anything to worry about. It's them that needs to make the decision, not you.'

We mulled this over for a whole hour and at the end of the session Jason said, 'Okay, I'll go, but only if you come with me.'

And that is how I found myself standing in the pissing rain, on a cold and miserable November evening, holding a cup of tea bought for me by Jason's mother – that went instantly cold as the rain plopped into it – watching Jason run round a football pitch.

It was clear he wasn't the best player on the pitch but what I thought was more than clear was that he was trying the hardest. Wherever that ball went, Jason went and whenever he got hold of it, he did his very best with it.

Within ten days he received a letter saying he had been accepted on the first year of a three-year footballing apprenticeship.

I was absolutely thrilled for him. I had told him to always follow his dreams and just see how far he could get, and although he had overwhelming anxiety on the night, and nearly didn't go, Jason pushed through and made that dream come true.

Eventually, eighteen months later, all the charges were dropped by the Police, his mobile phone and computer were returned and he is now leading a crime-free life with a much better understanding of his ADHD and all the coexisting conditions. And playing football.

Luckily Jason had strong and supportive parents who fought hard for him, just like Alex. It's boys just like Jason and Alex, but who don't have mums and dads like this, who I'd worked with in the Prisons.

It's heartbreaking to see the difference between a family who can afford to send a fifteen-year-old to a private school, for private therapy, for a private ADHD diagnosis and get the best legal support when they run into trouble, and those who don't have the means to do any of that.

There is a chasm of difference between the outcomes for these kids who come from well-off families and those who have parents who can't afford any of that. They don't always end up in Prison but far too many of them do end up behind bars

I might not have been in a Prison, but I knew I was doing a pretty good job of keeping these ADHD kids away from the criminal justice system. And that made my heart happy.

Finding my niche, helping desperate parents and Thomas reappearing

It didn't take long for my reputation for being passionate about keeping ADHD teenagers out of Prison to spread. Soon enough, I was having teenagers from all over the UK being brought to me by desperately concerned parents. Like me, the parents did not want their children going down the criminal justice route and they needed somebody who understood their child's ADHD brain.

I soon realised that having the exact same ADHD brain as these kids was the key to them trusting me. Many had sat in front of Neurotypical Counsellors, Psychologists, Educational Psychologists, School Counsellors and lots of people in white coats, and were sick to the teeth of talking to people who didn't get where they were coming from or how their brain worked.

But then they came to see me in my ripped jeans and T-shirts, with my potty mouth, and not one of them didn't engage! The rapport was instant, just as it had been in the Prisons.

I had literally hundreds of ADHD teenagers tell me that they would only talk to me because I 'got' how their brain worked and all the different ways that ADHD brains think. I didn't blink an eye when they told me they hated their parents, hated their teachers, hated everybody in their school, and particularly hated their brothers and sisters. I told them I'd been exactly the same at their age and it wouldn't be how they would feel all their lives, so to just roll with it knowing that it would be over as soon as they were out of puberty.

I understood how the teenage years for an ADHD adolescent are bloody hard. Your emotions are ricocheting around your body far more than for Neurotypical kids because ADHD is a dopamine/hormone deficiency so puberty impacts ADHD kids much harder. You hate just about everybody and the whole world! Your anger, frustration, and often violence, spews out of you and there's not a lot you can do about it.

I had been told I 'had a dreadful attitude' all the way through my teens and, as much as there were numerous people I thought deserved a punch, I managed to be only verbally aggressive and hate the lot of them.

But most of these ADHD kids I was seeing had let the rage out and found themselves in some right pickles. And some very serious pickles. They had been arrested primarily for criminal damage, often just for chucking stones or kicking a neighbour's plant pot; fighting; affray, for shouting and kicking off in public; stealing, often trainers, tracksuits and gadgets they couldn't wait for; threats to kill, when their ADHD verbal filter was non-existent; and some ABH, when their angry fists got the better of them. There were no murders, kidnaps, rapes or arson, but all of these teens had become involved with the Police and Youth Offending Services.

The recurring theme was how good they were at different sports, and this completely resonated with what I had seen in the Prisons. So many of those Prison boys had been on the path to being professional footballers, and now I was meeting kids on the outside who were achieving hugely in just about every sport you could name, but were about to go off the rails.

I had client boys and girls on rugby, golfing, cricket and athletics apprenticeships, and of course loads on football apprenticeships. They were all mid to late teens, had achieved massively in their field and were on track to be professionals, but were just about to throw it all down the lavatory for a variety of reasons.

Some of the kids had been arrested and the parents had shipped them in to me as soon as they could. Some were just on the brink of giving up whichever sport they were excelling in, because it seemed too much like hard work and they wanted to spend time with their mates. And some thought cannabis was far more appealing than yet more training. But I had seen where this ended up and I fought like a Trojan to keep these teens on the right path.

You can imagine how much I loved working with my teenage ADHD clients. I knew what horrors awaited them in Prison if I didn't succeed in keeping them out. And I even had a helper. That helper was Thomas. Thomas from HMP Aylesbury – the one who, back then, was just about to get out and was desperate to buy a pint of milk. His nan had taken him in rather than let him go into care.

I had tried to help Thomas in several ways when he was released. I had housed him three times, helped him get onto a construction apprenticeship scheme and arranged work for him with friends who were gutting their house, but one day – when he wasn't living at my house – he did something very silly that involved a knife. I found myself visiting him in Wormwood Scrubs when he was on remand for something he insisted was silly and he didn't think it would even get to court. He convinced me this was something so trivial, because nobody had been stabbed or hurt, but I still insisted on going to be with him at the court hearing in Harrow. The Judge had obviously had enough of Thomas doing hundreds of petty things and literally threw the book at him. He gave him the absolute maximum sentence of sixteen years. This came as a huge shock to me as Thomas had assured me it was 'nothing to worry about'.

Thomas, however, took it on the chin and decided he would help me from the inside. He used to write beautiful letters to me, ring me regularly and send me emails through the 'email a Prisoner' scheme. One day I had an idea and that was asking Thomas if he would write, via me, to some of these teenagers who still thought that being a gangster and going to Prison every now and again was quite an exciting prospect.

This began years of Thomas writing letters to my teen clients, which I would read to them in my therapy room. His letters were so powerful – they told my risk-taking and thrill-seeking adolescent clients exactly what they had waiting for them if they went to Prison. Thomas poured his heart and soul into his letters and they massively hit home. Hearing me say Prison was dreadful and 'you really don't want to go down that route' was one thing, seeing a letter sent from a Prison, on Prison headed paper, from somebody actually sitting in a Prison, was way more powerful. Thomas' letters changed the life path of so many teenagers.

Just one of these teen ADHD clients was a boy called Henry, who was fifteen and doing all sorts of dodgy things, like climbing into building sites at night, nicking anything he could sell and getting arrested. His mother brought him over to see me one day, from over two hours away, and I read him the letter Thomas had written to him directly. 'Dear Henry,' it began ... then four pages of Thomas telling him how to not screw up his life.

The mum texted me when she arrived home and said, 'I don't know what was in that letter but Henry was dumbstruck and didn't utter a single word the whole journey home.' From that day to this he has never committed another crime. That was the power of Thomas' letters.

It was at this point I changed the company name at Companies House. Headstuff Therapy became Headstuff ADHD Therapy, because that was literally all I was providing. And I was loving every minute of keeping those ADHD kids as far away from the criminal justice system as I possibly could.

How undiagnosed ADHD coexisting conditions creates the School-to-Prison Pipeline

I was also counselling older ADHD adults, especially ones like me who hadn't found out they were ADHD until their 30s, 40s, 50s and even 60s.

One thing I was not expecting from this was to understand more about myself. I thought my own moderate to severe Combined ADHD diagnosis in March 2015 explained everything. But it didn't.

The more time I spent working with adults who had other diagnoses it made me realise I had had other struggles, which hadn't been identified at school, at home, or by any GP or Consultant that I had sat in front of for decades.

So, in my mid 50s I went on to be diagnosed privately with three coexisting conditions. This blew my mind and explained my childhood even more. Much more importantly for me, it explained why so many of these boys in Prison struggled – it was because their coexisting conditions hadn't been identified either, let alone their ADHD in most cases. Struggling in school, getting kicked out or leaving education early featured in so many Young Offenders' stories and I was now beginning to see why.

My own personal cocktail now included severe dyspraxia with 1% processing and 1% motor skills, Sensory Processing Disorder, OCD, and the one that had completely ruined my education (and no doubt an awful lot of other peoples' as well) dyscalculia – which is the 'numbers version' of dyslexia.

I was expected to sail through my 12+. I was always in the top 11 out of 31 in my class at junior school and 16 of the 31 passed to go to the grammar school. Having come 4th, 8th, 10th and 11th out of 31 in all our end of year exams I should safely have been on my way to the grammar school.

However, what I didn't know was I had ADHD. I also didn't know I had dyscalculia. And I didn't know that dyscalculic-brains cannot work out problems. And those of you in the UK who are old enough will know that the 12+ was made up of ... problems!

So when I looked at these questions about people owning so many oranges, apples, pears, grapes and bananas, and was being asked to work out how many green ones somebody had and how many red ones somebody else had, my brain just came to a full stop. That's the best way I can describe it. My brain wouldn't even attempt to work this nonsense out. It just didn't know how to. Zero attempt whatsoever to work this out. Brain just would not go there.

So I did what any bored, under-stimulated undiagnosed/unmedicated ADHD eleven-year-old would do and I wrote lots of random numbers on all the answers. Anything from three million, to three hundred and sixty thousand, to twenty, to whatever number I fancied. I thought it was a ridiculous test. Why didn't they ask me serious questions rather than questions about bananas?

This subsequently caused a furore behind the scenes, which I had no idea about. Before the results were given to parents my lovely junior school headmaster had put in a major appeal to the Local Education Authority insisting that I absolutely must go to the grammar school.

When the results did come out publicly and I had failed, my mother, together with the headmaster, put in another appeal. This got them precisely nowhere, because the Education Authority told them that I had failed 'so spectacularly' (with my '3 million' answers no doubt!) that they couldn't possibly put me through. So that was me sent off to the local crappy secondary school, where I was bored stupid but came first out of 132 girls in every subject at the end of the first year.

It wasn't until my sixteenth birthday that my mother chose to tell me, at the end of that first year, the headmistress had rung her and said, 'Your child shouldn't be at this school. I've managed to get her a place at Dr Challoner's, the local grammar school.' This was a very good grammar school, but it was two towns away from where we were living. My mother asked if there was a place at the grammar school much nearer where we lived, but there wasn't.

She was sent the new school uniform list for the very good grammar school but, as she had forked out for a whole new school uniform the year before, she turned the place down. She told me the list was 'full of hockey sticks and lacrosse sticks' and she just couldn't afford it twice in one year.

So that was my education ruined. And how many of those boys, and the small percentage of girls, in Prison, had been let down in exactly the same way? Pretty much all of them I guessed.

Once I understood how badly I had been let down by nobody recognising my pretty obvious ADHD and then exploring the coexisting conditions, it fired me up even more to help the boys in Prison. Especially the ones like Aidan, who hadn't learnt to spell his middle name till he was in HMP Aylesbury. I could pretty much guarantee he had dyslexia. If somebody had picked that up when he was at school, would he have had such a tragic life in the care system?

I could now understand why ADHD teenagers had often felt such a failure at school, to the point they stopped going altogether roundabout the age of fourteen or fifteen, and it was then that they started to get into trouble. If nobody was bothering to work out why they were struggling, with undiagnosed dyslexia, dyscalculia, dysgraphia, dyspraxia and numerous other ADHD coexisting conditions, I could so easily see why they had thought, 'Stuff it. I'll swerve the humiliation, won't go and I will find something interesting I can do in town,' which before long included nicking a drink from Tesco, a sandwich from Greggs, and they were already on that criminal justice system slippery slope.

I was angry about my own screwed-up education as a consequence of not being diagnosed ADHD, but at least I had managed to get through on my ability to write. Thank the Lord I didn't have dyslexia as well or it could've been a very different story.

But the thought of tens of thousands of people sitting in Prison due to undiagnosed ADHD and undiagnosed coexisting conditions, meaning they hadn't completed their education, was unbearable.

I was beginning to get angry and I was starting to know I had to do something about this.

Becoming the UK ADHD teen-offending specialist and gathering an amazing team

The more swamped I became with teenage ADHD clients the more I knew I needed to expand. Much as I wanted to help every single one of them myself I just couldn't handle this huge influx on my own.

So, after two or three years of keeping hundreds of ADHD kids on the straight and narrow, I started to look for other therapists who were diagnosed ADHD and shared my passion. I turned away more than I took on, but eventually built up a fantastic team of passionate, fully qualified counsellors. We all cared about helping late-diagnosed ADHD adults and especially wanted to keep ADHD kids away from the criminal justice system.

I set up a separate company to focus on ADHD kids, adolescents and adults who were fighting addiction or involved in any kind of offending behaviour. I built up a brilliant team of addiction therapists and people experienced working in the Prisons, Probation or Youth Offending Services. That organisation was 'Headstuff ADHD Liberty' – Fighting For Your Freedom From Addiction and Crime.

Every single day we had new clients – teenagers and young adults who were finding themselves in some seriously difficult and frightening predicaments. We built relationships with ADHD Specialist Psychiatrists, Psychologists and Paediatricians and lost only one client to the criminal justice system as we fought to the death to keep them all out of Prison.

The 'one' particularly broke my heart. He was an eighteen-year-old boy who had been accepted at two universities in the September, but because his ADHD had been unmedicated he did something too risky with four mates, was caught, again by the bloody 'Joint Enterprise' charge, and sent to a Young Offender Institute on an eight-year sentence instead. He came to us many months after he had committed the offence, when the legal process was in full swing, or I like to think we could've kept him out of Prison. If only we had got our hands on him sooner.

We became very well known in the UK with numerous charities referring ADHD kids to us, who they couldn't help, and became the experts in keeping ADHD children, adolescents and young adults out of Prison.

Thomas kept writing letters whenever I asked him and many a teenager was turned away from dabbling in crime due to the horrors Thomas told them was waiting for them in Prison if they carried on with their current behaviour.

Thomas told them how he had gone two years without even seeing me because he was so frightened of being attacked in the Visit Hall. How he had watched grown men too terrified to go to the servery to get their lunch because they feared being attacked. How he had seen numerous Prisoners permanently disfigured by being 'hot watered', meaning they had boiling water from a kettle thrown at them, combined with sugar so it stuck to their skin. Thomas never held back on what these offending-for-kicks teenagers were throwing away and told them to appreciate their freedom while they had it, to listen to me and to accept the help when it was being offered to them. He also told them how he bitterly regretted having nobody to give him this sort of help as a teenager.

Now I had this fantastic team around me, who I could trust with my precious teenage ADHD clients, I had time to return to those HMP Aylesbury boys, because I was pretty sure there was undiagnosed ADHD in some of them and I was still determined to help them.

Aylesbury boys and Angel Psychiatrists

So I went right back to the very beginning. To Dante. You might remember him. He's the one where we had to call the Foreign Office liars and had managed to keep him in Hertfordshire rather than downtown Paris! It wasn't really the Foreign Office man's fault. More the Prison's for not updating Dante's thirty-three qualifications on his OASys records.

I'd kept loosely in touch with Dante and his steadfast girlfriend, Katie, over the years. At their request. Katie was desperate for me to stay in touch to keep him on the straight and narrow. She had never committed a crime and didn't want him to again either. They were still together, still living in Hertfordshire, and Dante was working full-time. I was so proud of him. He started off training to be a plumber and was loving it on the building sites but then decided to get into scaffolding, where he remains to this day.

I kept thinking back to how he had always insisted that 'he thought differently'. Was this what he meant? He had asked me to screen him for autism so he had been close to working himself out, just not close enough. He'd never mentioned the word ADHD, but then neither had I, and I was still years off my own diagnosis when I was working with him. I remember vividly though that nothing was ever enough for Dante, that he only started dealing drugs because he wanted brand-new trainers and brand-new tracksuits, and had no patience to save up, which was very ADHD – 'wanting everything now'. I remembered so clearly him telling me in numerous sessions how he always felt he was falling behind his peers – that's a sign of an ADHD internal motor, wanting you to push on and on at speed.

So I arranged to meet him in one of our regular Hertfordshire Tesco's car-park eateries and started to grill him. Not literally. He wasn't served up on a plate as a well-done burger! But I went through all the ADHD traits I had learnt about and Dante was nodding vigorously to practically all of them.

After all those counselling sessions and all that time in the Immigration Removal Centre, finally I was understanding Dante's brain. And surprise, surprise – it would appear he had the same one as me.

So I immediately booked him in with one of the ADHD Psychiatrists we were doing a lot of work with. Dr Khaled Helmy was, and is, a wonderful, kind man and Dante was the first of many of my ex-Prison clients who he insisted on assessing for ADHD completely for free. What an angel of a man. Khaled had been late-diagnosed ADHD himself, so he really understood and empathised with these boys whose ADHD hadn't been identified at school, meaning they so easily fell onto the slippery slope and had ended up in Prison. I begged him to let me pay him but he wouldn't hear of it. He wanted to help these boys in Prison, and to keep the boys out, just as much as me.

I went with Dante for his assessment and it was a revelation. It was so satisfying to hear Dante be understood, not be judged for his past, and to have his risk-taking and thrill-seeking teenage years explained to him with compassion and kindness by Khaled. And sure enough, at the end, he was diagnosed, exactly like me, with Combined ADHD.

I was so happy Dante now had the answers as to why he thought differently. But I was growing more and more concerned at the amount of ADHD I was seeing in these people who had come out of Prison, and I was even more concerned than that about the amount still trapped behind bars. Just how many of them had undiagnosed ADHD as well?

I tried to find my second Aylesbury client, Keiran, but I couldn't. This really frustrated me because he was the one with terrible IBS, appalling sleep, his mum was a drug addict, his father was a heroin addict, and he had been in care. He had told me about the 'buzz' and 'excitement' he would get going out robbing, and if they weren't indicators of ADHD, I was the Pope. But to this day I've never been able to find him, and I just hope that somebody managed to get hold of him and explored whether all of that was connected to ADHD, which I strongly suspect it was. And I hope to goodness he isn't back in Prison, because nobody had identified what I now see as pretty obvious ADHD in him.

Thomas was my third Aylesbury client and he was already diagnosed ADHD so I moved onto Barney, who was client number four. I hadn't seen any indicators of ADHD in him but then he was the one who wanted to talk about porn most of the time rather than himself, which might explain why! He was back living in London so we arranged to meet.

Barney had lost his alcoholic mum when he was sixteen, had committed crime from a young age himself, and his father had serious alcohol and drug issues as well as getting banned from numerous football grounds for violence. Barney himself had reached 20 stone from binge eating and his mum obviously had itchy feet as she dragged her kids, including Barney, around the country all the time. He was also the one who had taken cocaine with the chef at the posh London hotel, so there were loads of possible ADHD indicators there, but Barney came over as the most placid, calm, non-hyperactive client and I wasn't entirely sure if I was barking up the wrong tree with him.

However, I was now well aware that ADHD presented very differently in people, so we arranged to meet in London. I took him for a slap-up dinner. And once again, as with the other boys, when I started to explain what adult ADHD was, Barney ticked just about every box. He told me his brain never stopped – he might appear placid and calm on the outside but in his head he was in constant turmoil. He told me his sleep was still terrible and he could go three or four nights with absolutely no sleep at all. And much as he didn't show it, he had a lot of anxiety inside, especially social anxiety. There were so many things he just couldn't do and places he couldn't go. Even in the restaurant I took him to, he looked extremely uncomfortable despite me making sure we had a booth to ourselves away from most of the other diners.

So while in the Prison Barney had looked strong, confident and relaxed, as soon as he was on the outside he was an anxious wreck.

So back again we went to see Khaled, who was still refusing to let me pay for these boys who had been in Prison. I once again sat in on the assessment and it was a revelation to see how this boy suddenly understood himself. Barney had a way bigger problem with alcohol than I had ever been aware of in the Prison, because he wasn't drinking in there. As Khaled the Psychiatrist specialises in addiction as well as ADHD, hearing him talk to Barney about how not only his own alcohol problem but his mother's and his father's had impacted all their lives, almost definitely contributing and leading to his mum's early death, was hard to hear.

Can you imagine sitting next to a twenty-three-year-old boy who is being told that, if only adult ADHD had been understood seven years before, his mum might not have died? It was gut-wrenching and painful stuff to listen to. But if we didn't want to repeat these patterns, these boys had to get the correct diagnosis and medication, and Barney gladly took it when it was offered. From that day on his life was transformed. Gone was the alcohol addiction, because he had no need to self-medicate his ADHD anymore, and he went on to be a hugely successful chef. I can even say I've tasted his cooking myself and I've never eaten food like it.

Client number five, Aidan, had also been diagnosed ADHD as a child, which just left number six – Junior.

A bit like Barney, he hadn't shown any outward signs of ADHD being very cool, calm and collected. I couldn't trace him either, but looking back at my session notes, and remembering that he had been sent off in his first two professional football matches, getting red cards, swearing at the referee and punching somebody – and had then gone on to be very successful on television – I imagine he could well have ADHD as well.

You don't get the sort of drive to be a professional footballer and then a professional actor, punch people and get sent off in your two first football matches with red cards, if there is no ADHD lurking there!

So that was my Aylesbury boys sorted. Now just what was I going to do about the rest of them in Prison when I was sure most of them had ADHD as well?

Support groups
and Police Officers

My eternally supportive and wonderful counselling supervisor, Lynda, came up with an idea that at first filled me with horror. She said, 'You really ought to set up an ADHD support group. It's fine for you because you are meeting all these ADHD clients, but they aren't meeting each other.'

At the time I was running round like a blue-arsed fly – recruiting new ADHD counsellors, until we were at the point of having nearly 100, dealing with an overflowing inbox every day of parents and adults looking for ADHD-specific therapy by diagnosed ADHD therapists, and sorting out all my old clients from the Prisons who needed an ADHD diagnosis. But, in the end, I decided to do it. Because Lynda was right. Everybody I was seeing in my therapy room felt very isolated with their ADHD, and if anybody was going to introduce them to each other then logically it would be me.

So I set up what I called The Bucks & Beyond Adult ADHD Support Group. Sixteen people turned up to the first meeting and as I write this we have just under one thousand members, so you can tell how well that went!

At every meeting I would have a rant about the amount of ADHD in the criminal justice system and I met many people who were involved in the CJS who agreed with me. But there was one defining moment and that was when a Police Officer, aged thirty-six, joined the group. At the very end of the meeting he came up to me and said, 'Sarah, I didn't mention this during the meeting because I wasn't sure how popular it would be, but I am actually a Metropolitan Police Officer and I agree with you. Pretty much everybody I'm arresting seems to have ADHD.' I could have wept with joy. If the Police were realising the same as me, then surely something could be done to change the situation?

Daley Jones was that Police Officer, and he very soon started up a support group of his own, but with a difference. His was called The ADHD Alliance and the group aimed to support not only Police Officers but others in the emergency services who had ADHD. There was another member of the Support Group who was also in the Police and it was he and Daley, both ADHD, who set up The ADHD Alliance.

Daley thought that by doing this they would raise awareness of not only the number of staff who had undiagnosed ADHD, but how many of the people they were arresting also did.

They held regular online meetings with more and more people joining his group every day. He asked me if I would like to do a presentation at one of these meetings on ADHD in the criminal justice system? Obviously, I bit his hand off.

Daley sent out an announcement to Police Forces UK-wide and the day before I was due to do the presentation he texted me and said, 'Are you sitting down?' He then told me that the maximum they had had at any one of these meetings was eighteen people. But so far 440 Police Officers had signed up to hear me talking about ADHD in the criminal justice system! This was obviously a topic that was resonating with an awful lot of members of the Police.

I did my two-hour presentation the next day and the enthusiasm and positive reaction I received was heartening. These Police Officers, a lot of them ADHD themselves, were recognising ADHD in so many of the people they were arresting. They knew something had to be done about it. They just didn't know what or how.

But I did. I knew exactly what we could do about this situation and I set about making it happen.

Around this time, I received a telephone call out of the blue. A female voice said, 'Are you the Sarah Templeton who is angry about the amount of ADHD in Prisons?' This was unusual! But I answered, 'Yes, most definitely that's me. Why?' She then went on to explain that she was a Neuro Consultant in a UK hospital and was seeing some patients over and over again. They were all boys and men being brought into her hospital from the Prisons – all with head injuries from fighting and violence.

This had been going on for years and she had begun to realise it was the same ones over and over because they were all ADHD – all undiagnosed and therefore all unmedicated – so repeating the same emotionally dysregulated fighting, melt downs and kick-offs, and nothing was changing.

Being qualified to diagnose ADHD, this consultant had asked her superiors if she could diagnose and medicate them – saving her time and the NHS a fortune. Then came the bit that made her angry. She was told, and I quote, 'No. They're not worth it.' This had incensed her to the point she tracked me down. She'd been told they weren't worth it because they were Prisoners. I shared her outrage and disgust. This HAD to change. How dare anybody pass judgment on these Prisoners who had been appallingly let down by nobody screening, assessing or diagnosing them for ADHD and multiple coexisting conditions. Not worth it? This outraged me as much as it had her.

They were more than worth it and we damn well owed them an apology.

Brothers and mothers

ADHD people are drawn to each other, both in relationships and friendships.

One of my friends was a relatively new friend I'd only known for about ten years. I knew Chrissie well but hadn't met any of her five grown-up children. I knew she had one son who, by the age of twenty-nine, had been in Prison fifteen times. I might have never met him but I was always saying to Chrissie, 'I'm sure there's ADHD in that boy', but Chrissie wasn't convinced.

She herself had been very many stones overweight and by her own admission was a compulsive eater who just couldn't stop. I understood that because I'd been exactly the same before I was diagnosed and medicated for my ADHD, but Chrissie just couldn't see that hers might have had anything to do with ADHD.

I knew that addiction, offending and obesity featured in other members of Chrissie's family and used to tell her all the time that you don't find a family with obesity, offending and addiction present and no ADHD! But she was absolutely adamant that there was zero ADHD in her family, to the point she told me, 'We shouldn't talk about it any more or we will fall out!' So I shut up and said nothing more.

Until the time the son who had been in Prison fifteen times was arrested again, for something very minor which also involved his younger brother, and at that point I couldn't hold back anymore.

I messaged her and said, 'Please, please, please, let me meet Damon, because I just can't believe there isn't ADHD in that boy.'

She told me that Damon had an absolute aversion to therapists and counselling and there was no way she could convince him to come to my therapy room. I said that didn't matter. I would meet him anywhere. In a park, pub, coffee shop – I didn't care, but I wanted to talk to him to find out if there was any ADHD lurking beneath.

It was eventually arranged that I would meet Damon in a pub. When I arrived, he was obviously anxious. I tried to put him at ease as best I could, but for the first forty-five minutes he was very guarded. He really didn't want to tell me anything about himself, so I said, 'That's fine. Let me tell you about my ADHD and then you can tell me whether any of this resonates with you.'

I started to tell him all the ways people with ADHD think, lots of the traits, all the cock-ups I had made in my life, how I struggled with loads of things, and after a good while of this he looked at me sideways and said, 'Do you really do all this stuff?' And I replied, 'Yes, absolutely. This is all ADHD and I do it all.'

From that point on he admitted that just about everything I was saying was exactly how he was too, and then we had an intensive good two-hour chat about him and not me!

It turned out a lot of his crime, if not all of it, had been self-medicating what he didn't know was his ADHD. So his crimes were always minor and the sentences were never for more than six months. They were all around alcohol: stealing it, being drunk and disorderly, causing criminal damage when drunk, getting into fights when drunk and not much else.

Because he had been arrested for affray along with his younger brother Dean, I didn't want to let this boy go back to Prison for yet another short and silly sentence when I was now convinced he was ADHD. So we agreed we would meet in the pub again, but next time with his mum because he couldn't remember a lot about his childhood and he knew that she would.

So the next time, Chrissie joined us, purely to fill me in on the childhood stuff Damon had forgotten. When I asked Damon a question, he would nearly always answer, 'Yes! But she does that just as much as me,' pointing and laughing at his mother. This session went on for nearly three hours and I had as much information as I needed to know that there was no question Damon had undiagnosed ADHD.

Bearing in mind he had been in Prison fifteen times and was a prolific self-harmer, so had been in Health Care in his own words 'almost every day', I asked him, 'Did this ever come up in Prison? Did anybody ever ask you or screen you for ADHD?' He told me that no it never had. Nobody in Prison had ever mentioned the possibility of ADHD to him and I was the first person ever to bring it up.

Damon also told me even if they had mentioned it he wouldn't have admitted any of the things he had admitted to me, because he 'didn't want to be nutted off'. This was the first time I had ever heard that expression and I asked him what it meant. He whispered, 'Sent to a loony bin. I could deal with going to Prison but not to a Psychiatric Hospital.'

What I wasn't expecting was when we all said goodbye, and Chrissie hugged me as normal. She giggled in my ear, 'You were right. I have got ADHD.' I'd known it all along.

So within a very short space of time, we were back at Khaled the Psychiatrist's, where Damon was diagnosed not only with Combined ADHD but, as he left the room, the Psychiatrist showed me the paperwork. He said to me, 'Look at that,' showing me a lot of charts and graphs.

With my dyscalculia, I had no idea what I was looking at – we can't read charts and graphs – so I asked Khaled what it meant. He said, 'You are looking at the most severe case of ADHD I've ever seen.'

Damon was prescribed ADHD medication, which immediately and dramatically changed and improved his life. Shortly afterwards we had Chrissie diagnosed and although she wasn't keen to try the medication, I told her it was worth a go. She didn't think she would benefit from it in any way, having managed to get the compulsive eating well under control and losing two-thirds of her body weight on her own. I thought I was fighting another losing battle, but told her, 'You just don't know until you try it.'

A few days later, Chrissie phoned me. She thanked me for encouraging her to go on the medication and said, 'Until I took that medication I didn't know I had a huge ball of anxiety in my chest and now it's gone.' I was thrilled for her.

Meanwhile, there was Damon's younger brother. With all this ADHD in the family I wanted to meet him as he had been charged with affray the same as Damon and it was his first ever offence. He was also nervous about it but agreed to meet me in the same pub.

This boy was even more anxious than his brother. But, yet again, the traits were all there. What was incredulous about Dean was the fact that he had only ever been to school in the mornings. When I asked him why he said, 'Because I couldn't sit still long enough, so they only let me go to school in the morning,' and he had been to the local school for kids with behavioural difficulties! What in God's name had stopped those teachers from realising he couldn't sit still because he was hyperactive and had ADHD? I was being shocked every day by the number of kids who had been let down, especially in schools. Surely a teacher in a school for kids with behavioural problems would've been trained to look into why a child could only sit still long enough to be schooled in the mornings? Hello? Did it not enter their heads to look into why?

I also knew that Chrissie's one daughter, Laura, had been to see her local adult ADHD mental health services and had been told that she didn't have ADHD. I 100% now believed that this was incorrect, knowing that she too had been much bigger in previous years, I suspected from compulsive eating just like her mum. So off Laura went to see them again, with all this new-found knowledge about her family's ADHD, and she finally received the correct diagnosis. Combined ADHD.

Then off we went again to see Khaled the Psychiatrist, where Dean was diagnosed with ADHD. So this meant both brothers had been diagnosed with ADHD AFTER they had committed this very minor crime. Dean's was a first offence, and Damon's more serious because he had been in Prison fifteen times before, but I knew from experience that if you had committed a crime when you were not diagnosed or medicated for ADHD you were considered to be 'not of your right mind', which was mitigating evidence and showed reduced culpability. So I assured Damon that, as long as we presented the information to the court, he would not be going back to Prison.

I had been in this situation with so many clients, I knew I was right. Damon and Chrissie put me in touch with Damon's solicitor as Damon had been awarded Legal Aid and I wanted to use it for reports on how his undiagnosed and unmedicated ADHD had been responsible for his behaviour.

I thought I was in for an easy ride. I knew what I was doing here. How wrong could I be?

Solicitors, Barristers, Judges and Christmas

I set to work straightaway on writing two reports for Damon, in conjunction with his solicitor. I had done this numerous times before for other clients who had found themselves in trouble with the law and I was very confident this would work.

It's clear in law – if you are not diagnosed or medicated correctly for any mental health condition or neurodiversity, then you are 'not deemed to have been of your right mind' at the time of any offending behaviour. This has to be used as mitigating evidence and usually shows reduced culpability.

With Damon, it was very clear. He had not been diagnosed. He was not medicated. And not only that, but he had a very severe case of ADHD as indicated by the Psychiatrist.

For several years now, I had been helping a deluge of ADHD clients who found themselves in trouble with the law, determined to keep them out of Prison, but Damon was my friend's son, so I poured extra of my heart and soul into these reports. The first report was all about Damon, his childhood and his past. How he had gone undiagnosed for twenty-nine years, resulting in fifteen Prison sentences and all those sentences had been due to his undiagnosed condition. This report was to illustrate how his undiagnosed ADHD had impacted him.

The second report was on how he was now diagnosed, medicated and had absolutely transformed his life. How he was working full-time, in a settled relationship and had daughters he adored. And, very importantly, Damon hadn't committed one crime since diagnosis and medication. As all his offending had been due to self-medicating his severe undiagnosed ADHD, he was now teetotal and attended AA meetings several times a week to make sure he stayed that way.

After numerous delays due to the Covid pandemic, eventually the court date arrived. We all travelled over to Aylesbury Crown Court knowing we had done everything we possibly could to make sure the Judge understood how different Damon was, now he had the right diagnosis and medication. I went to court with his mum and partner fully confident that these reports would do what they had done in every other case I'd worked on and we would be coming home with both Damon and his brother Dean.

Outside the court I spent a lot of time talking to Damon's barrister, who hadn't had any idea about ADHD but he was fascinated by everything I was telling him. He had no idea that an ADHD brain is 'impulsive' and 'does everything without thinking of the consequences' – until it is medicated. He seemed like such a nice man and said he could've talked to me all day about it, because he found it so interesting and relevant for most of his clients as he had only recently become aware the majority of them had ADHD.

There were three people in the dock that day. Damon, his younger brother Dean and the third person who had been involved in the affray.

Things didn't seem to go well from the off. The Judge appeared to be muddled and focused on the first report about Damon's previous criminal record, without taking into account the second report showing how the diagnosis had transformed his life and behaviour. We weren't getting a good feeling, but we were absolutely sure this was because the Judge didn't understand the case fully. This was extra frustrating because we weren't allowed to talk and explain to the Judge that it was the second report that was by far the more relevant.

When it came to the sentencing, Damon's younger brother Dean was given community service because it was his first offence.

The third member of the party also didn't have a long criminal record, so was given community service.

But when it came to Damon the Judge said, 'based on his previous,' he was going to sentence him to eighteen months in Prison. At that point all hell broke loose.

Damon's mother flew out of the court as she couldn't bear to watch her son get taken away. Damon's partner and I both burst into tears and rushed to him in the dock, and Damon himself was in a dreadfully emotional state, crying and clawing at the glass dock window. It was a very traumatic scene.

Damon's partner was frantically pushing his ADHD medication through the gap in the dock glass as she knew how crucial it was he stayed on it for his emotional regulation and to stop him self-harming. I took the opportunity to talk to the two Prison Officers who were now putting Damon in handcuffs, telling them how critical it was he was kept on this ADHD medication. I told them how he now relied on it and it was only ADHD meds that had stopped his prolific self-harming.

One very nice lady Prison Officer asked me, 'Does he have mental health problems?' and I said, 'Yes, he is severely ADHD. He was not expecting this sentence and we will be appealing it immediately, but until then he must be kept on his medication.' She very kindly said she would make sure this message was passed on wherever he was taken. It really was a heartbreaking scene and one I was 100% not expecting.

Immediately the next day we put two plans of action into place. One was I spoke to my huge team of 100 therapists and told them this had happened, and if anybody wanted to write to or email Damon to support him, I knew he would welcome it. Loads of them did.

I said the same to the thousand-strong Bucks & Beyond Adult ADHD support group, who all knew and liked Damon. He had been several times. Dozens of them wrote letters, emails, sent him pictures of their dogs, and, along with his family, we swamped him with support in Prison and assured him we were doing everything we could to get him out. He was sent to Prison in the September and we had no idea how long it would take to right this very wrong decision.

The same day, his mum and partner contacted Damon's solicitor and demanded an urgent appeal.

I went to visit Damon in Prison several times and told him that we had asked for as urgent an appeal as possible and were doing everything we possibly could to get him out.

Then started a constant daily flow of reports, appeals and paperwork flying backwards and forwards between the solicitor, Damon's mum, his partner, me and the Court of Appeal.

Three months later, finally, his case was to be heard and, thank God, it was agreed the Judge had got it badly wrong. Damon was released from Prison the same day.

So instead of eighteen months he served three, which he should never have served at all. But, focusing on the positive, he was out six days before Christmas and spent that whole Christmas with his partner, daughters and family.

And he is still out. Still working full-time. Still taking his ADHD medication daily. Still regularly attending AA meetings to ensure he stays sober. And hasn't committed one crime in well over four years.

That's the power of getting the right diagnosis for a prolific offender and the power of the right medication. Not only does it transform their lives but it reduces crime, protects the public, reduces Prison numbers and saves the taxpayer money.

New starts, bad girlfriends and sensible Judges

One of my Aylesbury boys, Barney, the one who preferred talking about porn to talking about himself, came back into my life in a very random way. He needed to get out of London. I didn't ask too many questions but I could imagine why, and one day he pitched up living in the park opposite my house.

On the slide to be precise. He had found a nook and cranny at the top of the slide and was living there.

I couldn't have him in my house, because there wasn't room, but I certainly couldn't have him living in a park, so I straight away contacted the local homeless organisation I had been initially counselling, and then supervising other counsellors, for. Very soon they had him in a B&B. I switched back into mentoring mode and before long Barney had a job in a pub as a chef, was living in a caravan on a friend's farm, and everything was going well for him.

Then, overnight, it went really bad when his girlfriend from London pitched up. It takes a lot for me to not like somebody. As you've probably gathered, I like most people, whatever their past, but this girl put my back up right from the beginning. For starters she had never worked a day in her life, and at that point she was twenty-five. It was only because Barney had a good heart that he let her into his caravan. From which he was promptly evicted because it had been let strictly as a caravan for one.

I helped both of them get housed and he carried on working as a chef, while she sat at home on her lazy backside.

Before I knew it, I was getting a message from her to say that Barney had been arrested. I was livid. I was absolutely sure this would not have happened if she had stayed away from him – he was doing fantastically on his own, earning a good salary as a pub chef and making friends with other ADHD people in the area until she arrived and screwed the whole thing up.

So there was I back to Prison visiting. The even more random thing was that Barney was in the same Prison as Damon. They were both in Health Care one day and Damon was telling Barney how he had somebody on the outside who was helping him with his appeal and her name was Sarah. Barney, who had known me for the best part of ten years at this point, said, 'Not Sarah Templeton? She was my counsellor.'

They hated each other at first and both told me they didn't like the other one. But in the second email from each of them they'd changed their minds and decided they did like the other one!

On a visit to Barney, I found out it was this wretched girlfriend who had managed to put him back behind bars. If I thought I'd disliked her before, I absolutely despised her now.

She had been recording him and videoing him when he had lost his temper with her. She'd secretly taken numerous recordings and videos of him shouting, and the one time he touched her she decided it was assault and he was arrested. He'd allegedly bent her little finger back.

I couldn't believe it and I was so angry and felt for Barney. He informed me his solicitor had told him he was looking at a seven-year sentence, primarily due to his previous.

I wasn't having him going back to Prison for seven years! I asked him what I could do to help. His solicitor wanted character references, so I set about getting every character reference I could for him. I think I ended up with five, all saying that he was a perfectly lovely boy and it was only the girlfriend who brought this side out in him.

I also did a witness statement stating I'd seen how demanding and draining this girlfriend was, and I liaised with his solicitor to give him the very best chance in court. I wrote a letter explaining that he hadn't been on his medication at the time, because he had been diagnosed privately and was still waiting for the NHS to medicate him. This was also during a worldwide ADHD medication shortage so there was no guarantee he'd have been on them anyway.

I went to court that day. Barney was there by video link and because he had not been medicated for his ADHD at the time, helped by some very strong character references, heaven be praised his sentence was reduced from seven years to seventeen months. He'd already served six of those on remand so he didn't have long left to serve and, thankfully, the Judge barred the girlfriend from seeing him for ten years. Something Barney and I agreed on equally – we both wished the Judge had made it for life.

I've seen how a good girlfriend, like Katie with Dante, can transform these boys' lives. But this is the first time I had seen a bad girlfriend try to destroy one.

Crying clients, imposter syndrome and big surprises

While I was busy counselling literally hundreds of ADHD teenagers, who I was managing to keep on the straight and narrow, I was very often counselling their parents as well.

All these parents were absolutely petrified their kids were going to end up in Prison and they knew they had found an ally in me as I was desperate to keep everybody with ADHD out of Prison! And luckily, I understood completely how their kids' brains worked.

I would literally have parents coming from three hours' drive away on a regular basis to sit in my therapy room, telling me of all the risk-taking and thrill-seeking activities their teenagers were getting up to. When we couldn't get the teenager into my therapy room, I was supporting the parents and giving them the best ways I knew of keeping their teenagers away from taking drugs, dealing drugs, being excluded from school, fighting and most definitely from all other offending behaviour.

Some of the stories I heard in that therapy room would make your toes curl. There were teenagers who had left home, but were still choosing to hide their drugs in their mum's kitchens knowing that was a pretty safe place. Parents who were finding knives hidden in their garages. And parents who had found drugs in the boot of the car after their teenager had borrowed it.

Most of the parents were at the absolute end of their tether. They had spent fortunes and thrown everything at it they could to give their children the best education and the best support, but things were spiralling out of control and now they felt absolutely helpless. I loved supporting them and Thomas's letters were still proving to be life-changing for a lot of their wayward teens .

One mum, in particular, I had a very soft spot for. Julia had a nineteen-year-old son, Jacob. Julia herself was a counsellor and had been in practice for many more years than I had at that point. But she still came to see me about Jacob, because she had serious concerns about him and had almost gone beyond the end of her tether. She was dangling by a thread.

Ever since the age of fifteen Jacob had been getting into trouble and had come into contact with the Police numerous times. Julia was one of the mums who did find drugs hidden in her house. Jacob was seemingly unemployable as he walked out of every job within two or three days. He had tried ADHD medication, but had experienced too many side effects to continue with it and was now refusing to try it again. Julia frequently found herself in my therapy room crying as she just didn't know how to keep him away from the Police and potentially Prison.

I spent hours explaining how Jacob's brain worked to her. How telling him what to do would never work. How he had to think that everything was his idea if he was going to run with it. I explained how he had this constant need for adrenaline and excitement and, although he had been a brilliant sportsman in his younger teens, now he had stopped playing sport he was replacing that adrenaline with all sorts of illegal activities.

One day as Julia stood on my front doorstep about to leave she said, as she wiped away her final sniffles with a tissue, 'If only I had known all this stuff since he was a small child, I honestly think I would've brought him up completely differently and we wouldn't be in this situation now.'

That comment stayed with me. I was giving the same 'ADHD traits' and 'different ways of thinking' information over and over to these desperate parents, who I felt so incredibly sorry for, and all of it was coming as a shock to them. Nobody had explained to them how an ADHD brain works, let alone an ADHD teenager's brain. They didn't know what works better when you are interacting with an ADHD brain, or all the other dozens of things I was telling them.

I was sitting at my friend Ruth's house one day telling her this and she said, 'Well the answer is obvious.'

'Is it?' I said, not believing for a moment she had the answer.

'Of course it is. You need to write all this down in a book. Then they will not only have all the information you are giving them in therapy, but they will have it in writing to refer back to.'

I was fifty-seven years old. I had never written a book in my life. But over the next few weeks she kept on about this until in the end I thought, 'Okay. I will.' I only expected it to be useful to my clients, but I thought I would write all this stuff down in a book and keep copies in my therapy room, and then if clients wanted it, clients could have it.

I spent approximately nine months, once a week, sitting in Ruth's house writing a book. I felt like a 100% imposter even saying I was 'writing a book' – that seemed like absolute nonsense – but I did structure all the information in what I thought would be a helpful format for parents to read. I decided to give it a funny name rather than calling it *Yet another book about ADHD parenting*!

When it was released, in 2021, I thought we might as well put it on Amazon in case any parents of other ADHD kids wanted a copy. The name of it caused a minor rumpus as I had decided to call it *How NOT to Murder your ADHD Kid: Instead Learn How To Be Your Child's Own ADHD Coach*.

It was a bit of a gamble, but I banked on people having a sense of humour and 99.9% of the public did think the title was funny – including kids and teenagers, because I asked them in my therapy room! Every single one of them laughed. But I did get a bit of flack from people lacking a sense of humour. One had the audacity to mail my publisher and demand I change the title! However, I also had several bigwigs in the ADHD world who told me, absolutely, to not change the title, because it was a clear representation of how parents did feel at times – and it didn't take away from the fact that they loved these kids, despite wanting to murder them when they were hiding drugs in their kitchens!

Nothing could have prepared me for what happened next. I will simply say the book took off and was massively more successful than I could have ever dreamt about. Not just in my therapy room and not just in the UK. But across the world! That blew my brain. I would have laid my life on the fact that that would never have happened.

Then what happened next was a lot of parents telling me they were giving the book to their child's teacher – because I was explaining the ADHD brain and how to interact with their ADHD child, and they thought it would help the teacher to understand as well.

This went on for about six months before I thought it just wasn't good enough. There was a lot more information I could put in a book for teachers who were working with ADHD kids, which would be of help to them in the classroom. So I decided to write a second book! I was still feeling like an imposter, but thought that if I could help one teacher of one ADHD kid then it had to be worthwhile.

That took the best part of another year and I released *TEACHERS! How Not to Kill the Spirit in Your ADHD Kids: Instead, Understand Their Brains and Turbocharge Our Future Leaders & Winners.*

Here's just one example of how that book helped: one mum bought a copy for her son's form teacher, and her son told her that it had completely changed how his teacher dealt with him, and how life at school was suddenly a lot easier. So the mum ordered another ten copies to give to every single one of her son's teachers!

All I wanted was to help these kids be understood, to not be told off for natural ADHD traits, to be accepted for their ADHD, and not constantly be pushed to act like Neurotypical children. I firmly believe every ADHD child has the right to be their natural ADHD self, just as every Neurotypical child has the right to be themselves.

I followed this up with a book on parenting ADHD teenagers, because they are a breed all of their own! I was finding that I loved writing. It had been my best subject at school and now I could write to help people. All my life I had wanted to help people and suddenly I was finding that by writing everything I had learnt, from my own brain and from counselling hundreds of ADHD clients, I could actually be of help to other people.

How Not to Damage Your ADHD Adolescent: Instead Coach them Through their Turbulent Teens to Win at Life was my third (and I think!) final book on helping parents of ADHD kids.

Ultimately, my goal with all of these books was to have ADHD children understood properly from the start, so that the end didn't involve the criminal justice system. It was as simple as that.

Scarily, around this time, I received a telephone call one day at 5:10 p.m. It was from an ADHD Psychiatrist who had only recently started work at my local NHS Adult ADHD Service. He told me who he was, then went on to say it was after five so he could say anything! He'd seen how many of my complaint letters about misdiagnosis were 'littered throughout the department'. He said he'd followed up every case and realised I'd been right every time.

He also said he'd only been working there three months and 'had already completely lost faith in them'.

Grief. So it wasn't only Prison Mental Health teams who weren't trained up in ADHD, it was the National Health Service too.

One in four people in Prison have ADHD, 'personality disorders', poorly trained SENCOs and other nonsense

I'd been shouting about the amount of ADHD in the criminal justice system, specifically the Prisons, since 2015 – a lone counsellor with ADHD herself who had realised that pretty much everybody in Prison had the same brain as her. Nobody was interested in me. And I didn't blame them.

It wasn't until my books were published, and I had delivered the presentation for The ADHD Alliance to 440 Police Officers, that things started to take off.

Suddenly, there was interest in how many people we were locking up with 'Neurodiversity', as it was now called. I had been telling everybody for years that eight or nine out of ten people in Prison had ADHD. I then came across a Mental Health nurse who had worked in the Prison system for twenty years. She herself had ADHD and told me she had been keeping an 'unofficial record' for years, and 85% of Prisoners had ADHD, as far as she could tell.

Somewhere along the line, somebody had come up with a figure that 'one in four people in Prison have ADHD'. I truly do not know who this was and I don't know where they plucked the figure from – it certainly hadn't come from research, because nobody was screening people in Prison to find out. Possibly, the number referred to those who had been diagnosed ADHD before they went into Prison, but that wasn't taking into account the high ratio in Prison already who hadn't a clue they had ADHD. I knew the 'one in four' was absolute nonsense, and I would get very angry every time I heard somebody say it.

Very soon I started to be invited onto podcasts, webinars and radio stations, and asked to write articles for dozens of newspapers and magazines about the amount of ADHD in the criminal justice system. This was exhausting, but I wasn't going to say no to anybody – I was so passionate about people understanding that the Prisons were chock-a-block with ADHD.

I also started to get invitations to do training by different Probation teams and Neurodiversity Managers in Prisons. This thrilled me – I could help those working in Probation and Youth Offending Services understand that most of their clients did have ADHD, and until it was diagnosed and medicated they had very little chance of turning their lives around.

Then I was invited into schools to train teachers and parents of ADHD kids. This honestly made me so happy because the more teachers understood ADHD children, and how their brains worked, the more chance they had of keeping them in school and not losing them to the School-to-Prison pipeline.

What staggered me was how little teachers knew about ADHD. Just one example: I trained the teachers of three infant and junior schools in North London in 2023, all in the same hall. At the end, teachers were queueing up to buy my teachers' book. The last lady said, 'I just had to stay to thank you personally, because I am the SENCO (Special Educational Needs Co-Ordinator) at this school. For starters, you've told me everybody with dyslexia has ADHD, and I've realised that both me and my two daughters are not only dyslexic but also have ADHD. But, more importantly, I've been having SENCO training for the last twenty years and everything you've just taught us, in the last two and a half hours, I have never heard before. So thank you so, so much. I can now go back and do my job properly.'

She was a kind and caring lady who was very grateful that she now understood ADHD. What has stayed in my brain ever since is – what in God's name are they teaching SENCO teachers that in twenty years this poor lady didn't know anything about ADHD, until I did a presentation on it? To the point she didn't even know she had ADHD herself!

I'm guessing they're telling them about hyperactivity, inattention and distraction, and not a lot else.

So I began travelling all over England, Scotland and Wales to train as many people as I possibly could. The more ADHD kids were understood, the less of them would end up in Prison.

I was now beginning to understand that ADHD services in Prisons were very random to say the least. I met a wonderful Psychiatrist who told me he had spent six years in Leeds Prison diagnosing Prisoners with ADHD all day long. There were pockets in the Prison system where ADHD services were working, but there were many more Prisons where they were not. So the next thing we started to do was offer ADHD and autistic assessments in Prisons where clients couldn't get the right diagnosis. Far too many of them were being palmed off with ridiculous 'personality disorder' diagnoses, when in actual fact they had ADHD.

We placed an advert in the Prison newspaper, *Inside Time*, offering our services to people who couldn't get the right ADHD or ASD assessment inside. Since then we've been helping hundreds of people in different Prisons access the right diagnosis.

Some Prisoners were on remand and desperate to get the correct diagnosis before they went to court. Some wanted to get the right diagnosis so they could appeal their sentence. But, in most Prisons, they were being told that the staff were just not able to diagnose ADHD. What a crazy situation!

Health Care teams, Psychologists and Psychiatrists working in Prisons were unable to diagnose the condition that around 85% of the Prison population had? That to me was just as crazy as putting Neurodiversity Managers into Prisons and banning them from screening people! I had numerous meetings with some absolutely lovely Prison Neurodiversity Managers who were frustrated beyond belief because they knew their Prisons were full of ADHD, but they had been told by the Ministry of Justice not to screen them.

I've always been the sort of person who thinks if something isn't being done properly, then just do it yourself. For the last two years me and my team have been working hard to offer ADHD assessments in numerous Prisons, so these boys and girls behind bars do actually get the correct diagnosis, and can at last begin to understand themselves, giving them a much greater chance of not going back to Prison.

The chapter I never wanted to write

While all this was going on, Thomas, on his sixteen-year sentence, where he would have to serve at least twelve years inside, was doing amazingly well. I thought he would go into a deep, dark depression so I engaged his services immediately as my 'ADHD man on the ground' in the Prisons. I told him he had a new job title and that was 'ADHD Liberty Prison Representative'. I think he loved this and he took his new role very seriously.

Definitely plural Prisons there, because he was moved so many times I found myself visiting him in HMP Bedford, HMP Lowdham Grange in Nottinghamshire, HMP Swaleside in Kent, and probably a few others I have forgotten.

I sent him a copy of all my books and he spent his days visiting Prisoners in their cells, talking to them about their potential undiagnosed ADHD being behind their repeat offending – helping numerous people finally understand why they had always felt and behaved differently to others.

He did exactly the same with the Prison Officers. He would pick out paragraphs from one of the three books and then go and see a particular Officer and explain why this was relevant to an incident that had just taken place. He told me proudly how he would often invite different Prison Officers to come into his cell to read the books with him, so they could understand the Prisoners they were working with. He told me every Officer found it fascinating and couldn't understand why they'd not been trained in ADHD when so many inside had it.

Thomas had also realised that he needed to go back on ADHD medication himself. He was one of the teenagers who had been told he had outgrown ADHD in his late teens. The more he learnt, the more he realised that this sixteen-year sentence was because he had still been risk-taking and thrill-seeking and most definitely not thinking of the consequences. Had he been on the medication, a sixteen-year sentence might not have been the outcome.

I was writing to him regularly, and emailing him, and he used to phone me roughly once every two weeks, where we would have a major chat. He ended every single phone call, letter and email with, 'Love you millions.' This went on for years and years.

Our relationship changed and I was no longer his counsellor, but I counted him as a very good friend. He helped me more than anyone to spread the ADHD word in the Prison system – so much – telling so many people that just because you hadn't been diagnosed with ADHD as a child, it didn't mean you hadn't got it.

Then, to my absolute horror, he set fire to himself. I knew his mental health was fragile. I had been writing to the Prison he had previously been in, and the current one, explaining how his emotions were dysregulated because he was not on ADHD medication. It was even more imperative he be properly medicated now he had set fire to himself. I received nothing back.

When I saw Thomas on my next visit, he hoicked his sweatshirt up to show me the awful effect of him setting fire to himself. It was keloid scarring, so about an inch deep and very red, and went all the way from the top of his left leg, up his trunk and chest, and down his left arm. It wasn't only awful to look at, but he told me it was very painful.

During the peak of the Covid outbreak I hadn't been able to see Thomas because all visits to Prisons were cancelled, but we still kept in regular touch by phone, letter and email. After Covid he managed to get an 'accumulated visits' move from a Prison in Nottinghamshire to a Prison in London. I went to visit him and took my partner with me. He had met Thomas before and liked him very much. We spent the whole visit talking about his release, which was now possible in the next two years, and how he had options. Those options included going to Africa, where my partner is from, to live and work on a farm. My partner thought it might be good for him to get away, get some sun, and have guaranteed accommodation and work – but it was just an option. And we spoke about other options at the same time. He was definitely looking forward.

Once Thomas had decided he wanted to go back on ADHD medication I started to contact the Prison Mental Health teams, asking if he could please be put on it. I didn't get a response and neither did Thomas. I wouldn't have minded me not getting a response if somebody from Health Care had gone to see him, but apart from one Mental Health nurse, who he spoke very highly of, there was no movement when it came to medicating him for his ADHD. Apparently, this one Mental Health nurse also felt she was banging her head against a brick wall.

Thomas was definitely on a downhill slope when it came to his mental health. I could tell from talking to him and he would tell me that his mental health was 'bad'. I started to send safeguarding risk letters into the

Prison, saying that I really did fear for him if somebody didn't take responsibility for medicating him for his ADHD. Again, I received no response.

After seeing Thomas on the accumulated visit in London, my life became very busy and sad all at the same time. My mother, who had battled Parkinson's for thirty-five years, was taken into hospital after a fall. Her partner couldn't drive because he had cataracts and was waiting for an operation, so for the last seven weeks of 2022 I spent every single day picking her partner up and going into the hospital to see my mother. She died on 30 December 2022.

After organising her funeral and finalising her financial affairs, because I was her next of kin, I decided I needed four weeks away as I was on my knees with exhaustion. So I went to Africa for a month.

I wanted to switch off from literally everything, but now I bitterly regret that decision.

When I came back from Africa, I sent Thomas an enormous email explaining why I had been out of action for pretty much three months and updating him with everything. He knew my mother had been very ill. I think it ended up being a five page email and as always I paid for a reply. Thomas always replied to my emails and they were always long and gushing with love. But this one – I didn't get a reply. I didn't understand that, because I knew if he had been moved to another Prison they would have forwarded the email on, but still I heard nothing.

I was very conscious of time passing and thinking 'this is not right', and I checked my doormat daily for his spidery handwriting, but no letter arrived on the doormat.

The email hadn't been responded to and while he had known I was going to Africa for four weeks he would now have known I was back, but the phone calls had stopped coming too.

I was still wondering what to do about this when I received a message on Facebook Messenger from somebody saying, 'Are you the Sarah that knows Thomas?' This message came through about eleven o'clock one evening so, although I replied immediately, I didn't get a response.

I was so concerned that the next morning I rang this person, who turned out to be an aunt of Thomas' and who I had actually met once or twice before. She told me the worst news I've ever received. That on 6 March 2023, Thomas had hung himself and was dead.

I was absolutely destroyed by this. I had just lost my mother at the end of December and then just over two months later Thomas had taken his own life. He is the only client, both inside and outside, that I have ever lost to suicide. He actually took his life on the exact date he would've been thirty and a half. I'm sure that was more coincidence than intentional.

When I spoke to his aunt, I asked if there was going to be a funeral and she snapped, 'Yes. Tomorrow. Family only.' There was so much I could've said to that.

Where was his family when he needed them? Why didn't they go and visit him when he came down to London on accumulated visits? Why, still, hadn't they bothered to go and see him when he managed to extend the accumulated visits from four weeks to eight weeks? Why had they stopped his sister going to see him when she had wanted to, but had been told it wouldn't be fair on her because she would see him that time and then not for ages. He was in Nottinghamshire. Not Timbuktu.

Why was it up to me to house him three times when he came out of Prison, because his mother wouldn't have him in her house? But I said nothing. And I just wept.

Barney was as devastated as I was. Barney and I had probably been Thomas' best and closest friends. And at least we had each other to cling to over this absolute tragedy.

I knew I wouldn't get any information out of the family, nor the Prison, as to what had actually happened and how Thomas had died, but luckily I had two boys in the same Prison who both telephoned me with exactly the same story, so I'm 100% certain it's true. Apparently, Thomas had had some sort of ADHD meltdown during the day and to punish him in the evening the Officers had turned his electricity off.

This meant he had no light, of course, but also no television and no kettle, and absolutely nothing to occupy himself with. I received a letter from somebody who had sat with Thomas that night for five hours trying to talk him out of hanging himself, and the person who wrote was so apologetic for not being able to talk him out of it.

But he did say that Thomas had spent the last hours of his life telling him that he was ADHD and to get in touch with me on the outside and I would help him. So Thomas spent his last hours on this earth trying to help somebody. That was just so typical of him.

And in September 2024, I found myself sitting in the Coroners' Court listening to a Coroner talk about not only Thomas' suicide in that Prison, but two other Prisoners as well. And I found out that this particular Prison has an appalling record for turning people's electricity off to punish them. In the month Thomas died, there were three suicides alone in that one Prison. Of course not one member of his 'Family only' turned up to the inquest. But I was there for him.

From my third client at HMP YOI Aylesbury, who just wanted to get out to buy a pint of milk, to sitting in a Coroners' Court.

Thomas received more attention and news coverage when he was dead than he did when he was alive. He hit the national papers, including *The Guardian* and the *BBC News*. The inquest, which included two other men who had died by suicide in HMP Lowdham Grange in March 2023, went on for three full months.

I had given a five-hour statement to Nottinghamshire Police. I gave them copies of the five safeguarding risk letters I had sent to HMP Whitemoor and HMP Lowdham Grange, pleading with them to medicate Thomas. I had gone into a great amount of detail about why he desperately needed to be on ADHD medication, how he was quite severely ADHD and needed to be medicated for it and how not being on ADHD medication meant he had dangerously dysregulated emotions.

But when the Coroner's Report and the Prison Ombudsman's report came out there was absolutely no mention of my five safeguarding risk letters, or of

Thomas' ADHD. It was like they were talking about a completely different person.

Absolutely no mention of Thomas having adult ADHD, despite Nottinghamshire Police's final pointed question to me being, 'Do you think if Thomas had been on his ADHD medication he would be alive today?' and my answer had been a very firm, 'Yes'.

Instead, the reports talked about Thomas having EUPD, as in the much misdiagnosed Emotionally Unstable Personality Disorder. He did not have EUPD. They also admitted that they had been giving him antipsychotic medication, which never works for people with ADHD and in some cases is actually quite dangerous – causing severe depression and suicidal thoughts. I had worked with one private client who had been given this diagnosis before he came to me and told me that he had never felt suicidal until he took the antipsychotic medication. We went on to get this client diagnosed with ADHD and he threw the Quetiapine antipsychotics down the toilet, where they belonged.

There was also absolutely no mention of the fact that Thomas had been told he would have to be re-diagnosed with ADHD and he had completed part one of the assessment when he was in HMP Whitemoor. Thomas told me himself that, because he was then moved to HMP Lowdham Grange, the second part of the ADHD assessment never happened. So where was that hidden? Why did it not come out in the inquest that he had had part one of an ADHD assessment, but because of the Prisons not liaising he had never had the second part? Absolutely no mention of that in pages and pages of two reports.

As I read these reports I became angrier and angrier. They had never even known Thomas properly, let alone medicated him for his ADHD, despite my very lengthy five safeguarding risk letters.

So you can imagine how fired up I was after that to change things in the Prisons. Ignorance around ADHD and how severe the dysregulated emotions can be killed one of my most precious friends.

The one thing I know Thomas would've wanted more than anything is for me to use his story to educate everybody working in the criminal justice system about ADHD.

And that I will do, because one Thomas was one too many. Far, far, too many. I am heartbroken that I have lost him and I will love him millions forever more.

Reasons and why's

You may well be wondering why the words ADHD or Attention Deficit Hyperactivity Disorder don't appear on the cover or in the title of this book. That's because when I went into the Prisons in 2004, I was still eleven years off my own ADHD diagnosis and I had absolutely no idea the Prisons would be so full of ADHD.

I had known that I was drawn towards Prisons and Prisoners since an incredibly young age, but it took nearly another forty years before I realised that was because I had the same brain as most of the residents.

And I'm not alone. I think most people in the world have no clue just how full of ADHD Prisons actually are.

I believe there are a couple of reasons for this. One is that, in the UK at least, adults were not diagnosed with ADHD until 2009. Up until then we were told that ADHD was a childhood behavioural disorder that you outgrew in your late teens. So we are playing catch-up when it comes to understanding the condition in adults.

The second reason is that tens of thousands of adults do not realise they have ADHD. So people who have been prolific offenders for thirty or forty years are still sitting in Prison right now, not knowing that their ADHD traits have led them there.

But why do so many people in Prison have ADHD? I think once you understand the traits it's very easy to know why – there are simply so many ADHD traits and ways of thinking that can lead people down the wrong path.

An ADHD brain, until it is medicated, acts impulsively and doesn't think of the consequences. It's quite breathtaking when you start ADHD medication and you think of a consequence for the first time. This happened to me when I was fifty-five years old. Up until that point I hadn't been aware I wasn't thinking of the consequences of anything! But it became abundantly clear the very first time I did think of a consequence – purely because I was on medication. Those two traits alone account for a huge amount of offending.

Having worked with hundreds of ex-offenders I would say the other big traits that bring ADHD people into contact with the law are: a high propensity to boredom; hyperactivity and the need to get out and do something; not liking authority; always thinking we know best; and having no patience, so wanting everything now. That combo has led to many Prison sentences.

But there are many other traits added into the mix. Having a heightened sense of justice is an incredibly strong trait. If an ADHD person feels they have been wronged, they will not be able to let it go. Their heightened sense of justice will be raging until they take some sort of revenge.

Rejection Sensitive Dysphoria, and the perpetual fear of being humiliated or rejected, can see people become angry and violent without understanding why. They just know it's painful and they need to lash out at somebody to make themselves feel better.

Until an ADHD brain is medicated, emotions are dysregulated. But what does that actually mean? It means the part of our brain that should regulate our emotions – or choose the correct emotion and level of emotion appropriately – doesn't. And that can be any emotion, ranging from anger, outrage, frustration, and irritation, right through to being hypersensitive, easily upset and very emotional. Emotions, and the fact that we can't regulate them, play another huge part in why people cross the line into criminality.

Lack of strong parental guidance is also a big factor. Bearing in mind that ADHD is now accepted to be nearly always hereditary, many Prisoners have come from either violent, abusive, neglectful, chaotic or addiction-impacted homes. If these teenagers and adolescents were most often missed and undiagnosed, what chance did the generation before them have? Very little chance that they were diagnosed and medicated. In fact, I would go so far as to say that absolutely none of them were diagnosed and medicated. I've certainly not come across one Prisoner who had a parent, or two parents, diagnosed and medicated for their own, often severe, ADHD.

So the sad fact is, our juvenile Prisons, Young Offender Institutes and adult male and female Prisons are rammed to the rafters with primarily undiagnosed, and always unmedicated, ADHD. We are looking at people with a psychiatrically diagnosable condition, a lot of whom also have autism. In Victorian times we called these institutions lunatic asylums. Now we simply call them Prisons, and many people believe that the Prison system is the biggest psychiatric unit we have. I agree with them.

So how on earth do we tackle this?

You'll be pleased to know, I have the answer – absolutely nothing to do with the fact that I am ADHD and always know best! Honest. I'm just somebody who has worked in the Prison system, has ADHD, recognises the overwhelming amount of people with it and has the answer.

The subject nobody likes to talk about, but avoiding it is more dangerous

Before I explain how easy it is to sort out this whole mess, I'm going to give you the best reason, ever, why we have to change the education and criminal justice system in this country (and probably everywhere else, but I don't like to assume) when it comes to screening and identifying ADHD.

A little story to demonstrate this. During all my time working in the Prisons I had never worked with a sex offender. And I knew it was an area I was lacking experience in. A Sex Psychologist friend of mine at the time recommended I get in touch with an organisation called Circles. Very simply, Circles provides circles of support around a sex offender when they leave Prison. They also offer very good training, which I did and learnt a huge amount from.

The circles usually number three or four people and are often made up of people like me – Counsellors, Trainee Psychologists, Magistrates, Retired Probation and Police Officers – and people with an interest in helping people, learning more about sex offending, while at the same time protecting the public.

After my training, I was put in a circle with two other people and given one client to work with. This one client was in his mid 50s and had just spent ten years in Prison doing, in his words, 'every single course I could to find out why I did what I did, because I am disgusted with myself'. Not one of these courses had helped him find out why he did what he had done.

We had had two or three meetings with this man, who told us it was his fifteen-year-old stepdaughter who had reported him for sexually inappropriate behaviour, and this was why he had served the ten year sentence.

He seemed desperate to understand himself. He told us that he was the regular babysitter for his huge family, loved kids, and until this point had never had any thought of this kind of activity. The one phrase he did use over and over again was 'the buzz'. That he had got a huge 'buzz' from it. He wasn't proud of the buzz, but he did keep using the word.

Having an ADHD brain that never stops, it actually came to me in my sleep. The buzz, the buzz, the buzz. I wonder if that's the adrenaline he was seeking? Could he possibly have undiagnosed ADHD?

The next week I took in an ADHD screener. We completed it with him, because he struggled with reading and writing, and he scored incredibly highly.

I took this information back to Circles, who weren't terribly interested in it. I think they had their own ways of seeing things and working with people and weren't interested in a potential 'excuse'. ADHD is never an excuse, but it is very often the reason.

So instead I spoke to his Probation Officer, who was a lot more receptive. I explained in detail how an ADHD brain lacked adrenaline and risk-taking, thrill-seeking and sexual promiscuity could sometimes play a part. The Probation Officer was fully supportive and asked me what needed to happen next. I explained to her that we needed to get this client an urgent ADHD assessment and, as a Probation Officer, she actually had a lot of clout in making that happen quickly. Sure enough, after she had contacted this particular county's adult ADHD mental health services, the client was given an ADHD assessment within two weeks. He asked me to go with him.

This was one of the most heartbreaking assessments I ever sat in on. It turned out this client had been in a special needs boarding school for his entire education as his father was in the forces. He had always struggled with reading and writing and most of what was taught went over his head. But nobody in all those years of education had picked up that he had ADHD.

The assessor was so kind and non-judgmental with him, and diagnosed him at the end of the assessment with severe Combined ADHD and learning difficulties.

So he had spent a decade in Prison trying to find out what the root cause of his behaviour was, and hated himself for what he had done, yet had he been screened in school and medicated it is very unlikely that he would've still been risk-taking and thrill-seeking to the point he had to spend ten years in Prison. At a very rough estimate it cost us £500,000 to keep this man in Prison for ten years, and that didn't include the cost of all the courses he was taking.

This completely correlates with all the Prisons I am now liaising with. I don't think there is one Neurodiversity Manager in a Prison, that I have spoken to, who hasn't said something along the lines of, 'We think there is more ADHD on our sex offender Wing than any other.' And I strongly suspect they are right.

There are a lot of people in the ADHD world who don't like to link ADHD with sex offending, but as I tell them all, 'ADHD isn't always pretty.' And we can't just ignore sex offenders with ADHD if we want to protect children.

And if more proof were needed I, myself, at the age of ten, was on the end of family sexual abuse. Thankfully mine was extremely mild, but it was by somebody who at the time was diagnosed schizophrenic. We now know that person had undiagnosed ADHD, because two of his children are diagnosed with ADHD.

So if we are going to protect children from undiagnosed ADHD sex offenders, stop the School-to-Prison pipeline (which is full of ADHD), reduce suicides and self-harm in Prisons, save on the expense of building new Prisons, and empty the current Prisons of ADHD and autism all in one go, what needs to happen?

Sort it out! It's not hard

The one message I hope I have got over in this book is that the Prisons are not full of those nasty, evil, vicious people I thought they were when I was eight.

In fact, it's truthful to say that the nastiest piece of work I ever met in a Prison was a member of staff! And I think you know which one! #Paperclip!

I'm going to bullet point it to show you how easy it would be to transform our Prison system from the dire, failing, life-threatening, haemorrhaging money mess it's in right now.

Another positive of ADHD is we get straight to the point – we don't have time for sugarcoating and we can very often see the blindingly obvious answer to a problem when Neurotypicals can't.

So here are my answers to our failing Prison system – which doesn't serve the public by rehabilitating Prisoners, and also fails those serving sentences by not identifying mental health conditions and neurodiversity, which is the only thing that is going to stop them re-offending.

My answers to this situation come with a guarantee. And you can hold me to it.

1. Screening all children in school to be mandatory from the age of five and at every transition i.e. to junior school, to senior school and to college. For ADHD and all the coexisting conditions. This doesn't cost a penny and will wipe out the School-to-Prison pipeline. ADHD and all neurodiversity to be included in all teacher

training, so teachers feel fully equipped to identify red flags for all neurodiversity in their classroom. Clear pathways for children to receive early intervention, assessment, diagnosis and, if applicable, medication. And the necessary support put in place to allow them to achieve their full potential.

2. Screening for ADHD to be mandatory in every Police station. To catch kids at the youngest age possible when they go off the rails for the first time.

3. Screening for ADHD and the coexisting conditions to be mandatory in addiction, homelessness, Probation and Youth Offending services. When a new client is taken on, an ADHD screener should be part of the initial assessment to find out if ADHD is at the root of the problem. There is a huge crossover between addiction, homelessness and offending, and if we cover all bases less people are going to end up behind bars.

4. Screen for ADHD and the coexisting conditions on the Induction Wing of every juvenile Prison, Young Offender Institute and adult male and female Prison.

Then, in the Prison system, it's even easier to see what's wrong and how it could be so simply resolved.

1. Every Prison should be run like a residential college. All Prisoners to be in full-time vocational training or education every weekday from 9 a.m. to 4:30 p.m. At weekends sporting and creative activities should be obligatory for the same amount

of hours. And mandatory. No more ambling round a Prison yard with nothing to do. Keep everybody active seven days a week.

2. Nobody to leave Prison until they are at least a qualified barber, chef, plumber, builder, or whatever other vocational training they have undertaken. And training qualifications should be equal to those on the outside – not the worthless certificates many are given now. At the moment, there is little motivation for Prisoners to train when sessions get cancelled constantly and qualifications aren't worth the paper they are written on. Professionalise all Education and Training services in Prison, with Prisoners knowing that they will not be released until they are qualified in a minimum of one vocational skill. This must be something they can use immediately to get work on the outside. They will then have motivation to attend and finish training courses.

3. On the rare occasions when somebody is in Prison and already fully qualified as, for example, a roofer, they should spend the same amount of time each day 9 a.m. to 4:30 p.m. in therapy. Each Prison to have a Therapeutic Wing for those not needing education or for those who complete their vocational training and still have time to serve.

And that's it. Not difficult is it? At the moment we are doing the polar opposite of this. We are locking people up for up to twenty-three hours a day, destroying their mental health, and not rehabilitating them or preparing them for life on the outside at all.

On top of that we have Mental Health teams, Psychologists and Psychiatrists who aren't qualified to diagnose ADHD or autism, when they are overwhelmingly the conditions people inside have. So the whole lot of them need to be trained in ADHD and autism, which takes less than a week to train each clinician, and several can be trained at the same time to be able to assess for ADHD and autism. And the words 'Personality Disorder' need to be banned. There is always a reason for every behaviour and that is never that you were born with, or developed, the wrong personality.

And the guarantee?

- ✓ We won't be locking up people with mental health conditions and neurodiversity.

- ✓ Self-harm and suicide rates in Prison will dramatically fall.

- ✓ There will be no need to waste taxpayers' money on building new Prisons.

- ✓ The School-to-Prison pipeline will be at the very least massively reduced, if not completely eradicated.

- ✓ Sexual offences will reduce, and children will be protected and much less likely to be traumatised for life from childhood sexual abuse.

- ✓ The public will be safer as crime rates will fall.

- ✓ Government spending can be redirected from the criminal justice system into schools and the NHS.

And you know I said – if nobody's doing it right, do it yourself? Well I am. Headstuff ADHD Liberty became a registered charity in 2021. ADHD LIBERTY was born. I am the CEO of the charity and I have the most amazing team around me, who are all equally passionate about this disgraceful situation regarding ADHD in our Prison system.

We are in the process of setting up ADHD Support Groups in every Prison and Young Offender Institute in the country. It's a mammoth task, but me and my team have already started. These Support Groups will help those diagnosed support each other, help those wondering if they are ADHD to find out more information, and our thirty professionally filmed info-videos on all aspects of ADHD will help Governors, Officers and Mental Health teams understand all about ADHD, it's link with offending and addiction, and all other aspects of the condition.

We have also been liaising with National Prison Radio and have a one-year contract planned with them to raise ADHD awareness throughout the whole Prison system.

Bite-size excerpts from the thirty videos will be played regularly on a loop. There will be additional two-minute segments at the top of every hour for a whole year, detailing a different ADHD trait to help Prisoners recognise ADHD in themselves. We will be holding a monthly write-in surgery where people can send any ADHD questions in and I will answer them. The radio station will focus on playing music by ADHD singers, songwriters and producers.

On top of this, the charity will be funding ADHD awareness posters, ADHD trait flyers and more detailed trifold leaflets to be available in every Young Offender Institute and every Prison.

All of this starts in 2025. The same year I am releasing this book. This is a big job, but I will make it happen because one Thomas was one too much. I cannot bear the thought of people taking their life in Prison because they weren't aware enough of their own ADHD and the staff weren't trained enough to diagnose them correctly.

My time at HMP The Mount, HMP Guys Marsh and HMP Portland were the happiest of my life. And I include in that the boys from Aylesbury – just not the supposed 'professional' who was sketchy with the truth (and that's being kind) on official counselling qualification paperwork, never mind the self-serving act of unceremoniously booting me out of Aylesbury when it wasn't in the clients' best interests. AND when I had only done what I had been asked to by an Officer and stuck rigidly to what he asked of me.

I'll never know who was behind getting me evicted from HMP Portland, but they were definitely from Aylesbury and I wouldn't be surprised at all if they had been twirling that paperclip in their hair as they tried to ruin me for a second time.

Karma. I'm a big believer in it. Maybe they'll be buried under a random deluge of paperclips. I'm beyond caring.

But never beyond caring about those boys, girls, men and women trapped in Prisons with ADHD. For them, and those headed in that direction, I've devoted my life for ten years so far, and I have absolutely no intention of stopping.

For me – caring can NEVER be a crime.

Some big sloppy thank yous

Feel free to skip this page or have a large bucket to hand as it might be a bit sickly.

The first person I have to thank is my very good friend Ruth, who I met on a Halifax advert in the 1990s, standing in a big green cross, back when acting was my 'thing'. If it wasn't for Ruth there wouldn't have been one book, let alone four, as all of my books have been written in her warm, cosy lounge. And without her boot firmly up my bottom, I would never have entertained the idea of writing a book in the first place. She is literally my inspiration.

Secondly, I have to thank another friend who goes even further back, and without whom Headstuff would come to a grinding halt. Sindy and I met when we were children living in a caravan park, and lost touch for about thirty years, but now she keeps me and a hundred therapists in line. I appreciate her more than she will ever know.

Sophie is my book PA. When it comes to Amazon, eBay, dealing with printing, publishing and anything whatsoever to do with the books – Sophie is the Queen. She also puts all my presentations together and I would be absolutely lost without her.

Louise is my CJS PA. She has her finger on the pulse when it comes to who is doing ADHD screening pilots, and thankfully is one million times more organised than I am when it comes to filing emails away and finding them again. She's my right hand and irreplaceable.

I have had the joy of loving my niece Isabel for twenty-four years. It's only in the last couple of years that she told me my social media presence was crap and she would take it over!

She is now an integral part of the team and responsible for all the pretty infographics you see telling people off for getting things about ADHD wrong! I am so privileged to have her in my life.

Sara Donaldson had the unenviable task of being my new editor. Sara put up with the thousands of amendments I made and kept smiling when we sailed past the first edit, past the second, and onto the third! She's been an absolute joy to work with and I am so grateful for the care and attention she has taken with this book.

Olli Tooley also deserves huge praise. Buried away in the depths of North Devon he took the flack when my first book was slated on Twitter because of its title, so sadly I couldn't publish with his publishing house as intended. But, hallelujah, he agreed to do the typesetting and formatting for all my books anyway! There is nothing he doesn't know about publishing and he has guided me through the maze patiently and with good humour. He is an absolute diamond and I appreciate him so much.

And finally. But very importantly. My ADHD Liberty and Headstuff teams.

We started off as a random group of police officers, probation officers, addiction therapists and prison counsellors, who were all livid that nothing was happening about the amount of ADHD in prisons. Now we are quite the team – we scrub up well! To every single person who plays a part in the charity, and Headstuff, the biggest thank you, because without you, quite simply, none of this would be happening.

Resources

It's au revoir, not goodbye! There are loads of other ways I can help you, and some ways you can help me (cheeky I know, after you've already forked out for this book!).

WEBSITES

ADHDLiberty.org

If you want to see change in the criminal justice system, so do we! We are a registered charity and gratefully receive donations, large and small. We guarantee every penny will go towards helping people stuck behind bars with ADHD – or towards keeping ADHD adolescents headed for Prison OUT.

SarahTempleton.org.uk

This is where you can find everything about me and links to useful media. Please pass this website link on to anybody who can further our campaign to stop the ADHD School-to-Prison Pipeline.

HeadstuffADHDTherapy.co.uk

Fully qualified ADHD counsellors, children's counsellors, family mediators, coaches and addiction therapists, all diagnosed ADHD themselves. Based in the UK and working internationally. All hand-picked by me, so guaranteed to be the best!

ADHD training for Schools, Police Forces, Probation, Prisons, businesses, addiction services, homelessness services and anybody wanting to understand ADHD.

MY BOOKS

How NOT to Murder your ADHD Kid: Instead Learn How To Be Your Child's Own ADHD Coach!

My first book on parenting younger ADHD kids aged up to about eleven.

How NOT to Damage your ADHD Adolescent: Instead Coach them through their Turbulent Teens to Win at Life!

This book will help you understand everything your ADHD teenager is going through, and definitely keep them well away from the criminal justice system.

Teachers! How Not to Kill the Spirit in Your ADHD Kids – Instead, Understand their Brains and Turbocharge our Future Leaders & Winners.

To help teachers understand ADHD children's brains. If you are struggling to have your child understood at school, this book should help